I0885359

"*Femicide, Criminology and the Law* captures the distinctive nature of femicide and lays out its components with sophistication critical to comprehending its exceptionality. I believe the authors' interdisciplinary methods for effectively addressing femicide have significant potential for global applicability, and I strongly recommend their book."

Justice Yosef Elron, *Israel Supreme Court*

Femicide, Criminology and the Law

This book offers an interdisciplinary perspective on femicide, using Israel as an illuminating case study, given its diverse communities and common-law-based legal system. Utilizing analytical alongside practical perspectives, the book offers a novel crimino-legal approach to femicide. In addition to its interdisciplinary novelty, the book presents originality in going beyond the more usual focus on the central victims and the common legal tools. Here, the authors extend the analysis to secondary victims of femicide and examine the applicability of second-tiered relevant legal tools, mostly tort law, as a means to gain justice for the victims. This explorative journey culminates with the authors' definition of femicide as a quintessential "crime of distinct nature." In the context of current international pledges to better understand and consequently better fight femicide, this work allows readers to comprehend the phenomenon and the ways to abolish it. The book will be an invaluable resource for academics, researchers and policy makers working in the areas of criminal law, tort law, family law, criminology and gender studies, as well as for legal theorists and criminologists seeking integration of both disciplines.

Hava Dayan conducts research in the field of criminal law and society, with a focus on gender and crime, at the School of Criminology, Faculty of Law, University of Haifa, Israel.

Yifat Bitton is President of Achva Academic College for Science and Education in Israel. She is a legal academic and social activist for equality.

Femicide, Criminology and the Law

Hava Dayan and Yifat Bitton

Routledge
Taylor & Francis Group
LONDON AND NEW YORK

First published 2023
by Routledge
4 Park Square, Milton Park, Abingdon, Oxon OX14 4RN

and by Routledge
605 Third Avenue, New York, NY 10158

Routledge is an imprint of the Taylor & Francis Group, an informa business

British Library Cataloguing-in-Publication Data
A catalogue record for this book is available from the British Library

ISBN: 978-1-032-36687-6 (hbk)
ISBN: 978-1-032-36688-3 (pbk)
ISBN: 978-1-003-33327-2 (ebk)

DOI: 10.4324/9781003333272

Typeset in Galliard
by Apex CoVantage, LLC

To all women who could have been alive but for their gender, and to all the voiceless and invisible secondary victims left tormented for life by these women's deaths.

Contents

Foreword by Justice Yosef Elron, Israeli Supreme Court

> "Last but not least, I will add that only a few days ago, on November twenty-fifth, Israel, alongside other countries throughout the world have commemorated the International Day for the Elimination of Violence against Women. In the case before us, the appellant has murdered his late wife viciously . . . while in her home – a space they shared that was supposed to be her safe haven and a fortress. This case is a typical example – however extraordinarily brutal – of this same heinous phenomenon, that has become a social epidemic, crossing through groups, denominations and nationalities, that has taken the lives of 24 (Israeli) women this past year."
>
> (ISC 2333/17 Doe v. People (2.12.2018)).

These words, taken from one of the many femicide cases I've tried, encapsulate the outrageous and grievous elements of femicide – the killing of a woman due to her gender – precisely the way this book does. Serving the Israeli legal system for many years mainly as a criminal justice judge, most notably as former President of the Haifa District court and currently as a Supreme Court justice, I have come to realize that these cases cut across cultures, ages, and societies, on the one hand, yet carry common denominators, that warrant their own category and analysis, on the other hand.

Common knowledge teaches us that while most homicide cases are committed in circumstances of escalating conflicts between men within non-domestic spaces, homicide cases of women represent another set of characteristics, primarily of gendered relevance. Rarely committed by women, these homicides were often perpetrated by men, who were almost always closely related to the victim before or during the killing. For the victimized women, these domestic characteristics signified danger rather than safety. These striking differences between "regular" homicide and women's homicide with their correlated particularities nurtured my realization that these cases warrant reconceptualization, whereby gender will be taken into consideration in trying them. This book fills this void.

As its name suggests, the book stands as a thought-provoking interdisciplinary research project on femicide, using Israel as an illuminating case study, given its diverse communities and its common-law-based legal stratagem. Utilizing both legal and criminological analytical and practical perspectives, the book offers a systematic and innovative approach to femicide. Apart from its interdisciplinary novelty, it presents originality in its shifting paradigm: Instead of focusing, as expected, on the crime's center-stage victims (the women) and center-stage effective legal tools (criminal law), it offers a more holistic approach, expanding its analysis also toward secondary victims of femicide and to the utilization of second-tiered relevant legal tools (mostly, tort law) as means to do justice with the victims and to effectively fight this atrocity.

Utilizing criminological theory to identify crimes in order to determine their legal consequences, I find great value in the book's interdisciplinary promise. Crimino-legal interdisciplinary works are rare in general, and yet to be performed in the growing field of femicide. The authors noticed this lacuna and decided to venture on this unexplored terrain. Throughout the book, criminology and law are exercised reciprocally to enrich the field, to better understand its complexities and to better design the means required to effectively address its multifaceted implications.

Among the diverse array of essential issues discussed in the book, two were of unique interest to me. Throughout my judgements on femicide, it was impossible to ignore the many ramifications femicide has had on the women's children and family members, for whom the legal system could hardly offer comfort. It was apparent that femicide leaves an abundance of personal, psychological, social, financial, mental and at times even physical injuries to those left behind in a way that was different from that observed at non-femicide homicide cases, for many reasons, as the book elaborates. The need for legal tools that will address this peculiarity of femicide is dire. Take, for instance, the fact that the killing scene for many femicide cases is the home, where the children reside. In a case recently tried, I've used the presence of the woman-victim's minor children in the murder scene as a means to establish the "special cruelty" circumstance required by the criminal code to issue mandatory life sentence on a man who slayed his wife (ISC 3168/19 Doe v. People (26.1.22)). The cruelty, I opined, was embedded in the characteristics of this murder being a femicide: Having the victim's children witness it and the murder being committed inside her home, where she and they were supposed to be safe. In this respect, this book's treatment of femicide's secondary victims cannot be overstated.

The second issue that intrigued me most was the book's critical crimino-legal analysis of the difficulties encountered by criminal law in doing justice with femicide cases where crime-scene staging has been entertained, as due to its domesticity, femicide often lack witnesses and is perpetrated within the scope of the couple's intimate circles. Femicide scenes suspected to have been tampered with and staged to look as if the woman committed suicide or died of some other unfortunate unnatural death are not a rare sight. In such cases, judges struggle and may be torn between their inner instincts and feelings of justice, and their being shorthanded given current criminal-law doctrines pertaining to circumstantial evidence. Luckily, in some of these cases, it's either the murderer's own negligent staging or the police's persistence that makes him eventually confess and allow us to convict him, though it still warrants special justification for countering his lies (ISC 1330/19 Shoa v. People (27.12.20)). The authors' insistence on illuminating the inherent vulnerability of femicide scenes to staging and its further effects on the ability to establish murder convictions are therefor of important use to judges.

The book captures the distinctive nature of femicide and lays out its components, with a level of sophistication crucial to understanding its exceptionality. I myself have used every femicide case decided by me as an outlet for emphasizing the idiosyncratic elements it features, such as the victims' paralyzing fear of their proximity to the perpetrator that prevents them from complaining; the usual execution of the crime in the victims' homes where their safe haven should have been; the harm inflicted upon their family members, especially children – who often lose both parents due to the crime; their inevitable presence in many of the murderous acts; the fact that these murders are personal, but reflect a social phenomenon of a gendered nature, etc. (see, e.g., ISC 2333/17 Doe v. People (2.12.2018)). These are but a few of the reasons this crime should be given separate scholarly attention, which will provide, the way this book does, means and tools to address them with the utmost efficacy.

Aimed at distinguishing femicide from the general category of homicide, the book's journey culminates with its signature definition of femicide as a quintessential "crime of distinct nature," by virtue of its crimino-legal peculiarities and complexities. To this end, the book does more than challenge and criticize the "law on books." Instead, it proceeds to introduce new tools and public-policy recommendations intended to more effectively combat femicide. Its authors insist that their scholarly and theoretical contribution to the field be accompanied by a set of tools accessible for usage by relevant agents of change within the criminal-justice system, such as prosecutors, judges and legislators. The global prevalence of femicide and its main subtypes, combined with the authors' comparative analysis, render their insistence worthwhile, as I find great potential for many of their suggestions being roughly applicable throughout the world and becoming relevant to the fight against the femicide pandemic worldwide.

Preface

When Andi was eight years old, she fell in love with the "king" of the classroom and invited him to be her playmate one nice autumn afternoon. They played volleyball on the small patio at Andi's home, and things were going pretty well between them. They had a nice time. Life seemed to be smiling at Andi.

Alas, that casual and lovely atmosphere was suddenly shattered when the door facing the patio where the two kids were playing opened wide and Andi's mother burst into the yard, pleading with Andi to fetch Mrs. Rosario, their longtime, well-to-do widowed neighbor. But Andi's father wasted no time. Dashing to Andi's mother to prevent her from escaping, he grabbed her by her hair, slammed her to the floor, and dragged her back into the room, straight back to what would be a dark and gloomy fate, shutting the door Andi's mother had barely managed to open.

Back in that room, he continued unleashing hell on Andi's mother. It was a noiseless horror in a way. He did not yell while beating Andi's mother. And her mother kept silent while being beaten. She did not utter even a single sound. She quietly faced that brutal, merciless battery, subdued in deafening silence. But Andi could hear the recurring, evolving cycle of blows, creating a chilling, chronic rhythm of punctual, violent strikes that reached a crescendo – hellish music to her ears.

Andi stood there, stiffly stunned. She did not run, as urged by her mother, to fetch the neighbor for assistance. Appalled and unable to move, she stood in front of the door, which for a split second had swung open to reveal the horrifying monstrosity occurring inside. "Is your father beating your mother?!" exclaimed the surprised boy. Andi managed to regain her composure: "Nope," she vehemently argued, "not at all!" Andi hid her extreme turmoil and resumed an ordinary façade, continuing to play with the boy she loved. Her tiny body stoically resumed the volleyball game, yet deep inside, an eternal flaming inferno scorched her soul, forever.

After what felt like hundreds of years, both her father and the boy finally left. The boy Andi loved left for good, apparently shocked by the surprising events that unfolded during what should have been a playful, loving afternoon. It was time to check on her mother. Andi's mother faced the aftermath of the wild beatings in the same way: Silently. She did not utter a single word about the dreadful event Andi has just witnessed. Instead, she sat with Andi to drink tea together. Andi still remembers the smell of the dry biscuits they speechlessly simmered in their teacups. It was only then that Andi's mother asked Andi in a hushed tone: "Why didn't you run to call for help?" Andi kept quiet. She lowered her head, feeling fully ashamed of herself and utterly flooded with guilty feelings. Andi did not answer. She did not have an answer. Why hadn't she run for help?! Andi never had an answer for that disturbing, tormenting question. Although she was the middle child between two siblings, all three extremely close in age, Andi was always considered the older one. The one everybody could always absolutely trust and count on. Andi felt she had behaved in a completely selfish, inexcusable manner, and that she was, in fact, a terribly bad and rotten person. Filled with remorse and self-contempt, she never forgave herself for having disappointed her mother and herself in such a reprehensible way.

Andi saw her mother's terrible bruises, spread all over her abdomen, and a spot of blood on her mother's pillow, probably left there by her bleeding nose. Or maybe he had tried to suffocate her with the pillow, as he had already done in a prior horrible event unknown to Andi at that time. Despite being a huge, tall, well-fed and strong man, her father enhanced that ruthless beating by an everyday items: He struck Andi's mother so badly that he managed to break several wooden hangers on her relatively tiny body.

For Andi, this was the first time her father had beaten her mother. Alas, as she later learned, it was not the first time. Andi did not know of all the prior beatings, because they occurred at night, when Andi and her siblings were fast asleep. They did not hear those horrific events because Andi's mother never uttered even the slightest sound, not even once, while being ferociously beaten. She kept quiet to avoid disturbing her three little sleeping kids. This time, Andi was aware of the beating because it was not at night and because her mother tried to escape, pleading for Andi's help. Andi was thus very aware this time of her mother's beating. Sure enough, she had never forgotten it. In fact, that beating she witnessed was the reason Andi was thereafter suspicious of her father.

She was especially suspicious of him when, about two months later, he suddenly and unexpectedly arrived for a visit. He used to visit them irregularly, because Andi and her siblings were the unplanned and abandoned outcome of one of his many extramarital affairs, probably the one that had gone the most utterly wrong from his point of view. On that day, he arrived about ten minutes before Andi's mother was supposed to return from work. Andi's mother had a daily routine of finishing work, taking a long bus ride, and then walking several kilometers to their home. Being the sole provider with no extended family to assist her, she had no choice but to work.

The children were already used to feeling lonely while at home, waiting for Mommy to return from her low-paying job, where she earned barely enough to keep them from starvation. At the time of his unexpected visit, Andi was playing with her little sister when she suddenly heard the noise of a key locking the door that led from the inner part of the house where she was playing with her sister to a small patio that then led to the house's entrance. Having made sure the children would not interfere with his plans, he had managed to secure sole access both to the house's patio, the place where he has decided to execute his plan, and the house's entrance door, the very door through which Andi's mother would enter any minute now.

Wary of his rare arrival and strange maneuver blocking Andi from reaching the patio and the house's entrance, Andi stopped playing with her sister and quietly tiptoed to the inner door's keyhole. Peeping through, Andi saw what would be for her the most frightful sight she would ever witness in her life. Appalled, Andi saw her father hiding in a tiny niche in the small patio, only few meters from the entrance door. Well-hidden in that tiny niche, he would be unseen by anyone entering the house. Standing still, he held a big hammer in his right hand. He stood steady, the hammer raised high in the air, ready to surprise Andi's mother and strike from his hiding place. Andi's mother was supposed to enter the house any second now, and Andi was destined to see through the locked door's keyhole her mother's skull being cruelly, savagely, and brutally cracked into pieces.

This time, Andi wanted so badly to rush and call for the neighbors' help. This time, she was not stiffly paralyzed. She was ready to dash and call for help. Alas, she was locked away from the scene where a heinous crime was about to occur. Andi wanted to shout from her tiny lungs, to scream so loud that she would be heard from a long distance and be able to warn her mother not to come any closer to home. But Andi did not yell. "Don't you dare scream!" she hushed herself, suppressing as much as she could her tremendous urge to shout at the top of her little lungs. She did not utter a single sound. She knew very well, even at that young age, that if she shouted or screamed for help, her murderous father would open the locked door, kill little Andi, and then continue to execute his deadly plans for her mother.

Andi was also too young to know by heart any prayer that could have helped her mother. All she could quietly whisper in her mind was: "God, God, God, God, God, God, God." She continuously repeated that word for a few minutes while standing behind the keyhole, staring at her father holding the big hammer in his right hand, ready to kill in a blitz of atrocious hammer strokes. "Please – please God, my mother is about to come home any second now – please," she whispered. "Please, help."

In a sudden, unexpected, miraculous turn of events, the doorbell sounded. Clear and loud. Had she imagined it? No, the house's bell had surely rung. It could not have been Andi's mother, she thought, because her mother had her own set of keys to the entrance. That ringing bell was the sweetest sound Andi would ever hear. She stopped breathing and gazed at her father. He waited for whomever was ringing the bell to figure out that no one was home and decide to leave. But the bell kept ringing. "Please, whomever you are, please do not leave. Please keep ringing the bell," wished Andi. The person on the other side of the door was not going to leave anytime soon – they kept ringing, waiting for someone to answer the door.

Andi stared at her father in his criminal hiding niche. He hesitated for a few moments, then lowered the hammer and made his way back to the inner door that he had locked Andi behind. Andi quickly left her spot at the inner door's keyhole and ran back to her seat, looking as ignorant as she could, as if she had spent all that time playing with her little sister, unaware of the pending tragedy. "Look as if you know nothing!" she mumbled to herself. "Don't you dare disclose in any manner the horrible sight you just witnessed," she thought. "Watch your words, movements, and facial expressions!" she reminded herself. Andi was so scared he would see in her face that she knew about his terrible plans. Andi lowered her head, trying to appear fully focused on the game she allegedly was playing with her little sister. "You should do everything to avoid him looking at your horrified face," she said to herself, "or else Mommy will very soon die."

Unlocking the house's inner door, her father nonchalantly entered the room where Andi sat playing with her little sister. In a very clear and instructive voice, he commanded Andi to attend to the person ringing the doorbell: "Open the door, do not let anyone come in, and say to whomever it is that no adult is currently at home. Then, immediately close the entrance door and return straight back to this room. Do you understand what I have just ordered you to do?" he asked. Of course, Andi did. She understood very well that he was a murderer who was going to kill, any moment now, her Mommy

Realizing that this was probably the sole incredible, miraculous chance she would ever have to save her mother from being killed, Andi tried to grab her little sister's hand to take her, too, to the entrance door. Alas, unaware of the tragically dangerous situation, Andi's little sister refused to stop playing. Andi was afraid that if she firmly insisted on taking her little sister with her, her father would sense in her voice, behavior, or facial expression that she was aware of his vicious, murderous plan. But Andi was not going to leave her little sister with him. Not even for one split second. She tightened her hand, firmly clasping her little sister's, and pulled her, to supposedly attend to the person ringing the entrance doorbell.

Holding tightly to her little sister's hand, Andi opened the door to find an old man whom she had never seen before. He turned out to be the house's landlord, who probably knew, too, that her mother was supposed to return home any minute now. The angry landlord stood there, waiting for her mother to hand him the overdue rent for the past few months. Andi did not intend to engage in a conversation of any kind with whomever had miraculously rung the bell. She quickly told the angry landlord that her father was inside and didn't wait for his reply. She dashed as fast as she could, before anyone could stop her, to the neighboring Mrs. Rosario to tell her about her killer father's vicious plan.

Mrs. Rosario instructed Andi to run as fast as she could to the bus stop where her mother would arrive any second now and do everything she could to stop her, at all costs, from approaching the house. Meanwhile, Mrs. Rosario added, she would stand in the street right outside the entryway to Andi's house to prevent her mother from entering the house, in case she happened to arrive home from some other unexpected route.

Andi grabbed her little sister's hand and ran as fast as she could to the bus stop. It was the longest, most excruciating, terrifying, and tormenting run of her life. Breathless, she reached the bust stop on a central boulevard, where literally hundreds of people descended every evening from numerous buses, rushing on their way back home. Andi was so afraid of not spotting her mother among the many people leaving the buses, which all seemed to stop at once.

What if she had already missed her mother, who went directly, like a sheep to the slaughter, back home? She stood there, torn between wanting to run back home to check whether she missed her mother, sending her straight to the killer's hands, and the need to comply with Mrs. Rosario's instructions to stay still at the bus stop and prevent her mother from approaching their home at all costs. So many people continued to descend together from the conjoined buses – "What if I miss spotting Mommy and don't prevent her from being murdered?" she tormented herself. Andi figured that the best way to screen the masses of people exiting the many various buses all stopping at once was to focus on scanning people's legs, while standing a few meters away from the bus stop. Better still, she thought, would be to stand at a spot near the bus stop, a spot leading toward her home. "This way," she thought, "I can focus on screening only people who are dashing in our home's direction." She focused on screening as many people as fast as she could, all while holding her little sister's hand. "Please mommy, hurry, please come quickly, please, quickly . . ." whispered Andi.

Andi stood there for three agonizing, endless hours. She kept holding tightly to her little sister's hand while scanning the crowd, like the best lookout ever. Andi screened hundreds of people's legs dashing home along the capital's central boulevard from her carefully chosen vantage point. Yet Andi's mother was nowhere to be seen. Daylight began to fade, and twilight gave way to full darkness. The early evening hours turned into a chilly night. Dazzled by the sudden lustrous flashing lights that came on when the buses alighted, Andi's eyes blurred. She could hardly be sure she could spot her mother amid the jumble of shadows as travelers made their way home, vaguely disappearing into the darkness. Andi strained her eyes to see properly. The scene became a vicious cycle of a blurring collage of intertwining colors, which then gave way to overwhelming darkness that blanketed the street. Time and again, the darkness was shattered by the blinding, shining bus lights. Within the plethora of colors and flickering lights, people's shadows appeared for a split second, then vanished quickly into darkness. "I am doomed," Andi thought. "I will never be able to spot Mommy this way." Years later, she could still remember how the passengers threw their bus tickets to the pavement, a sight that looked, once night's darkness took over the boulevard, like little Christmas snowflakes spinning down slowly and gracefully.

At last! Three hours later than her usual arrival time, Andi's mother descended from a bus. Hallelujah!!! In that moment, Andi was the happiest child in the whole world – she ran quickly to her mother and told her what she saw behind the locked door's keyhole. To Andi's utter surprise, without hesitating, her mother believed her. They all took a bus to the police station, which turned out to be the very same police station where Andi's mother had spent the past three hours as Andi waited for her at the bus stop, struggling to persuade the police forces, to no avail, that her life was in real and tangible danger due to her husband's persistent attempts to kill her. Escorted by the police, they all returned to their home.

The would-be killer was still waiting all those hours, adamant about finishing what he came to do. But as soon as he saw the police car approaching, he jumped over the house's tall fences and ran away, leaving his bag with its incriminating evidence behind.

Assisted by the police, they entered home and opened the bag that lay next to the niche where he hid. The big hammer was still there, as was a very expensive bottle of whisky, underwear, and clothes. "Hmmm – probably to clean himself after his bloody plan to crush my mommy's skull and leave the premises clean-handed," Andi thought. A thick, long rope was also found in his left-behind bag. Andi sensed that the rope was meant for her and her siblings. Indeed, he never planned to kill himself. Andi knew all too well that he was too full of himself to do that. Andi guessed that he had intended to kill her mother by cracking her skull with the hammer. And the rope – the rope was meant to strangle all three unwanted, lousy, rejected, and meaningless extramarital little children.

After that horrifying night, Andi and her siblings began to improvise a barricade every night, pushing heavy furniture toward that inner door, piling it up, then removing it each morning, so they could leave the self-imposed prison that shielded them and prevented Andi's father from sneaking in at night to try once again to kill their mother. When one evening he managed to crack that improvised and ultimately futile barricade, they wandered each night to a different location, seeking a safe shelter to spend the night. They slept at neighbors' houses, hospital emergency-room corridors, lighted public gardens, and other such places. After each erratic night of sleep, they returned home at dawn, dressed for school or work, and continued the façade of their lives as ordinary people, as much as they could. Eventually, mainly thanks to their Jewish origins, the community's rabbi, who had learned about the bigamous man and his violent temper, urged their prompt evacuation, sending them all to Israel.

Twenty-five years later, Andi managed to locate her quasi-killer father, living under a false identity. He was never indicted for his many violent deeds – still a charming, good-looking narcissist, still a well-fed, healthy, strong man. Andi was forever skeptical that she had witnessed that nearly tragic event, despite the remnants left in her memory. Curious as she was, she wanted to know: Did it all really happen? Or had she fantasized and invented this unbelievabe, unimaginable, preposterous unfolding of events? After all, she was the only one stuck behind that locked door, peeping through its keyhole and witnessing it all. Maybe it never happened? Maybe it was all only in her mind?

Andi dared to ask him whether what she witnessed behind that locked door's keyhole had indeed happened. To her utter surprise, not only that he did not deny the event, he also started bragging about how creative he was on many other various occasions when he tried, yet failed, to kill her mother. "Well," Andi thought to herself, "I wouldn't brag that much if I were you, mister big-shot quasi-killer. After all, you managed to fail at all those attempts, didn't you?" At the same time, awkwardly enough, Andi was happy to realize, hearing him confirm her shocking memories and brag about the many other occasions on which he attempted to kill her mother, that she was mentally well. She did not invent that terrifying event that she had solely witnessed locked behind the door and peeping through its keyhole.

Yet Andi was still ill at ease. "What was is that you planned to do with us, the children?" she asked him. "After all," she added, "you knew very well that we only had Mom to raise us and take care of us three kids while you were with your legal family." Andi's quasi-killer father gazed at Andi's perplexed face. His eyes were empty. "Was there anyone there at all, behind those vacant eyes?" she asked herself. He looked as if he did not even begin to grasp or understand what Andi had asked him. Or perhaps he did understand what she asked, all too well. Andi could see in his blank eyes the answer to her query. Us kids, she told herself, were destined to be killed as well. After all, we were nothing to him. Nobody to care for, and nobody to worry about. It took Andi an additional split second to understand the nature of her and her siblings' sad and invisible, yet very true, immaterial existence to him. She was nothing more than a nuisance, a troubling ghost from his forgotten past. Andi lamented asking him that question. After all was said and done, his empty gaze upon hearing her question was one of the most heartbreaking, saddest, loneliest moments of her life.

The events that brave little Andi recounted are neither the beginning nor the end of her life story. But they do offer a glimpse into what seem to be profound and elementary characteristics of the femicide phenomenon, to the point of being its most common denominators: Its domestic nature; its gendered social and physical power asymmetry; the alarming fact that all too often, when women are spared from femicide, they are saved by mere trivial, incidental chance; and its ingrained bitterness, entrenched in the fact that in some way or another, the women's children, even when they do not become orphans due to femicide, are doomed to be fully immersed in eternal, ever-tormenting and tragic victimhood.

Femicide takes various shapes, forms, and manifestations. Each femicide pattern embodies different particularities, yet all forms share the same sad, heartbreaking outcome. Not all women are as lucky as Andi's mother, who was, to use the well-known phrase in a femicide context, figuratively and literally "saved by the bell." Some underlying elements of femicide are the same and worthy of being studied and understood. How many women survive femicide? How did they manage to survive? How many times and in what ways were they almost killed? How many of those women were ultimately killed? And if they miraculously survived, were they able to feel safe again anywhere?

Additional puzzling questions pertain to children and femicide. Where were the women's children during the recurrent killing attempts or final executed killing? Were they locked in a separate room where they could hear and imagine the horrors of their mother being slaughtered? And what if they were at the scene as their mother's killing unfolded, yet did not manage to save her? How do such events affect these femicide orphans? What does it mean for a child to keep engaging with their killer father, who is all too often also an abusive father? Do they ever feel they are, at least genetically and biologically, the descendants of a killer? How does such a realization affect their self-identity, self-esteem, and self-image? Do these kids share with anyone their tragic stories of being femicide victims?

Many more questions pertain to the long-term effects of such a phenomenon. Do women and children of failed attempts ever recover? How do these experiences affect the intergenerational relations between the femicide-surviving mother and her children? What about intragenerational relations among the surviving siblings? Do such women and children share their heartbreaking and gloomy experiences with anyone? What are the long-term effects of such bitter experiences? How do such horrifying sights affect children's ability to trust others? How do such experiences affect children's ability to choose for themselves, in due time, a non-abusive intimate partner? Are they ever able to be intimate with someone? Do they trust this world, at least enough to raise children of their own? Do such children and femicide survivors manage to sleep at night? Or do horrifying sights, sounds, and smells taunt them every night? Are we talking about a multilayered, vicarious and complex traumatic phenomenon that afflicts a tremendous number of people? Could we be talking, in fact, of a transgenerational phenomenon that affects huge numbers of people and lingers for decades and generations?

These and many more questions await future rigorous and comprehensive victimological studies. This book does not, and cannot, address them all. It offers a crimino-legal glimpse into various aspects of this sad, dreadful phenomenon, with the goal of demonstrating that despite taking Israel as a case study, femicide and its many awful ramifications share global similarities and are, lamentably, all too common throughout the world.

Hava (Andi) Dayan
Israel, 2022

Part I

An Overview of Femicide

1 A Theoretical Overview of Femicide

Introduction

The phenomenon of femicide cuts across cultures, time and societies. Criminologically speaking, femicide is conceptually situated in the broader perspective of violence against women. Such violence is a form of gendered violence, targeted at women or girls.[1] The phenomenon of violence against women is perceived to be part of a larger social phenomenon of male patriarchal dominance achieved and maintained through coercive control.[2] Such violence may take various forms (physical, visual, verbal, emotional, economic, political or mental), and may occur at various stages of a woman's life cycle. Violence against women may take place in different spheres of life (at home, at work and in the social arena) and may be embedded in and performed through various social spheres (political, legal, racial, religious, ethnic and cultural). The nature of the violence itself may have varying degrees, forming a continuum with nonphysical harassment at one end and fatal assault at the other.[3] The violence may be explicit, formal, and organized but also discrete, sporadic, and covert. While recognizing that violence against women is a multifaceted and complex issue, this book limits the scope of its discussion to a particular subtype of gender violence: Femicide. Femicide (or feminicide) is a homicidal form of violence targeted at women and expressed through their actual killing. The socio-criminological definition of this homicidal form refers to the act of killing a woman or girl because of her gender.[4] It is the major cause of unnatural death of women globally and the seventh leading cause of premature death for women globally.[5] Like the larger gendered violence stratagem to which it belongs, femicide spans the woman's life cycle. Women are persecuted from womb to dirt: Female fetuses are the target of intended abortions due to the pursuit of male offsprings, female infants and children are murdered due to

1 Radford and Russell, 1992: p. 10.
2 Ibid, p. 4.
3 Ibid, pp. 3–4, for a description of the notion of a continuum of violence against women.
4 Ibid, p. 3.
5 Campbell et al., 2003; Weil, 2015, 2016: p. 7.

DOI: 10.4324/9781003333272-2

being sexually abused, and adult women are murdered mainly through domestic violence at the hands of their current or former intimate partners.[6]

Women are usually not murdered by women. Most often, they are murdered by men. The men who kill women are only rarely strangers. Women are typically murdered either by their intimate former or current partner or other male family members, as in cases of Arab women femicide. Indeed, scholars agree that the socio-criminological features of femicide are distinct from other forms of homicide and deserve a gender-specific framework of analysis.[7] For example, as opposed to the common thread of homicide, whereby the victim is killed at the hands of a stranger, women are significantly more likely to be killed by an intimate partner or close family member and frequently in the context of a continuing abusive relationship.[8] Patterns relating to the murder of women display empirical proximity to the family arena: The women are primarily murdered in the framework of "their family"; i.e., by their partners, usually "after lengthy periods of prolonged physical violence accompanied by other forms of abuse and coercion."[9] Men, on the other hand, are most likely to be killed by strangers or acquaintances.[10] Neither can it be equated with the homicide phenomenon of "honor" killings, because femicide targets women because of their gender whereas "honor" killings encompass a wider range of family killings, male killings included.[11] Femicide is also different than other forms of gender-based violence: Whereas prevalent domestic violence motives and victims suggest that this is a controlling strategy targeted at both women and children, femicide is often the result of deliberate action intended to bring about ruin for the woman and more specifically, her death.[12]

The average number of femicides in Israel is about 25 women per year.[13] In other words, a woman is killed in Israel almost every two weeks.[14] However, the actual number of victims related to this phenomenon is much higher. The actual victims of femicide are not restricted to the officially reported number of women being killed. To the numbers of the women killed (as primary victims), we should add at the very least two kinds of secondary victims: The victim's children (in 40% of these killings, they are present at the murder scene, either watching or being injured or killed by the perpetrator);[15] and the perpetrators themselves, who in about 20% of the killings commit suicide in conjunction with and pursuant to

6 Laurent et al., 2013: p. 4.
7 Landau and Hattis-Rolef, 1998: p. 76; Taylor and Jasinski, 2011: p. 342.
8 Smith and Brewer, 1995: p. 176.
9 Dobash et al., 1992: p. 81.
10 Rosenfeld, 1997.
11 Kressel, 1981: pp. 145–146.
12 Ben Ze'ev and Goussinsky, 2008: pp. 197, 208–211.
13 Dayan et al., 2022.
14 Excluding femicide cases in Gaza, West Bank, and East Jerusalem.
15 Dobash and Dobash, 2012: pp. 662–667.

the killing.[16] To these secondary victims, we should add the victim's extended family (parents and siblings), the victim's close friends, her new intimate partner, bystanders, and society at large.[17]

The Crimino-Legal "Emergence" of Femicide

Femicide has gained growing global notice in recent years, alongside efforts toward its eradication.[18] Alarmed by the fact that femicide was increasing throughout the world, the Academic Council of the United Nations held symposiums in 2012, urging member states to undertake steps to prevent femicide.[19] The United Nations Vienna Declaration on Femicide, in conjunction with the Commission on Crime Prevention and Criminal Justice (in 2012), refers to various modes of killing of women in different social, political, cultural, and religious circumstances. According to the declaration, these practices can take the form of, inter alia: (a) Murder of women as a result of intimate partner violence; (b) torture and misogynistic slaying of women; (c) killing of women and girls in the name of "honor"; (d) targeted killing of women and girls in the context of armed conflict; (e) dowry-related killings of women; (f) killing of women and girls because of their sexual orientation and gender identity; (g) killing of Aboriginal and Indigenous women and girls because of their gender; (h) female infanticide and gender-based sex-selection feticide; (i) genital-mutilation-related deaths; (j) killings related to accusations of witchcraft; and (k) other types of femicide connected with gangs, organized crime, drug dealing, human trafficking, and the proliferation of small arms.[20] Different types of femicide reflect the threat to women's lives throughout their life span. They include female feticide (the killing of female fetuses), female infanticide (the killing of female infants), uxoricide (the killing of spouses), sororicide (the killing of sisters), and matricide (the killing of the female parent).

The term *femicide* was first coined by Russell and introduced in a book she wrote with Radford and published in 1992. In their seminal book, femicide is defined as the misogynous killing of women by men[21] that takes many different forms shaped and changed by culture and context.[22] Russell and Radford argued that these diverse forms may refer to racist femicide, homophobic femicide, lesbicide, marital femicide, femicide perpetrated by strangers, serial femicide, mass

16 Dayan, 2021.
17 See, for example, Connolly and Gordon, 2015.
18 Corradi et al., 2016.
19 Corradi et al., 2016: p. 983.
20 Laurent et al., 2013: p. 4.
21 Radford and Russell, 1992. Russell emphasized the idea that men commit femicide with sexist motives, and she chose to replace the word *woman* with *female* to show that girls and infants can also be victims of femicide. See, generally, Russell and Harmes, 2001: pp. 13–14; Russell, 1990: pp. 104–108.
22 Radford and Russell, 1992: p. 7.

femicide, and the deliberate transmission of AIDS that results in death. Radford preferred an expansive definition of femicide, one that does not refer exclusively to intentional killing of women, but rather "situations in which women are permitted to die as a result of misogynous attitudes or social practices."[23] She mentioned a broad spectrum of practices embedded in patriarchal gender-based violence: The death of women and girls resulting from botched abortions, unnecessary surgery on women and misogynous neglect or starvation of female infants and women.[24] According to Russell, femicide is the end result of various forms of terror against females that result in death:

> Femicide is on the extreme end of a continuum of anti-female terror that includes a wide variety of verbal and physical abuse, such as rape, torture, sexual slavery (particularly in prostitution), incestuous and extra familial child sexual abuse, physical and emotional battery, sexual harassment (on the phone, in the streets, at the office, and in the classroom), genital mutilation (clitoridectomies, excision, infibulations), unnecessary gynecological operations (gratuitous hysterectomies), forced heterosexuality, forced sterilization, forced motherhood (by criminalizing contraception and abortion), psychosurgery, denial of food to women in some cultures, cosmetic surgery, and other mutilations in the name of beautification. Whenever these forms of terrorism result in death, they become femicides.[25]

Femicide as a concept and term was promoted as an alternative to the gender-neutral term *homicide* to highlight the killing of women primarily for the reason of being women. According to Radford and Russell, the term *femicide* had a political purpose, intended to alter the prevailing understanding of the violent death of women. They argued that naming the phenomenon "gives women's experiences and understandings priority over men's intentions and as such is consistent with one of the basic tenets of feminism – women's right to name their experience."[26] Thus, the coining of this term for the phenomenon was part of feminist action and theory to find, create, and redefine words that reflect and record women's experiences in general and violence against them in particular. It was the feminist notion that "names provide social definitions; make visible what is invisible; define as unacceptable what was accepted; make sayable what was unspeakable"[27] that spurred the intentional coining of the term and naming of the phenomenon.

The naming of femicide was, of course, declarative and not constitutive. Women were killed long before the phenomenon was named and delineated.

23 Op. cit.
24 Op. cit.
25 Russell, 2011.
26 Radford and Russell, 1992: p. 3.
27 Kelly and Radford, 1996: pp. 19–20.

However, the gender-neutral term *homicide* lacked the gender-sensitive element of terminology crucially needed for the realistic and fact-based description of particular gender-based fatally violent events. The new term for the old phenomenon of women killing aimed to reconceptualize the homicide phenomenon and reconstruct women's social experience by voicing what was until then unvoiced: The recognition that the violent death of women is a crime in and of itself, not to be confused with gender-neutral homicidal crimes termed *homicide*, *killing*, *murder*, or *manslaughter*.[28]

The term *femicide* was not only coined for the sake of describing reality as such. Reframing the term as a social and political problem had a constructivist purpose.[29] It aimed to reconstruct a social reality as emanating from patriarchy, using a gender-sensitive perspective. The practice of naming and renaming this gender-based violent social phenomenon was part of a larger feminist goal and practice from the 1970s onwards, aimed at revealing the nurtured nature of it while mobilizing society and producing social change by raising awareness and making visible something that up to then had been invisible. According to Radford and Russell, it was vital to begin by coining the term, because "naming an injustice, and thereby providing a means of thinking about it, usually precedes the creation of a movement against it."[30] Thus, the term *femicide* also had a political purpose, to ignite a process that would eventually transform the social order that had legitimized or tolerated gender-based killings at that time. In Radford and Russell's words, "by going beyond an academic discussion of the evidence, by making the fight against femicide a major theme of this anthology, we hope it will play a strategic role in consolidating feminist resistance to femicide."[31] According to Corradi et al., "the groundbreaking contribution of Radford and Russell in coining the term was to emphasize that homicide deletes from the sociological eye that special, gender-based evidence of woman-killing, which is different from the murder of men," and to reframe it as a unique social and political problem.[32]

Whereas Radford and Russell's naming of femicide enabled its criminological characterization and sociological politization, Catherine MacKinnon's legal framing of femicide underlined its compelling normative account. MacKinnon's work tremendously influenced the legal understanding of gender-based violence against women, given her emphasis on women's suffering and experience of hurt, mainly in relation to feminine life experiences such as sexual harassment, rape, pornography, and prostitution. MacKinnon based her work on Marxist theory, adapting its basic ideas to the gender-relations experience. Arguing that "sex is for women what work is for the Marxist theory," she conceptualized women's

28 Corradi et al., 2016: p. 977.

29 Ibid, p. 978.

30 Radford and Russell, 1992: p. xiv.

31 Radford and Russell, 1992: p. 7.

32 Corradi et al., 2016: p. 978.

sexuality and autonomy as capital belonging to women, confiscated from them by men, who use it to gain control over women for their own enjoyment.[33] These exploitative relations persist through the coerced and violent commodification of women's sexuality and the subjugation of their autonomy to men's desires, as phenomena such as rape and pornography reflect.[34] This theory is particularly illuminating with regard to femicide committed by men against their intimate female partners (past or present), acting on the notion of their right to dominate and control their female spouse. Male perpetrators who commit femicide express their dominance in the ultimate manner, whereby the pure existence of the female partner is dependent on the man's will and decision, allowing her no sense of agency whatsoever.[35] Femicide is the epitomized form of MacKinnon's dominance theory: Intimate-partner femicides usually occur when the man concludes that he is losing his power to dominate and control what he sees as his possession – namely, when the woman threatens or attempts to leave the relationship.[36] The killing is normally preceded by growing acts of violence aimed at physically establishing dominance and that eventually allow the men to exercise dominance to the fullest.

MacKinnon's monumental work, alongside other prominent feminist theories,[37] serves to warn us against evaluating society's gendered lives and deaths as neutral. She pointed to women's subjugation to male dominance, rendering them more prone, susceptible, and vulnerable to harm induced by gender-based violence. Her work illuminates the fact that femicide by intimate partners is likely to resemble this oppressive framework, without needing to behave in an exceptional manner normally expected from "regular" criminals. This realization resonates with characteristics identified in intimate-partner femicide perpetrators: They are much more ordinary people than "regular" man-murdering perpetrators. Namely, they are not people who hold a history of violence. Normally, they are not involved in further criminal activity, except for domestic violence, and they are less likely to come from a background of poverty, family dysfunctionality, drug and alcohol abuse or addiction.[38] This oppressive vulnerability framework led MacKinnon to question the law's basic commitment to women's lives, by sincerely asking: "Are women human?"[39] Her provocatively put question resonates the neglect of the law to protect women against different forms of femicide, although they violate basic human rights regularly protected under both national and international law. Her account of this legal neglect has been furthered by her more recent observation that violence against women is a form of terrorism. Analyzing the new and

33 MacKinnon, 1983.
34 MacKinnon, 1979; MacKinnon & Dworkin, 1997.
35 Adams, 2007; Goussinsky and Yassour-Borochowitz, 2012.
36 Farr, 2002: p. 268; Messerschmidt, 2017.
37 For other feminist works underpinning the feminist approach to femicide, see Corradi et al., 2016: pp. 5–6.
38 Dobash et al., 2004.
39 MacKinnon, 2006.

transformative legal order structured by the international community to eradicate terrorism, MacKinnon advocated the need to equally fight against the terror of gender-based violence. The post-9/11 international shift proved the flexibility of the law in fighting terrorism, empowering governments to entertain extreme legal measurements to prevent and eliminate it. This international solidarity stood in sharp contrast to the unwillingness to apply comparably effective legal tools in waging the fight against gender-based violence or even femicide. Arguing for independent international intervention to protect women's rights, MacKinnon demanded to incorporate a gendered point of view on international law to render gender-based violence a violation of international law's corpus on human rights.

Drawing on her lifelong legacy, this book introduces innovative ways to realize MacKinnon's vision of gender equality: (a) To exercise it as a substantive imperative rather than as a formal pledge and (b) to ensure those derogating women's lives are held accountable.[40] Utilizing both legal and criminological analytic tools, our work acknowledges women's vulnerability to femicide as emanating from the patriarchal order and shapes crimino-legal means aimed at alleviating the discriminatory effect of this vulnerability, even if postmortem.

The Roadmap to the Book

Notwithstanding the different backgrounds and motivations related to femicide, this book focuses on the main form of femicide prevailing in Israel and other societies worldwide: The criminal homicide of an adult woman by a family member, most often but not exclusively her intimate partner. The book presents femicide's various socio-criminological aspects relevant to a broad range of such acts: Intimate-partner femicide (killing by spousal and non-spousal female intimate partners); "honor" killing (killing of women on account of family "honor"); femicide–suicide (killing of women followed by the immediate suicide of the killer); concealed femicide (killing of women staged as a noncriminal death); femicide secondary victims (victim's parents and offspring); and aspects of the state's role and liability regarding femicide phenomenon and victims.

The various aspects characterizing femicide are explored using an interdisciplinary framework of analysis that considers criminological and legal perspectives, along social-theory lines. Interestingly, the conceptual proximity between the legal discipline and the discipline of criminology may cause one to perceive them as redundant to each other, which might explain the dullness of such interdisciplinary pursuit. In this book, however, the distinctiveness of each discipline nourishes the other. The criminological account provides the detailed analyses of the elements that femicide is comprised of. It seeks to identify the structural, systemic and peculiar characteristics that warrant femicide a crime of special importance to society. It further provides the analytical context upon which the notion of femicide can and should be differentiated from other types of lethal violence. The

40 MacKinnon, 1983.

legal account of the book, on the other hand, provides the implications for legal liability and accountability that the criminological features of femicide delineate. Consequently, legal analyses of femicide presented in the book are informed by the criminological notion of femicide being a crime of distinctive nature and serve to criticize the limits of existing legal tools to fight femicide. The book further exhibits a combined empirical and theoretical account of femicide, utilizing both criminological analysis of femicide and critical analyses of its various legal aspects. This multilayered exploration of femicide, though focusing on Israel as its case study using relevant case law and legislation, offers observations and accounts of femicide that are generalizable to the phenomenon worldwide.

The book is composed of three main parts, each representing its interdisciplinary-rich composition. Methodologically, it employs qualitative and quantitative research methods alongside critical theoretical analysis. Regarding content, it employs multidisciplinary and interdisciplinary views, primarily criminological and legal and always social. The first introductory part provides a theoretical and empirical overview of femicide in general and in Israel in particular. Utilizing a methodological review of related empirical evidence, the second part of the book analyzes primary criminological aspects of two prevalent femicide subtypes in Israel – "honor" killing and femicide-suicide. Additionally, this part utilizes a crimino-legal analysis to critically reflect on the usage of the "reasonable-man" legal doctrine to reduce criminal liability from murder to manslaughter in intimate-partner femicide subtypes and to introduce a much less common and less recognized subtype of femicide: Concealed femicide. Given the scarce research regarding this last subtype, it is analyzed using mainly quantitative tools. The third part of the book offers a critical analysis of the legal structure underlying femicide, problematizing its dire yet almost un-researched implications, mainly concerning secondary victims of femicide in the nuclear and extended family, and the role of legal apparatuses other than the criminal system in eradicating the phenomenon. The roadmap to the chapters in the book's three parts is hereby laid out.

Part I of the book is composed of two chapters, with the current chapter being the first in the book, introducing the theoretical overview of the phenomenon and a basic overview of femicide's subtypes. This chapter is followed by Chapter 2, which offers an empirical overview of the phenomenon nurtured by observations and insights on criminological characteristics of femicide in Israel. The empirical chapter draws on current scholarly interest in seeking possible links among social, cultural, and ethnic characteristics that shape the killing of women as a social construct. This quest is ingrained in the criminological account of cultural as well as socio-structural factors such as race, ethnicity, and religion that shape the differences in rates and modes of violence, rendering some crimes more prevalent in some sectors of the population than in others,[41] and femicide

41 Landau, 1984.

is no exception.[42] The fact that femicide rates vary across regions and that cross-national variations have been reported widely suggests plausible links between femicide and sociocultural aspects, which calls for further inquiry, particularly given the dull body of studies in this peculiar field.[43]

Chapter 2, thus, relates to a major methodological problem in the study of femicide. Many femicide scholars have recently delved into the understanding of the phenomenon, contributing to the identification and exploration of various related aspects and patterns of the perpetrators, victims, and modus operandi. However, because most studies on femicide were conducted in Western populations, the generalizability of various noted observations are questionable regarding non-Western societies in general and Israel in particular.[44] The empirical and theoretical shortcoming of femicide studies' overreliance on Western populations should be addressed by studies in non-Western societies in general and among ethnic minorities in particular.

Israel is a suitable society to analyze non-Western femicide patterns not only because of its Middle Eastern qualities, but also because it is a hub for various distinct ethnic minorities: Israel-born Jews, Ethiopian-immigrant Jews, immigrant Jews from former USSR, and Arabs. In this respect, the research questions are tailored according to the victims' ethnic background and are likely to lead to a more nuanced and complex understanding of different patterns of femicide. For example, though many researchers on femicide of Arab women have collected and analyzed primary socio-criminological characteristics of such killings on victims – perpetrator relations, age, marital status, weapon and motives – empirical comparative analyses of femicide among different social groups are still direly needed. Such empirical comparative analysis would contribute to the understanding of sociocultural aspects of femicide and analysis, and this chapter endeavors to do so. To take yet another example, femicide among Ethiopian-immigrant Jews can teach us about non-Western characteristics of femicide. Indeed, the study of femicide among diverse cultural groups is crucial to its comprehensive understanding: Although Ethiopian-immigrant Jews make up only 2% of the population in Israel, they account for 37% of all femicide–suicide cases.[45] Studying such unique femicide characteristics should stimulate distinct questions that aim to unravel the particular Ethiopian sociocultural aspects of femicide vis-à-vis cultural notions and other possible social factors related to their immigrant social class and status. In presenting the femicide phenomenon in a sociocultural-sensitive framework of analysis and context, the chapter offers empirical nation-based observations on femicide in Israel, outlining the main characteristics of femicide relating to common Israeli perpetrators, victims and modus operandi.

42 Landau and Hattis-Rolef, 1998: p. 82; Sela-Shayovitz, 2010: p. 1425.
43 Corradi and Stöckl, 2014; Weil, 2016: p. 7.
44 Taylor and Jasinski, 2011: p. 347; Weil, 2016: p. 7.
45 Dayan, 2021.

Part II of the book presents theoretical and empirical aspects of common femicide subtypes in Israel and many other countries. It opens with Chapter 3, presenting a crimino-legal analysis that critically addresses the most common form of femicide in Israel: The killing of women by their current or former intimate partner. In doing so, this chapter deals with the chauvinist sociocultural perceptions nurturing the Israeli legal system's usage of the legal doctrine of provocation, which is statutorily entrenched in the country as a British criminal common-law transplant. The chapter discusses the sociocultural underpinnings of the doctrine by Israeli defendants who claim to have killed their wives while being provoked. Using case-law analysis, the chapter critically deconstructs Israeli femicide case law dealing with the British doctrine of provocation by problematizing its resonation with Jewish religious law that relates to gendered claims about the victims' infidelity and the killers' reasonably ensuing provocation and loss of control. Conceptualizing the critical deconstruction in gendered sociocultural predispositions, the chapter demonstrates how Israeli social norms, attitudes and beliefs toward sexual jealousy, matrimony, loss of control, morality, gender and homicide are entangled and intertwined in the structure and function of Jewish religious convictions, adapted as to affect Israeli criminal law. The chapter offers a critical analysis of the underlying discriminatory gendered basic assumptions that structure current application of the doctrine of provocation. It illuminates how such a socio-legal structure constitutes the Israeli "unfaithful" woman, shaping her corresponding killer as "reasonable" and "normative," so to speak. In post-separation intimate-partner femicide cases, the legal threshold of the reasonable sexually jealous male who loses control defines gendered norms that may border on normalizing such violence.

The chapter presents the only two femicide cases where a provocation claim was ever accepted in Israel. These cases show that sociocultural underpinnings of the concept of the Jewish Israeli "reasonable man" are entrenched in its legal conceptualization, and reveal a deeply rooted patriarchal male chauvinist norm. It normalizes violent possessive men by constructing them as reasonable and normative – and taints married women's resolution to terminate their intimate relationships with their would-be killers as provoking adultery.[46] Put simply, men are considered less morally guilty when they kill "unfaithful" women, as they are awarded lenient convictions and sentences for these killings compared to "regular" killings, where invoking the provocation excuse was never allowed by courts. At the same time, Israeli women are being blamed for morally instigating and provoking their own killing – thus, precipitating their gruesome, premature and undue death. In line with the Israeli legal doctrine requiring a normative, prescriptive, and objective standard of reasonableness, as well as the Supreme Court's rulings mitigating the aforementioned defendants' murder convictions,

46 Howe, 2004; Miller, 2010.

killers of former intimate partners are construed, sociologically, judicially and morally, as "reasonable (wife) killers."[47]

The second chapter of the book's Part II, Chapter 4, offers theoretical and empirical observations on femicide associated mainly with Israel's Arab community, a femicide subtype known for its linkage with the wider criminological phenomenon of "honor" killing. In the literature, femicide of Arab women is usually termed "honor" killing and regarded as a particular form of "honor" violence against women, wherein the killing of a woman is perpetrated by a member or members of her family disapproving of her social behavior in general and her sexual behavior in particular.[48] Scholars agree that key characteristics of F.H.K. relate to its familial, collective, and "honor"-related nature.[49] Although "honor" killings may be associated with the larger perception of honor as dominating Arab culture in general – hence, applicable to men and women alike – a particular gender-specific notion of "honor" – the Arabic term *'ird* – targets mainly women and seems to intersect with the larger phenomenon of femicide. Female "honor"-related 'ird refers to the women's sexual purity and chastity[50] and is an ascribed passive status[51] that can only be lost by the misconduct of an individual woman, allegedly staining the collective identity and social status of the family.[52] Though 'ird's gain or loss is a collective possession that affects the "honor" of the whole family unit,[53] it appears to be a personal possession, and each woman is strictly held responsible for her "honorable" corresponding behavior, affecting the larger family's "honor."[54] Taken with the central social importance of the family unit to the cultural organization of Arab society, female 'ird can be seen as a major gendered controlling mechanism.[55] By presenting current empirical criminological shifts in F.H.K. patterns regarding weapon of choice, the perpetrator's identity, alleged motives for killing, and the link to gender-based violence, the chapter focuses on the scholarly need to gain a better understanding of the boundaries of the intersections between F.H.K. and the four domains: Intimate-partner femicide, gender-based violence, domestic violence, and "honor" violence.

Keeping the book's second part's focus on femicide subtypes, Chapter 5 introduces the idiosyncratic form of femicide–suicide, a phenomenon accounting for the vast majority of homicide–suicide cases and a considerable share of femicide

47 Dayan, 2021; Spatz, 1991.
48 Abu-Rabia, 2011; Hassan, 2006; Shalhoub-Kevorkian, 1999, 2002.
49 Abu-Odeh, 1997; Chesler, 2010.
50 Awwad, 2001: p. 41.
51 Hasan, 2002: p. 6.
52 Hasan pointed to the absurdity of the social power matrix wherein "the passive woman, thought to be inferior in status, holds within her body the public worth of all her male relatives, worth which she can directly damage and diminish, but which she cannot augment" (Hasan, 2002: p. 7).
53 In the Arab social structure, this includes not only the nuclear and extended family, but also the super-extended family clan lines called *hamula*; see Pely, 2011: p. 211.
54 Dodd, 1973: pp. 40–41.
55 Dodd, 1973: p. 40.

cases, particularly those relating to intimate-partner femicide. It explores the theoretical and empirical characteristics underlying this subtype of femicide as a peculiar form of murder followed by a suicide of the murderer. Though the femicide–suicide phenomenon cuts across regions and societies, there is a dearth of studies on its patterns, motives and characteristics in non-Western populations. Most empirical observations are based on studies conducted in Western societies and are oblivious to different cultural settings. As Adinkrah indicated, very few studies have been conducted in non-Western societies, and our understanding of sociocultural patterns and variations of homicide–suicide is still in dire need of research.[56] This chapter, therefore, answers the imperative to further explore the overlap of the phenomenon with socio-structural circumstances and ethnic minorities, including immigrant ethnic minorities. Exploring empirical data from Israel and analyzing the sociodemographic and criminological characteristics of such killings, the chapter suggests that the distribution of the phenomenon varies across immigrant ethnic minority groups in the country. Furthermore, characteristics of the phenomenon among immigrant Jews exhibit similarities to patterns of femicide–suicide reported in other non-Western societies.

Committed to identifying less-acknowledged femicide subtypes, Chapter 6 offers a perspective on what is termed concealed femicide and is composed of cases that bear more elusive and inconclusive characteristics. This chapter offers an explorative analysis of Israeli femicide cases that have been concealed through homicide-scene staging, namely "concealed femicide."[57] Seeking to further examine this newly identified form of femicide, this chapter adds two layers to understanding this phenomenon. The first layer positions concealed femicide in a feminist theoretical framework, while the second discusses its evidentiary consequences.

Presenting cases in which Israeli women died under circumstances identified as elusive femicide, the chapter discusses overlooked femicide methods. Although femicide, as all other murders, can be concealed in various ways,[58] the chapter focuses on a rather sparsely analyzed means of concealment: Murder-scene staging in cases of intimate-partner femicide. Aspiring to shed more light on the peculiarity of concealing femicide, the chapter focuses on two primary characteristics of this phenomenon. First, it lays out this subtype's underpinning feminist theory. Emphasizing the vulnerability assigned to women's lives generated by gendered power relations, the analysis revisits the domesticity in which cases emerge as not only cultivating the male dominance brutally expressed in the femicide act, but also facilitating the concealment thereof. Second, the chapter concentrates on the evidentiary ramification that the domesticity of this subtype yields – the lack of direct evidence to prove the murder. The domestic circumstances of concealed-femicide cases lead prosecutors and judges to rely on circumstantial evidence as

56 Adinkrah, 2014: p. 365.
57 Bitton and Dayan, 2019.
58 Pettler, 2016.

the basis for convicting the intimate partner of the murder. Given the false yet well-entrenched perception of this type of evidence as inferior to direct evidence, this legal reliance inflicts on women a set of harms even in the process of revealing the true nature of their allegedly neutral death. This crimino-legal analysis of concealed-femicide cases broadens our understanding of both the prevalence of this subtype of femicide and the harmful consequences it holds for women beyond the obvious devastation of their demise.

Part III of the book, concentrating on femicide's secondary tier, offers an analysis of various victimo-legal aspects relating to issues positioned at the penumbra, rather than the core of femicide – namely, matters pertaining to the secondary-tier devastating effects of femicide. First are personas, the "secondary victims," introduced in the seventh chapter. Those victims who were not the main killer's target are barely considered as subjects of femicide research. Although secondary victims have not been physically injured during the femicide, these people nevertheless sustain a great deal of agonizing mental, emotional, economic, and social detrimental harms and difficulties as a result of the femicide. Second, and introduced in the eighth chapter, is a secondary substance matter that relates to the legal treatment of femicide. The fight against femicide is primarily waged by criminal law, yet it is seconded by tort law. Chapter 8 explores the contribution of this tort path to femicide victims and its importance to eradicating this phenomenon. This last part of the book illuminates such seemingly secondary issues that bear primary importance but remain in the shadows of scholarly research.

The first chapter in Part III, Chapter 7, introduces "secondary victims," who, unlike direct homicide victims, remain largely unknown to the public.[59] It reminds us that femicide produces two different types of victims: The woman who was directly murdered by the killing act and the people associated with her, or the "secondary victims." Secondary victims are usually the woman's children but can include other family members and friends who are left to cope with the trauma and aftermath of the murder. This chapter aims at shedding light on these secondary victims, because little information is available about the all-encompassing hurdles that they endure in addition to the fatal result of the crime. Children and the wider circle of secondary victims of femicide are forced to restructure family affairs and custodial matters; supervise the criminal proceedings to ensure that justice, however meager and postmortem, is done on behalf of the woman; seek compensation for their injuries; and more. Throughout these processes, they are fighting not only for their rights, but also for recognition of their idiosyncratic suffering, as the chapter reveals.

Chapter 8 presents the legal primacy of femicide and its supplement. Traditionally dominated by criminal law, femicide is perceived as a matter of, at most, public interest in harm and punishment, positioned away from the private realm of tort law and its compensatory role. This chapter challenges this common perception and uncovers the potential embedded in tort law to undertake both a

59 Costa et al., 2017: p. 3088.

compensatory and transformative role in waging the fight against femicide. Presenting the revolution tort law underwent in the last decades to protect women's needs, it demonstrates its aptitude to become instrumental in compensating women and their heirs for femicide and in holding accountable those enabling it. Given the strict nature of criminal law, tort law functions as a crucial, and at times sole, provider of justice to victims of femicide, even if this justice is meager and issued only ex post. Discussing the harmonious and disharmonious interplay between tort and criminal law regarding femicide, the chapter sheds light on the advantages and pitfalls of the growing utilization of tort law in femicide cases. Though second in line for legal exhaustion, tort law, as the chapter suggests, should categorically become a substantial tool in fighting femicide.

The book ends with a two-part ninth chapter dedicated to concluding remarks and presenting a meta-crimino-legal overview of the phenomenon. Based on the various criminological aspects discussed in this book, the chapter offers a crimino-legal model showing that femicide is "a crime of distinctive nature" by virtue of its intersection with various criminal phenomena and its multi-legal ramifications. This last chapter demonstrates the peculiar nature of femicide and accordingly focuses on two fronts: First, it establishes the criminological peculiarity of femicide as overlapping with many other criminal behaviors and acts; and second, it lays out guidelines for a holistic legal reform designed to answer the overarching implications of femicide based on recognizing it as "a crime of distinctive nature."

The first part of the last chapter offers a criminological meta-overview of the spatial positioning of femicide vis-à-vis other criminological phenomena. Reviewing the book's main chapters with the aim of positioning femicide, this part reveals that femicide crosses into no less than six other criminal phenomena: Homicide, "honor" crimes, domestic violence, intimate-partner homicide, homicide–suicide, and staged crimes. Of course, additional criminal intersections may exist, yet these six criminal intersections are the main ones found in adult femicide in Israel. These varied intersections are not new to the study of femicide, yet the exact contours and realms of intersections between femicide and these six criminal phenomena haven't been discussed in a holistic manner that renders femicide a crime of distinctive nature. Acknowledging the rather limited scope of our study, in the sense that we have chosen to focused on crimino-legal aspects of adult femicide alone, we try in the last chapter of the book to mark and delineate a detailed contour of adult femicide's intersections with these six criminal phenomena. In doing so, we describe the realms in which each of the criminal phenomena uniquely intersects with adult femicide, determining also the realms falling outside the scope of the intersection. We believe that such a mapping model better clarifies femicide and the particular ways in which it is, criminologically speaking, a multifaceted phenomenon of an idiosyncratic nature.

On the legal front, the second part of the last chapter extrapolates from the model's legal-analysis critical policy guidelines required for the promulgation of regulations aiming to eradicate femicide and reflect society's complete disapproval thereof. Our analytic point of departure stems from treating femicide as a crime of distinctive nature, not only by virtue of its criminological trait but also by virtue of its overarching legal implications. This idiosyncratic phenomenon, therefore, warrants specific legal rules and tools tailored to match its myriad peculiarities: The understanding of the risk factors for femicide victimization and perpetration in its penalty approach, implementation of investigative tools to ensure effective enforcement, attendance to the needs and necessities of the victim's family, and more. The law must be fashioned as reflecting the holistic approach with which legal mechanisms must address the multifaceted complexities of femicide.

Presenting femicide's peculiar characteristics and overarching implications, this book serves as a wakeup call stressing the imperative need to illuminate the want of relevance and effectiveness with which femicide is currently addressed in Israel as well as in many other democratic liberal legal systems.

To recapitulate, this book contributes to the fight against femicide by being among few of its kind in two main respects: First, it conducts a comprehensive criminological analysis of various femicide subtypes and their aspects that have rarely been analyzed and compiled into one expansive and encompassing treatise; and second, it offers a novel and interdisciplinary analysis of the phenomenon by examining both its criminological and legal aspects. Though utilizing primarily Israeli cases, the analyses of femicide presented in this book are of global relevance because this sad and tragic phenomenon in its main subtypes and underlying crimino-legal aspects are applicable, even if roughly, throughout the world. Furthermore, because the Israeli legal structure is deeply rooted in English common law, its substantive legal doctrines explored here are widely shared by many commonwealth countries around the globe and can serve as a fruitful ground for comparative analyses.

References

Abu-Odeh, L. (1997). Comparatively speaking: The '"honor"' of the 'East' and the 'passion' of the 'West.' *Utah Law Review*, *2*, 287–307.

Abu-Rabia, A. (2011). Family "honor" killings: Between custom and state law. *The Open Psychology Journal*, *4*, 34–44.

Adams, D. (2007). *Why do they kill? Men who murder their intimate partners*. Vanderbilt University Press.

Adinkrah, M. (2014). Homicide–suicide in Ghana: Perpetrators, victims, and incidence characteristics. *International Journal of Offender Therapy and Comparative Criminology*, *58*(3), 364–387.

Awwad, A. M. (2001). Gossip, scandal, shame and "honor" killings: A case for social constructionism and hegemonic discourse. *Social Thought and Research*, *24*, 39–52.

Ben Ze'ev, A., & Goussinsky, R. (2008). *In the name of love: Romantic ideology and its victims*. Oxford University Press.

Bitton, Y., & Dayan, H. (2019). "The perfect murder": An exploratory study of staged homicide scenes and concealed femicide. *The British Journal of Criminology*, *59*, 1054–1075.

Campbell, J. C., Webster, D., Koziol-Mclain, J., Block, C., Campbell, D., Curry, M. A., Gary, F., Glass, N., McFarlane, J., Sachs, C., Sharps, P., Ulrich, Y., Wilt, S. A.,

Manganello, J., Xu, X., Schollenberger, J., Frye, V., & Laughon, K. (2003). Risk factors for femicide in abusive relationships: Results from a multisite case control study. *American Public Health*, *93*(7), 1089–1097.

Chesler, P. (2010). Worldwide trends in "honor" killings. *Middle East Quarterly*, 3–11.

Connolly, J., & Gordon, R. (2015). Co-victims of homicide: A systematic review of the literature. *Trauma, Violence, & Abuse*, *16*(4), 494–505.

Corradi, C., Marcuello-Servos, C., Boira, S., & Weil, S. (2016). Theories of femicide and their significance for social research. *Current Sociology*, *64*(7), 967–974.

Corradi, C., & Stöckl, H. (2014). Intimate partner homicide in 10 European countries: Statistical data and policy development in a cross-national perspective. *European Journal of Criminology*, *11*(5), 601–618.

Costa, D. H., Njaine, K., & Schenker, M. (2017). Repercussions of homicide on victims' families: A literature review. *Ciência & Saúde Coletiva*, *22*(9), 3087–3097.

Dayan, H. (2021). Sociocultural aspects of femicide – suicide: The case of Israel. *Journal of Interpersonal Violence*, *16*(4), 494–505. https://doi.org.10.1177/0886260518792983

Dayan, H., Kugel, C., & Enosh, G. (2022). Sociocultural aspects of femicide: A population-based analysis. *Crime and Delinquency* (Forthcoming).

Dobash, R. E., Dobash, R. P., Cavanagh, K., & Lewis, R. (2004). Not an ordinary killer – Just an ordinary guy: When men murder an intimate woman partner. *Violence against Women*, *10*(6), 577–605.

Dobash, R. P., Dobash, E. R., Wilson, M., & Daly, M. (1992). The myth of sexual symmetry in marital violence. *Social Problems*, *39*(1), 71–91.

Dobash, R. P., & Dobash, R. E. (2012). Who died? The murder of collaterals related to intimate partner violence. *Violence against Women*, *18*(6), 662–671.

Dodd, P. C. (1973). Family "honor" and the forces of change in Arab society. *International Journal of Middle East Studies*, *4*, 40–54.

Farr, K. A. (2002). Battered women who were" being killed and survived it": Straight talk from survivors. *Violence and Victims*, *17*(3), 267–281.

Goussinsky, R., & Yassour-Borochowitz, D. (2012). "I killed her, but I never laid a finger on her" – A phenomenological difference between wife-killing and wife-battering. *Aggression and Violent Behavior*, *17*, 553–64.

Hasan, M. (2002). The politics of "honor": Patriarchy, the state and the murder of women in the name of family "honor". *Journal of Israel History*, *21*, 1–37.

Hassan, Y. (2006). Stove burning, acid throwing and "honor" killings. In K. D. Askin & D. M. Koenig (Eds.), *Women and international human rights law* (Vol. II, pp. 587–611). Transnational.

Howe, A. (2004). Provocation in crisis – Law's passion at the crossroads? New directions for feminist strategists. *The Australian Feminist Law Journal*, *21*, 53.

Kelly, L., & Radford, J. (1996). 'Nothing really happened': The invalidation of women's experiences of sexual violence. In M. Hester, L. Kelly, & J. Radford (Eds.), *Women, violence and male power*. Open University Press.

Kressel, G. M. (1981). Sororicide/filiacide: Homicide for family honour [and comments and reply]. *Current Anthropology*, *22*(2), 141–158.

Landau, S. (1984). Trends in violence and aggression: A cross-cultural analysis. *International Journal of Comparative Sociology*, *25*(3–4), 133–158.

Landau, S., & Hattis-Rolef, S. (1998). Intimate femicide in Israel: Temporal, social and motivational patterns. *European Journal on Criminal Policy and Research*, *6*, 75–90.

Laurent, C., Platzer, M., & Idomir, M. (Eds.). (2013). *Femicide: A global issue that demands action*. Academic Council on the United Nations System.

MacKinnon, C. A. (1979). *Sexual harassment of working women: A case of sex discrimination*. Yale University Press.

MacKinnon, C. A. (1983). Feminism, Marxism, method, and the state: Toward feminist jurisprudence. *Signs: Journal of Women in Culture and Society*, *8*(4), 635–658.

MacKinnon, C. A. (2006). *Are women human? And other international dialogues*. The Belknap Press of Harvard University.

MacKinnon, C. A., & Dworkin, A. (Eds.). (1997). *In harm's way: The pornography civil rights hearings*. Harvard University Press.

Messerschmidt, J. W. (2017). Masculinities and femicide. *Qualitative Sociology Review*, *13*(3), 70–79.

Miller, A. E. (2010). Inherent (gender) unreasonableness of the concept of reasonableness in the context of manslaughter committed in the heat of passion. *William & Mary Journal of Women and the Law*, *17*, 249.

Pely, D. (2011). When "honor" trumps basic needs: The role of "honor" in deadly disputes within Israel's Arab community. *Negotiation Journal*, *27*(2), 205–225.

Pettler, L. G. (2016). *Crime scene staging dynamics in homicide cases*. CRC Press.

Radford, J., & Russell, D. E. H. (Eds.). (1992). *The politics of woman killing*. Twayne.

Rosenfeld, R. (1997). Changing relationships between men and women. *Homicide Studies*, *1*, 72–83.

Russell, D. E. H. (1990). Femicide. In D. Russell & N. Van de Ven (Eds.), *Crimes against women: Proceedings of the international tribunal*. Russell.

Russell, D. E. H. (2011). *The origin and the importance of the term femicide*. www.dianaRussell.com/origin_of_femicide.html

Russell D. E. H., & Harmes, R. A. (Eds.). (2001). *Femicide in global perspective*. Teachers College Press.

Sela-Shayovitz, R. (2010). The role of ethnicity and context: Intimate femicide rates among social groups in Israeli society. *Violence against Women*, *16*, 1424–1436.

Shalhoub-Kevorkian, N. (1999). Law, politics, and violence against women: A case study of Palestinians in Israel. *Law and Policy*, *21*(2), 189–211.

Shalhoub-Kevorkian, N. (2002). Femicide and the Palestinian criminal justice system: Seeds of change in the context of state building? *Law and Society Review*, *36*(3), 577–606.

Smith, M. D., & Brewer, V. E. (1995). Female status and the "gender gap" in U.S. homicide victimization. *Violence against Women*, *1*, 339–350.

Spatz, M. (1991). A 'lesser' crime: A comparative study of legal defenses for men who kill their wives. *Columbia Journal of Law and Social Problems*, *24*, 597.

Taylor, R., & Jasinski, J. L. (2011). Femicide and the feminist perspective. *Homicide Studies*, *15*(4), 341–362.

Weil, S. (2015). Combating femicide in multiple ways: The cost actions IS1206 on 'femicide across Europe.' In *Femicide: Targeting of women in conflict: A global issue that demands action* (Vol. 3, pp. 139–141). ACUNS.

Weil, S. (2016). Failed femicides among migrant survivors. *Qualitative Sociology Review*, *7*(4), 6–21.

Weil, S., & Kouta, C. (2017). Femicide: A glance through qualitative. *Qualitative Sociology Review*, *13*(3), 7–12.

2 Empirical Criminological Insights on Femicide

Introduction

Having introduced the theoretical overview of the phenomenon and the basic overview of femicide's subtypes, this chapter offers an empirical overview of the phenomenon nurtured by observations and insights on the criminological characteristics of femicide in Israel.

The main framework of analysis in this chapter relates to femicide as a sociocultural phenomenon. Because cultural and sociostructural factors such as race, ethnicity and religion contribute to different rates and modes of violence that make crime more prevalent in some sectors of the population than in others,[1] femicide should therefore be no exception.[2] The fact that femicide rates vary across regions and that cross-national variations have been reported widely suggest plausible links between femicide and sociocultural aspects.[3] However, there is a lack of studies that focused on possible links between cultural, ethnic, and social background and the killings of women.[4]

Social aspects that were empirically noted regarding higher rates of femicide relate to immigration, poverty and ethnicity: Immigration has been linked to higher rates of femicide, linking social strain theories to the tendency of immigrants to resort to femicide when facing social constraints regarding assimilation in society and employment.[5] Also, poverty has been noted as a social factor influencing higher rates of femicide,[6] Islamic religion has been noted as a social factor linked to higher rates of femicide,[7] and variations in the rates of femicide were noted across various ethnic-minority groups. For example, substantial higher

1 Landau, 1984.
2 Landau and Hattis-Rolef, 1998: p. 82; Sela-Shayovitz, 2010: p. 1425.
3 Corradi and Stöckl, 2014.
4 Weil, 2016: p. 7.
5 Dayan, 2021; Landau and Hattis-Rolef, 1998; Sela-Shayovitz, 2010; Wallace, 1986; Weil, 2016.
6 Dayan, 2021; Della Giustina, 2010: pp. 125–126.
7 Chesler, 2010.

DOI: 10.4324/9781003333272-3

rates of femicide were found among African Americans across the United States,[8] Arabs across the Israeli population,[9] and Arab Bedouins across Arabs in Israel.[10]

A review of femicide studies conducted in Israel revealed that previous studies conducted with the entire population in Israel[11] concentrated on intimate-partner femicide, excluding femicide occurring in non-intimate relationships ("honor" killings, for example) and the killing of women who do not have an intimate relationship (single women, older widowed women, and foreign workers, for example). Studies that included all women killings in Israel were carried out only in the Arab population in Israel and did not extend to the Jewish population.[12] Even a comparative analysis between the two main ethnic groups in Israel, Jews and Arabs, was carried out only regarding a subtype of femicide – intimate-partner femicide[13] – leaving a gap in comprehensive and comparative research on various types of femicide across the two main social groups in Israel: The Jewish and Arab populations.

This chapter, thus, follows the scholarly quest to delve into the sociocultural and criminological variations and manifestations of femicide via population-based analysis, using Israel as a case study. In doing so, this chapter presents descriptive analysis of possible differences among femicide manifestations across various social groups in Israel.

Social and Ethnic Groups in Israel

The total population in Israel (excluding the West Bank, Gaza, and East Jerusalem) features 8.6 million people.[14] The main ethnic division in Israel is between the Jewish majority (78% of the population) and the non-Jewish minority, mostly Arabs of Muslim religion (20% of the population).[15] Israel was established as a homeland for the Jewish people and is often referred to as the Jewish State, whereby its social identity is widely considered an amalgam of national, ethnic, and religious identities with a shared history and cultural tradition defined also in religious terms.[16]

Nearly half of all Israeli Jews are descended from Jews who immigrated from Europe, whereas around the same number is descended from Jews who immigrated from Arab countries, including Iran, Turkey, and Central Asia.[17] National

8 Campbell et al., 2003; Della Giustina, 2010.
9 Landau and Hattis-Rolef, 1998; Sela-Shayovitz, 2010.
10 Dayan, 2021.
11 See Landau and Hattis-Rolef, 1998; Sela-Shayovitz, 2010. Shalhoub-Kevorkian (2002) conducted empirical research on FHK in the Arab population in territories often referred as Palestine – Gaza and the West Bank – territories that are excluded from this research.
12 Such as Edelstein, 2011; Kressel, 1981; Touma-Sliman, 2005.
13 See Landau and Hattis-Rolef, 1998; Sela-Shayovitz, 2010.
14 Israel Central Bureau of Statistics, 2016.
15 Israel Central Bureau of Statistics, 2016.
16 Waxman, 2006: p. 15.
17 Israel Central Bureau of Statistics, 2005.

military service is mandatory for any Jewish Israeli older than 18, but because many ultra-Orthodox Jews are exempted, the secular Jewish population is currently the only population group in Israel that has a mandatory military conscription for both men and women. Israel's Jewish population is a relatively highly educated social group, with almost half of all Israeli Jews holding postsecondary degrees.[18] In recent years, the Israeli high-tech industry has grown rapidly. The number of persons employed in industry in Israel continues to grow, with more than 25% of the industrial workforce employed in high-tech manufacturing.[19] These two social trends of high-level education and a high-tech industrial workforce have led to the ranking of Jews in the mid-upper sociodemographic stratum of Israeli society.[20]

From the 1990s onward, the Israeli Jewish population has been composed of three main social groups: Veteran (native-born) Israeli Jews and two groups of immigrants that arrived in Israel in two major immigration waves in the 1990s – immigrants from the former Soviet Union and immigrants from Ethiopia. Jewish immigrants from the former USSR comprise about 10% of the total population in Israel. Of the immigrants who arrived between 1989 and 1990, 60% were college-educated, many of them as engineers and doctors.[21] Upon arrival, many former USSR immigrants, including highly educated and skilled professionals, took menial and semiskilled jobs and lived in poverty, making about 60% of them rank among the poorest third of the Israeli population. High levels of personal and family distress and low-income crises were noted in the first years of their social adjustment.[22] However, equipped with skills and high-level education, former Soviet Union immigrants bounced back and adjusted relatively well to the new environment and by 2012, the average salary of an immigrant from the former Soviet Union was comparable to that of veteran Israeli Jews.[23]

An additional group of immigrants arrived in Israel from the 1990s onward: Immigrants from Ethiopia. This social group represents about 2% of the population in Israel. The adjustment of Ethiopian-immigrant Jews was much more challenging than that of former USSR Jewish immigrants. Coming from small rural communities with patriarchal family structures where hierarchy and authority were based on age and gender, Ethiopian-immigrant Jews felt alienated by the absorbing society. Not only did the Rabbinate, the official Jewish religious authority in Israel, question whether they were Jewish, but also their sociocultural adjustment was fraught with difficulties owing to their lower levels of formal education and their occupations that were no longer relevant in the modern

18 Israel Central Bureau of Statistics, 2016.

19 Israel Ministry of Foreign Affairs, 2013 (see www.mfa.gov.il/MFA/InnovativeIsrael/AboutIsrael/Spotlight/Pages/Advanced%20Agriculture%20as%20a%20Tool%20Against%20Desertifica.aspx)

20 Israel Central Bureau of Statistics, 2016.

21 Landau and Hattis-Rolef, 1998.

22 Landau and Hattis-Rolef, 1998.

23 Israel Central Bureau of Statistics, 2016.

economy.[24] Although in Ethiopia, women married at a young age and remained at home,[25] in Israel they demonstrated relatively faster acculturation than Ethiopian men, by joining the albeit low-skilled workforce, learning the Hebrew language, and engaging in social interactions.[26] These circumstances culminated in soaring unemployment rates among Ethiopian male immigrants, leading to loss of their patriarchal status and their downward social mobility.[27]

A gender perspective on the Jewish social groups in Israel reveals that most of the improvement of women's status has been incidental, a side effect of Israel's impressive socioeconomic progress as a welfare state for its citizens.[28] Israel's progress as a welfare state has improved women's life expectancy, level of literacy, marital age, and rate of employment. However, Halperin-Kaddari argued that despite the impressive amount of new reform-minded legislation promoting women's rights and well-being that was enacted from the 90s onward, disparities between women and men still remain and women still seem to face disadvantage in various fields of life, including the public sphere, workplace, wage equity, and educational opportunities.[29] These disparities are noted in high-ranking military positions and combat (and elite) roles;[30] discriminating patriarchal policies in religious courts in all personal status matters;[31] gross significant wage disparities between men and women;[32] women's concentration in the lower echelons of executive and managerial positions;[33] underrepresentation of women in prestigious technological fields and engineering and high academic positions;[34] and far fewer appointments of women to positions in representative government and parliament.[35] Prior studies on femicide in the Jewish population in Israel noted the underrepresentation of veteran Jews, a slight overrepresentation of immigrants from the former USSR, and a significant overrepresentation of Jewish immigrants from Ethiopia.[36]

In addition to the Jewish population, 20% of the population in Israel, about 1.3 million persons, is of Arab background. The Arab population in Israel is heterogeneous and composed of four main Arab subgroups – Bedouins, Muslims, Christians and Druze – that differ religiously, socially, culturally and geographically. This population (excluding the Arab population in the West Bank, East Jerusalem, and Gaza, often referred to as Palestinians) stands at about 18% of

24 Geiger, 2013; Landau and Hattis-Rolef, 1998.
25 Geiger, 2013.
26 Edelstein, 2011.
27 Geiger, 2013.
28 Halperin-Kaddari, 2004: p. 12.
29 Halperin-Kaddari, 2004: pp. 10–13.
30 Halperin-Kaddari, 2004: p. 153.
31 Halperin-Kaddari, 2004: pp. 227–228.
32 Halperin-Kaddari, 2004: pp. 133–134; Moore, 1993: pp. 323–334.
33 Berenstein, 1993: pp. 90–91; Halperin-Kaddari, 2004: p. 112, 132.
34 Halperin-Kaddari, 2004: p. 82, 95; Toren, 1993: p. 126.
35 Azmon, 1993: pp. 253–257; Azmon and Izraeli, 1993: p. 14; Halperin-Kaddari, 2004: p. 134–142.
36 Dayan, 2021; Edelstein, 2011; Landau and Hattis-Rolef, 1998; Sela-Shayovitz, 2010.

the citizens of the Israel state.[37] The Arab population in Israel is composed of a majority of 81% Muslims, made up of two main subgroups – Bedouins (21% of the total Arab population in Israel) and non-Bedouin Muslims (60%) – and two smaller groups, Christians (10%) and Druze (9%).[38] Several cultural characteristics are common to all four Arab social groups: Family and clan as the central unit of society, a collective identity, patriarchal and patrilineal social structure, and notions of family "honor" and female-related "honor." Patriarchal culture and the familial clan (*hamula*) social structure have remained despite economic, educational, political and social changes in Israeli Arab society in recent decades.[39] As a minority group in Israel, Arab society maintains social harmony through social interdependence and mutual responsibility of individuals, culturally preserving family ties and placing community interests ahead of individual interests.[40] Traditional marriage patterns are preserved (with women required to obtain the family's blessing and consent) and early marriage is common. Family problems are generally addressed and guided by older family members, who provide concrete and immediate solutions.

Since the founding of Israel, the Arab population has become a substantial minority in Israel. This is the result of its high fertility rate combined with decreased disease and mortality rates.[41] According to Al Haj, Arab society in Israel has undergone significant changes in different areas, of which the level of education is probably the most salient. The illiteracy rate among Arabs has decreased rapidly, along with a steady increase in tertiary education.[42] Nonetheless, the education level of Israeli Arabs remains lower than that of the Jewish population.[43] The livelihood of Arabs also underwent a radical change from agriculture to predominantly wage labor.[44] The Arab worker is situated at the bottom of the labor force ladder, mainly employed in the service and construction sectors in addition to manual jobs in industry.[45] Most Arabs reside in all-Arab towns, mixed towns where they constitute a minority, or villages.[46]

According to Sa'ar and Yahia-Younis, although Arabs' Israeli citizenship grants them certain equal rights in voting, welfare, education and so forth, they are overrepresented in poverty and concentrated in the lowest socioeconomic echelons, with soaring rates of unemployment.[47] Their residential areas are usually underdeveloped in terms of infrastructure, and they reside mostly in villages and

37 Israel Central Bureau of Statistics, 2016.
38 Israel Central Bureau of Statistics, 2016.
39 Landau, 1995.
40 Shalhoub-Kevorkian, 1999: p. 193.
41 Landau, 1993: p. 6.
42 Al Haj, 1995: p. 20.
43 Al Haj, 1995: p. 25, 84–85.
44 Al Haj, 1995: p. 28.
45 Op. cit.
46 Landau, 1993: p. 9.
47 Sa'ar and Yahia-Younis, 2008: p. 309.

remote small towns. Muslim Arabs do not own economically significant enterprises – industrial, financial, or commercial – and the average personal income of Muslim Arabs remains below that of the Israeli Jewish sector.[48] Most Arab-owned enterprises are family-operated: Capital is usually provided by the family and supplemented by small short-term loans, and the entrepreneur and workers are often members of the same family.[49] An additional economic problem relates to the unemployment of well-educated Arabs in jobs appropriate to their skills, with many university graduates facing severe unemployment and underemployment problems[50] and many graduates of secondary schools and universities working in blue-collar jobs.[51] Thus, despite the relative upward mobility of Arabs in the Israeli labor market, the gap between them and the Jewish population remains stable.[52]

A perspective on the various Arab subgroups reveals that they are heterogeneous in their socioeconomic status. Particularly noteworthy is the socioeconomic status of the Bedouin subgroup. As a nomadic society, the Bedouin had an economy based on agriculture and herding, with men working outdoors and women remaining at the tent site.[53] However, their unique sociocultural nomadic fabric disintegrated following the Israeli government's decision to relocate the pastoral nomads to planned urban settings. This led to the Bedouin's loss of land, herds, and agricultural fields[54] and culminated in an Arab social subgroup characterized by high rates of unemployment, poverty, illiteracy, drug addiction, crime, and violence.[55]

In contrast to the Bedouins, the Christian Arab subgroup in Israel is characterized by high education levels, employment rates, and social advancement.[56] Among the Arab subgroups in Israel, the Christians are economically strong, owing to their better education, prominence in liberal professions and relative wealth. Many are townspeople and few are farmers, preferring urban living to rural areas.[57] The percentage of university graduates among Christian Arabs is three times their share in the total Israeli Arab population,[58] and they hold proportionally more jobs that require training.[59] Thus, on a continuum with Bedouin Arabs at one end, in the lowest social strata with the lowest economic status in the Arab population in Israel, Christian Arabs are located at the opposite end, already modernized and members of the highest social strata with a relatively

48 Landau, 1993: p. 12.
49 Landau, 1993: p. 20.
50 Al Haj, 1995: p. 24; Landau, 1993: p. 15.
51 Al Haj, 1995: p. 24, 204–205.
52 Al Haj, 1995: p. 29.
53 Abu-Rabia-Queder, 2006.
54 Al Haj, 1989: p. 177.
55 Elbedour et al., 2006: p. 217.
56 Hlihel, 2008: p. 307.
57 Landau, 1993: p. 18.
58 Al Haj, 1995: p. 197.
59 Landau, 1969: p. 16.

high economic status compared with the other Arab subgroups in Israel. In between these two extremes are the (non-Bedouin) Muslims and the Druze, members of the middle social strata in terms of economic status and undergoing gradual modernization.

A gender perspective on the Arab social groups reveals that when compared to the social status of Jewish women, the social status of women in Arab society has always been considered inferior to that of men, with women's lives constrained and dependent on men financially, socially and culturally.[60] The socioeconomic change that the Arab population of Israel has undergone has affected women in terms of the rising age of marriage, mandatory education for girls, and women's higher participation in the labor force.[61] In the past 50 years, Arab women in Israel have registered dramatic changes: Their level of schooling has risen spectacularly,[62] the average number of children per woman has dropped significantly, and freedom of movement granted by women's families or husbands has increased.[63] At the same time, Arab women are rendered the exclusive jurisdiction of religious courts that discriminate against women;[64] exposed to domestic violence that is exacerbated by sociocultural and political conditions;[65] participate in paid employment at significantly lower rates; and hardly participate in formal politics.[66]

Another social group that has been growing lately in Israel is composed of foreign workers and illegal immigrants (asylum seekers). About 150,000 residents are foreign nationals: An estimated 100,000 foreign workers work mainly in agriculture and construction, of whom about 50,000 are women working in caregiving.[67] According to an OECD annual report, the phenomenon of worker abuse is very common in this sector; both labor and sexual abuse of workers occurs, mainly against women by employers or family members.[68] In addition to foreign workers, this social group consists of an estimated 40,000 asylum seekers originating mainly from Sudan and Eritrea, as well as other sub-Saharan countries, who arrived in Israel from 2006 onward.[69] According to Kalir,[70] most members of this community live in South Tel Aviv, a place that has hosted the poor, underclass residents of the city for decades. The area suffers from persistent neglect of its deteriorated public infrastructure, is notorious for the presence of drug dealers and street prostitution, and "has become the 'capital' of undocumented migrants

60 Shalhoub-Kevorkian, 1999: p. 194.
61 Glazer and Abu Ras, 1994: p. 276.
62 Al Haj, 1989: p. 188.
63 Sa'ar and Yahia-Younis, 2008: p. 309.
64 Halperin-Kaddari, 2004: pp. 258–259, 261.
65 Shalhoub-Kevorkian, 1999: p. 194.
66 Al Haj, 1989: p. 188; Sa'ar and Yahia-Younis, 2008: p. 309.
67 OECD, 2017: p. 31.
68 OECD, 2017: p. 42.
69 ASSAF, 2016: p. 5; Yakobi, 2010; Yaron et al., 2013.
70 Kalir, 2015.

who arrived from countries worldwide in search of a better life."[71] This social group is stricken with extreme high rates of unemployment, poverty, health problems and crime. Women in this social group are particularly vulnerable. Among asylum seekers, only some 7,000 are women; 3,340 of these women are registered as mothers, but it is unknown how many of them are single mothers.[72]

Constituting about 17% of the asylum-seeker community, women are considered to be a more vulnerable population. As status-less persons, they are denied welfare and health rights and are exposed to abusive employment; they are also an easier target for exploitation and abuse in both the asylum-seeker community and Israeli society. Consequently, about 60% has experienced domestic violence.[73] The problem of marital abuse in this community has been revealed by data collated by the Israeli Parliament, indicating that about 24% of all women murdered by their partners in Israel between 2009 and 2013 were foreign nationals.[74] Many women choose not to turn to the police for survival reasons: Should their violent partners be incarcerated, they might find themselves alone, often with children, yet ineligible for state-authority support. Sometimes they are forced to marry or enter a relationship with their creditors. These forced marriages lead to continued exploitation and abuse. As a result, many single mothers are dependent on support from others (for example, 70% of them do not receive any help from their ex-spouse and find themselves at the mercy of community members for financial support or a place to stay).[75] Many times, this dependence on others exposes them to exploitation and abuse – housing problems and lack of a safe space of their own render the mothers at risk of rape and sexual harassment in the domestic sphere, and according to ASSAF,[76] at times this means abuse and attempted control by relatives or a demand made by men for sexual services in return for free housing, low rent, or other types of assistance.

Israel's Policy toward Femicide

Gender-based domestic violence in Israel has been the target of broad reforms and extensive government attention and action – with little resulting improvement.[77] At least 11% of all adult women across all strata of society have been victims of violence by their spouses at least once.[78] The number of domestic-violence complaints filed continues to rise, and research has indicated that numerous

71 Kalir, 2015: p. 590.
72 ASSAF, 2016: pp. 5–6; Drori-Avraham, 2016: p. 3.
73 ASSAF, 2016: p. 1.
74 Knesset Research and Information Centre (Violence Directed at Women – 2013 Data).
75 ASSAF, 2016: p. 10; Drori-Avraham, 2016: p. 3.
76 ASSAF, 2016: p. 14.
77 Halperin-Kaddari, 2004: p. 176, 186.
78 19% among women with low-level education, 11% among high school graduates, and 5% among women with higher education. See Halperin-Kaddari, 2004: p. 196.

reforms addressing all stages of police involvement in domestic-violence cases have not been implemented, except for the initial stage of initiating a criminal procedure by filing a complaint with the police.[79]

A marked awareness in femicide led the Israeli parliament to pass the Law for the Prevention of Family Violence in 1991, according to which a woman can obtain an immediate court order barring a violent husband from the home for up to ten weeks.[80] Increased awareness of the femicide phenomenon led to the establishment in 1995 of a special Parliamentary Inquiry Committee on the Murder of Women by their Spouses. Following the committee's recommendations, the position of special domestic-violence police investigator was created and the position was filled in every police station, in addition to establishing hotlines for battered women and additional legal-service clinics.[81] Despite these preventive measures, femicide rates in Israel have not declined.[82] The following section describes contemporary patterns of femicide in Israel.

Socio-Ethnic Patterns of Femicide in Israel

Our following observations, extracted from our previous studies on femicide and corroborated with an analysis of national empirical findings of femicide in Israel in 2010 to 2015, reveal notable socio-ethnic patterns. These distinct patterns relate to various characteristics of femicide such as frequency, femicide subtypes (such as intimate-partner femicide, femicide–suicide, and "honor" femicide), killing scene and motive, and the nature of victim–perpetrator relations.

A socio-ethnic perspective on femicide frequency reveals intriguing patterns. Whereas Jewish women are underrepresented among victims, comprising 57%[83] of cases whereas their share among total population is 78%, both Arab and foreign women are notably overrepresented. Particularly striking is the share of foreign women among femicide victims in Israel, who comprise about five times their share of the total population (2% of the population, yet more than 10% of all femicide victims in Israel).[84] In addition, although the Arab ethnic group comprises 20% of the total population, Arab women account for 32% of all femicide victims in Israel. This higher rate of femicide in the Arab ethnic group suggests that socio-ethnic and cultural aspects may be related to femicide. In line with this empirical observation, F.H.K., usually termed "honor" killing, is further elaborated in Chapter 4, focusing on its unique sociocultural and criminological characteristics.

In addition to these ethnic patterns, particular femicide rates emerged when we analyzed the various social subgroups in the two main ethnic groups in Israel,

79 Halperin-Kaddari, 2004: p. 196, 199.
80 Landau and Hattis-Rolef, 1998: p. 81.
81 Sela-Shayovitz, 2010: p. 1426.
82 Sela-Shayovitz, 2010: p. 1426.
83 Percentages were rounded.
84 Dayan, 2022.

Arabs and Jews.[85] In the Jewish ethnic group, femicide frequency is most notable among two of its social subgroups: Ethiopian and former USSR immigrant Jews. Although Ethiopian Jews comprise about 2% of the total population, they account for 8% of femicide victims. Similarly, although former USSR immigrant Jews comprise about 10% of the total population in Israel, they comprise about a quarter (23%) of all femicide victims. A similar pattern is observed in the Arab ethnic group, with variations among its social subgroups. A high rate of femicide is noted in the Bedouin social subgroup, which makes up 13% of femicide victims in the total population, yet comprises 4% of the total population in Israel. The Christian Arab social subgroup, on the other hand, is underrepresented, with hardly any femicide cases, despite accounting for 2% of the total population.[86]

These femicide frequency patterns, whereby femicide rates tend to be higher in certain social subgroups of the two main ethnic groups, seem to coincide with the differential socioeconomic status of these groups in Israel. In our analysis of the unique socio-ethnic fabric of Israel in the first part of this chapter, we noted that the groups with the lowest socioeconomic status in Israel were Ethiopian Jews, Bedouin Arabs and foreigners. These three groups are the same socio-ethnic groups with the highest rates of femicide. This coincidence should come as no surprise, because previous studies on femicide have noted the possible link between the tendency to resort to femicide and economic strain.[87] An additional possible explanation for these frequency patterns is related to immigration patterns. Given foreigners are mostly low-skilled workers or illegal immigrants, a possible link between social strain related to immigration and its correlative social constraints such as lack of a social network, employment and language skills might explain the high rates of femicide in these groups. The fact that Bedouin Arabs are included in this group does not impede the applicability of the explanation regarding the link between immigration and femicide, because as we noted earlier, Bedouin Arabs "immigrated" to new urban settings based on the Israeli government's decision to relocate the pastoral nomads to planned urban settings.[88] Indeed, various scholars have attested to the link between immigration and its correlative social strain – and femicide.[89]

With particular relevance to the higher rates of femicide among immigrants, an additional notable femicide subtype exists among femicide cases in Israel, referring to the phenomenon of femicide–suicide, which seems to be more common, almost in an exclusive manner, in a particular Jewish social group: Ethiopian immigrant Jews. This femicide subtype seems to coincide with the number of casualties of femicide in Israel, which is higher than the number of women killed. Indeed, the higher number of femicide victims, in addition to the number of

85 Dayan, 2022.
86 Dayan, 2021a.
87 Cooney, 2014; Dayan, 2021b.
88 Al Haj, 1989.
89 Geiger, 2013; Landau and Hattis-Rolef, 1998; Sela-Shayovitz, 2010; Wallace, 1986; Weil, 2016.

women killed, relates to the fact that in about a fifth of the cases, the perpetrator commits or tries to commit suicide immediately after killing the woman (15% of perpetrators commit suicide, whereas 6% try but fail to commit suicide).

The phenomenon of femicide–suicide and its peculiar characteristics in Israel are further elaborated in Chapter 5, yet for the sake of this chapter's aim to present an empirical overview of femicide in Israel, we outline this subtype's notable socio-ethnic characteristics. Indeed, when analyzing femicide–suicide among socio-ethnic groups in Israel, notable patterns are noted. An ethnic pattern characterizes femicide–suicide cases, with the Arab ethnic population being virtually absent, whereas Jewish perpetrators and victims account for almost all such cases. Furthermore, as noted, a closer look at the various social groups in the Jewish population reveals that this femicide subtype is particularly identified with Ethiopian immigrant Jews, who are overrepresented in such cases. Accounting for 2% of the total population, Ethiopian immigrant Jews account for 32% of femicide–suicide cases.[90] These findings imply that femicide–suicide in Israel has both ethnic and social characteristics, because it tends to occur in the Jewish ethnic group in general and among Ethiopian immigrant Jews in particular.

Empirical observations reveal that an additional femicide subtype, that of intimate-partner femicide, seems to be a highly prevalent pattern of femicide in Israel, particularly in the Jewish ethnic group. In this regard, the fact that most femicide is perpetrated in the victim's home (comprising 56% of cases), whereas public or remote places are rare (7% and 3% of cases, respectively), speaks first and foremost to the domestic nature of the femicide phenomenon in Israel. This empirical finding coincides with various international observations, reporting that most femicide cases occur in familial circumstances.[91] Indeed, a substantial share of femicide cases in Israel are perpetrated by the victim's former or current intimate partner, against the backdrop of the victim's desire to end the intimate relationship. Although victims' former or current intimate partners comprise 50% of all perpetrators, familiar victim–perpetrator relationships (children, parents, uncles, etc.) comprise 38% of the cases. This observation differs along an ethnic perspective when comparing the frequency rates of victim–perpetrator relations between the two main ethnic groups in Israel: Whereas most Jewish femicide cases involve the victims' former or current intimate partner (70%), only about a third of all victim–perpetrator relations (35%) involve a current or former intimate partner among Arab victims.[92]

These notable ethnic differences in victim–perpetrator relations speak to the possible cultural relativity of the specific femicide subtype: Intimate-partner femicide. Indeed, such observation is exacerbated by ethnic differences regarding the motive for perpetrating femicide. When analyzing data on femicide motives across all subgroups in Israel, the most common motive for femicide relates to

90 Dayan, 2021.
91 Campbell et al., 2003.
92 Dayan, 2022.

the victim's decision to terminate an intimate relationship (26%). However, this observation differs across ethnic groups, because among Arab victims, the most common motive for femicide relates to family "honor" (37%), whereas the victim's decision to terminate an intimate relationship accounts for the motive only in 5% of cases. Therefore, it seems that intimate-partner femicide requires a special focus and analysis. Hence, in line with empirical findings regarding the higher frequency of this femicide subtype in the Jewish ethnic group and its very low frequency in the Arab ethnic group, we devote Chapter 3 to this topic. In that chapter, we focus on intimate-partner femicide in the Jewish ethnic group, along with an analysis of Jewish socio-legal underpinnings that seem to construe this particular femicide subtype in Israel.

Thus far, we identified three main femicide subtypes in Israel, which seem to correlate with Israel's socio-ethnic fabric. Could there be any additional possible femicide subtypes hidden in our empirical data on femicide in Israel? Yes. We believe an additional femicide subtype is hidden away, buried literally, beyond official femicide cases. We term these cases "concealed femicide,"[93] referring to femicide that exhibits elusive criminological characteristics due to the crime scene being staged by the perpetrator. Such femicide cases are usually staged as either a natural or nonnatural and noncriminal death, and thus will almost always be excluded from data on femicide and its accurate counting. A concealed femicide scene will be usually staged according to the death scenario the offender seeks to present. The staged death scenario may simulate a legitimate noncriminal death scenario, a non-death scenario, or a criminal death scenario that alters the identity of the suspected offender.[94] In a non-death scenario, the femicide scene will be staged as if the woman victim is a missing person. In a noncriminal death scenario, the femicide scene might be staged as if she died from a personal accident, car accident, fall from height, electrocution, fire, drug overdose, medically induced death such as terminal illness or natural death, or a self-induced death such as a suicide. In a criminal death scenario, the femicide scene will be staged to alter the offender's identity; for example, staging a death to appear as if it occurred during a burglary, break-in, sexual crime or during a self-defense act.

Because the epidemiological literature on such killings estimates their prevalence as possibly as high as 8% of all homicide crime scenes,[95] we believe that at least that share of additional undetected femicide cases construe empirical observations of femicide. Our estimation builds on prior empirical and theoretical observations of staged homicide crime scenes, implying that the prevailing form of such staging involves femicide cases. First, victims and offenders in these cases are usually involved in some sort of relationship (work, familial, intimate), typically a domestic

93 Bitton and Dayan, 2019.
94 Chisum and Turvey, 2011; Dayan 2022; Pettler, 2016.
95 Hazelwood and Napier, 2004; Keppel and Weis, 2004; Schlesinger et al., 2012.

relationship.[96] Second, most victims are female and most offenders are male.[97] Third, most scenes are staged in the home,[98] better facilitating staging, which requires the perpetrator to have unobstructed time alone at the site of the homicide. Fourth, an intimate-partner relationship is the most common victim–offender relationship in staged homicide scenes in Western societies, and most staged homicide scenes involve the killing of an intimate partner.[99] Finally, most such cases are perpetrated against the backdrop of circumstantial relationship dissolution.[100]

Thus, following these empirical and theoretical observations linking this particular homicidal subtype to femicide, we devote the last chapter in Part II of the book, Chapter 6, to presenting cases in which Israeli women died under circumstances identified here as proxies of a crime, as well as identifying and discussing other killing methods staged as noncriminal death and usually overlooked by both the criminal system and scholars researching the field.

Conclusion

The findings presented here seem to echo prior international findings on femicide; as noted in global reports, the most common femicide perpetrator in Israel is the victim's current or former intimate partner. Equally echoed are femicide motives, resonating with global findings that the most common motive for femicide is the victim's desire to terminate her intimate relationship with the perpetrator. Still, these international observations of femicide require a framework of analysis that is culturally sensitive. This is because the same femicide disparities noted by previous scholars between the two main ethnic groups in Israel – that is, Jewish femicide victims are slightly underrepresented, whereas F.H.K. victims are overrepresented[101] – prevail. The fact that a decade after these empirical observations were noted, we find the same general patterns of femicide frequency across the two main ethnic groups in Israel speaks to the dire need to study femicide with a perspective that considers its sociocultural context.

Looking at femicide manifestations as socioculturally relative, our observations seem to be in line with prior studies' reports on F.H.K. in Israel, indicating that Arab women are overrepresented among women killed in Israel. Indeed, although their total share in the population is about 20%, they constitute 30% to 40% of the women killed each year in Israel.[102] The same criminological patterns previously reported regarding this femicide subtype in the Arab population in

96 Dayan, 2021; Petherick and Ferguson, 2015; Pettler, 2016.
97 Bitton and Dayan, 2019; Dayan, 2021; Hazelwood and Napier, 2004; Keppel and Weis, 2004; Pettler, 2016.
98 Dayan, 2021; Eke, 2007; Pettler, 2016.
99 Dayan, 2021; Douglas and Douglas, 2006; Eke, 2007; Pettler, 2016.
100 Bitton and Dayan, 2019; Dayan, 2021; Eke, 2007; Pettler, 2016.
101 Landau and Hattis-Rolef, 1998: p. 82.
102 Edelstein, 2011; Landau and Hattis-Rolef, 1998; Sela-Shayovitz, 2010.

Israel[103] still prevail; similar to previous empirical reports, we found that F.H.K. perpetrators were most often from the victim's patrilineal family and that the most common motive for such femicide relates to notions of family "honor" for reasons of alleged sexual misbehavior.[104]

In addition to patterns previously reported, we highlight new empirical observations on the heterogeneous nature of femicide frequency in the various Arab social groups, with the highest femicide frequency among Bedouin Arabs and lowest rate of femicide frequency among Christian Arabs. These empirical observations imply that femicide in general and F.H.K. in particular do not solely derive from culture. Instead, in Israel, and probably in other societies, too, femicide frequency is closely linked to socioeconomic conditions. This empirical and theoretical observation is further emphasized by the fact that extremely high rates of femicide are noted in the foreigner social group. Together, the current patterns of femicide in Israel speak to the need to further study femicide, along social comparative frameworks of analysis.

When applying the same framework of analysis – that is, studying femicide as a socioculturally relative criminal phenomenon – to the analysis of femicide in various Jewish social groups, we note that prior intra-ethnic variations of femicide in the Jewish population still prevail. Indeed, in line with prior reports on femicide patterns in Israel in the 90s, we still see empirical indications of an underrepresentation of veteran Jews, a high overrepresentation of immigrant Jews (from both the former USSR and Ethiopia),[105] and a salient increase in intimate-partner femicide among Ethiopian immigrant Jews, particularly in the form of femicide–suicide.[106] This criminological observation will be treated separately, focusing on the criminological nature of the most common femicide subtype among Ethiopian Jews: femicide–suicide. These intra-ethnic variations in femicide frequency prompt our call for further studies of femicide using comparative frameworks of analysis that consider sociocultural contextual factors that seem to play a major role in this criminal phenomenon.[107]

In addition to the various sociocultural and criminological contextual factors of femicide that we wish to highlight, this book explores the understudied femicide subtype of concealed femicide, which in our opinion, is an endemic characteristic of femicide across various societies requiring rigorous and comprehensive empirical and theoretical exploration. In doing so, we present our socio-legal and criminological analysis of this type of femicide, hoping to contribute to its analysis in the framework of gender-based violence in general and fatal gender-based violence in particular.

103 As noted, Shalhoub-Kevorkian's (2002, 2003) research on femicide was conducted in the West Bank or East Jerusalem; therefore, her empirical observations are outside the scope of this research's population.

104 Edelstein, 2011: pp. 120–127; Kressel, 1981: p. 146; Touma-Sliman, 2005: pp. 184–187.

105 Landau and Hattis-Rolef, 1998: p. 83.

106 Edelstein, 2011: p. 171; Sela-Shayovitz, 2010: p. 1429.

107 Dayan, 2021, 2022.

Having outlined an empirical and criminology-based theoretical overview of femicide, the following part of the book, Part II, presents, from an intra- and interdisciplinary perspective, the four femicide subtypes previously introduced: Intimate-partner femicide, "honor" femicide, femicide–suicide, and concealed femicide.

References

Abu-Rabia-Queder, S. (2006). Between tradition and modernization: Understanding the problem of female Bedouin dropouts. *British Journal of Sociology of Education, 27*, 3–17.

Al Haj, M. (1989). Social research on family lifestyles among Arabs in Israel. *Journal of Comparative Family Studies, 20*, 175–195.

Al Haj, M. (1995). *Education, empowerment and control: The case of the Arabs in Israel.* State University of New York.

ASSAF: Aid Organization for Refugees and Asylum Seekers. (2016). *Annual report for 2016.* http://assaf.org.il/en/content/voices-assaf-annual-report-2016

Azmon, Y. (1993). Women and politics: The case of Israel. In Y. Azmon & D. Izraeli (Eds.), *Women in Israel: Studies of Israeli society* (pp. 253–268). Transaction.

Azmon, Y., & Izraeli, D. (1993). Women in Israel: A sociological overview. In Y. Azmon & D. Izraeli (Eds.), *Women in Israel: Studies of Israeli society* (pp. 1–24). Transaction.

Berenstein, D. (1993). Economic growth and female labour: The case of Israel. In Y. Azmon & D. Izraeli (Eds.), *Women in Israel: Studies of Israeli society* (pp. 67–96). Transaction.

Campbell, J. C., Webster, D., Koziol-McLain, J., Block, C., Campbell, D., Curry, M. A., & Sharps, P. (2003). Risk factors for femicide in abusive relationships: Results from a multisite case control study. *American Journal of Public Health, 93*(7), 1089–1097.

Chisum, W. J., & Turvey, B. (2011). *Crime reconstruction* (2nd ed.). Academic Press.

Cooney, M. (2014). Death by family: "Honor" violence as punishment. *Punishment and Society, 16*, 406–427.

Corradi, C., & Stöckl, H. (2014). Intimate partner homicide in 10 European countries: Statistical data and policy development in a cross-national perspective. *European Journal of Criminology, 11*(5), 601–618.

Dayan, H. (2021a). Female "honor"-killing: The role of low economic status and rapid modernization. *Journal of Interpersonal Violence.* Advance online publication. https://doi.org/10.1177/0886260519872984

Dayan, H. (2021b). Sociocultural aspects of femicide-suicide: The case of Israel. *Journal of Interpersonal Violence.* Advance online publication. https://doi.org/10.1177/0886260518792983

Dayan, H. (2022). *Ethnocultural aspects of homicide crime scene staging.* Homicide Studies.

Della Giustina, J. (2010). *Why women are beaten and killed: Sociological predictors of femicide.* Edwin Mellen Press.

Douglas, J., & Douglas, L. (2006). The detection of staging, undoing and personation at the crime scene. In J. E. Douglas, A. W. Burgess, A. G. Burgess, & R. K. Ressler (Eds.), *Crime classification manual* (pp. 31–44). Jossey Bass.

Drori-Avraham, A. (2016). *Abandoned single mother asylum seekers.* ASSAF. http://assaf.org.il/en/sites/default/files/Abandoned%20report%20summary_0.pdf

Edelstein, A. (2011). *Intimate homicide in Israel: Theoretical and empirical aspects.* Bialik (in Hebrew).

Eke, A. (2007). *Staging in cases of homicide: Offender, victim and offence characteristics* [unpublished doctoral dissertation, Toronto University].

Elbedour, S., Abu-Bader, S., Onwuegbuzie, A. J., Abu-Rabia, A., and El-Aassam, S. (2006). The scope of sexual, physical, and psychological abuse in a Bedouin-Arab community of female adolescents: The interplay of racism, urbanization, polygamy, family "honor", and the social marginalization of women. *Child Abuse and Neglect, 30*(3), 215–229.

Geiger, B. (2013). Ethiopian males account for the double acts of murder and suicide committed by males in Ethiopian families' post-migration to Israel. *International Criminal Justice Review, 23*(3), 233–252.

Glazer, I. M., & Abu Ras, W. (1994). On aggression, human rights, and hegemonic discourse: The case of a murder for family "honor" in Israel. *Sex Roles, 30*(3–4), 269–288.

Halperin-Kaddari, R. (2004). *Women in Israel: A state of their own.* University of Pennsylvania Press.

Hazelwood, R. R., & Napier, M. R. (2004). Crime scene staging and its detection. *International Journal of Offender Therapy and Comparative Criminology, 48*(6), 744–759.

Hlihel, A. (2008). Non-married women among Arab population: Factors enhancing the phenomenon in central and northern Israel. In A. Manna (Ed.), *Arab Society in Israel (2): Populations, Society and Economy* (pp. 283–312). Van Leer Institute.

Israel Ministry of Foreign Affairs. (2013). *Advanced agriculture as a tool against desertification.* www.mfa.gov.il/MFA/InnovativeIsrael/AboutIsrael/Spotlight/Pages/Advanced%20Agriculture%20as%20a%20Tool%20Against%20Desertifica.aspx

Kalir, B. (2015). The Jewish state of anxiety: Between moral obligation and fearism in the treatment of African asylum seekers in Israel. *Journal of Ethnic and Migration Studies, 41*(4), 580–598.

Keppel, R. D., & Weis, J. G. (2004). The rarity of "unusual" dispositions of victim bodies: Staging and posing. *Journal of Forensic Science, 49*(6), 1308–1312.

Kressel, G. M., (1981). Sororicide/filiacide: Homicide for family honour [and comments and reply]. *Current Anthropology, 22*(2), 141–158.

Landau, J. M. (1993). *The Arab minority in Israel: 1967–1991, political aspects.* Clarendon Press.

Landau, S. (1984). Trends in violence and aggression: A cross-cultural analysis. *International Journal of Comparative Sociology, 2*, 133–158.

Landau, S., & Hattis-Rolef, S. (1998). Intimate femicide in Israel: Temporal, social and motivational patterns. *European Journal on Criminal Policy and Research, 6*, 75–90.

Moore, D. (1993). Relative deprivation in the labor market. In Y. Azmon & D. Izraeli (Eds.), *Women in Israel: Studies of Israeli society* (pp. 323–340). Transaction.

OECD. (2017). *OECD expert group on migration annual report: International migration – Israel 2016–2017.* Institute for Immigration and Social Integration and Ruppin Academic Center.

Petherick, W. & Ferguson, C. (2015). False reports. In W. Petherick (Ed.), *Applied crime analysis: A social science approach to understanding crime, criminals, and victims* (pp. 121–143). Academic Press.

Pettler, L. G. (2016). *Crime scene staging dynamics in homicide cases.* CRC Press.

Sa'ar, A., & Yahia-Younis, T. (2008). Masculinity in crisis: The case of Palestinians in Israel. *British Journal of Middle Eastern Studies, 35*(3), 305–323.

Schlesinger, L. B., Gardenier, A., Jarvis, J., & Sheehan-Cook, J. (2012). Crime scene staging in homicide. *Journal of Police and Criminal Psychology*, *29*(1), 44–51.

Sela-Shayovitz, R. (2010). The role of ethnicity and context: Intimate femicide rates among social groups in Israeli society. *Violence against Women*, *16*(12), 1424–1436.

Shalhoub-Kevorkian, N. (1999). Law, politics, and violence against women: A case study of Palestinians in Israel. *Law and Policy*, *21*(2), 189–211.

Shalhoub-Kevorkian, N. (2002). Femicide and the Palestinian criminal justice system: Seeds of change in the context of state building? *Law and Society Review*, *36*(3), 577–606.

Shaloub-Kevorkian, N. (2003). Re-examining femicide: Breaking the silence and crossing "scientific" borders. *Signs: Journal of Women in Culture and Society*, *28*(2), 581–608.

Toren, N. (1993). The status of women in the academia. In Y. Azmon & D. Izraeli (Eds.), *Women in Israel: Studies of Israeli society* (pp. 125–134). Transaction.

Touma-Sliman, A. (2005). Culture, national minority and the state: Working against the "crime of family "honor"" within the Palestinian community in Israel. In L. Welchman & S. Hossain (Eds.), *"honor": Crimes, paradigms, and violence against women* (pp. 181–198). Zed Books.

Wallace, A. (1986). *Homicide: The social reality*. Bureau of Crimes Statistics and Research, Attorney General's Department.

Waxman, D. (2006). *The pursuit of peace and the crisis of Israeli identity: Defending/defining the nation*. Springer.

Weil, S. (2016). Failed femicides among migrant survivors. *Qualitative Sociology Review*, *7*(4), 6–21.

Yakobi, H. (2010). Let me go to the city: African asylum seekers, racialization and the politics of space in Israel. *Journal of Refugee Studies*, *24*(1), 1–22.

Yaron, H., Hashimshony-Yaffe, N., & Campbell, J. R. (2013). "Infiltrators" or refugees? An analysis of Israel's policy towards African asylum-seekers. *International Migration*, *51*(4), 144–157.

Part II

Femicide Subtypes

3 A Crimino-Legal Perspective on Intimate-Partner Femicide

The "Reasonable" Israeli Wife Killer

Introduction

Having introduced in Part I of the book a theoretical overview of the phenomenon of femicide and an empirical overview of its various subtypes, Part II offers an empirical overview of the phenomenon nurtured by observations and insights regarding the criminological characteristics of various femicide subtypes in Israel. This part of the book elaborates on four main femicide subtypes: Intimate-partner femicide, femicide of Arab women, femicide–suicide, and concealed femicide. This chapter offers a critical crimino-legal analysis of the most common femicide type in Israel, intimate-partner femicide.

This chapter follows our empirical observations regarding intimate-partner femicide being a femicide subtype more common in the Jewish population. The chapter explores how criminal law's application to femicide victims and perpetrators socially constructs the normative violent Jewish Israeli male when applying the doctrine of provocation. Femicide circumstances are directly related to the doctrine of provocation. This is because one of the English law categories recognized as meriting provocation as a partial defense for murder related to intimate relations is particularly relevant to allegations of female adultery. Demonstrating how Israeli social norms, attitudes and beliefs toward sexual jealousy, matrimony, loss of control, morality, gender and homicide are entangled and intertwined in the structure and function of Israeli religious and criminal law, this chapter offers a critical analysis of the basic underlying gender-discriminating assumptions that structure current Israeli application of the doctrine of provocation.

To answer these questions, the chapter critically deconstructs Israeli case law dealing with the doctrine of provocation by problematizing its underpinning Jewish religious law and the way it relates to gendered claims about the victim's infidelity and the killer's ensuing provocation and loss of control. As the chapter shows, the Israeli provocation partial defense for murder portrays and constructs the legal definition of the Israeli "unfaithful" woman and the "reasonable" and "normative," so to speak, Israeli wife killer. Such men are considered less morally guilty when they kill "unfaithful" women, and they consequently receive lenient

DOI: 10.4324/9781003333272-5

convictions and sentences.[1] At the same time, women are blamed for morally instigating, precipitating and provoking their own killing – thus, "deserving" their gruesome, premature and undue death.

The chapter begins by laying the theoretical groundwork of the Israeli doctrine of provocation, followed by an analysis of its application. It continues with a critical deconstruction of two Israeli femicide cases in which provocation claims have been applied. The chapter concludes by problematizing the socio-legal implications of such case law on lethal gender-based violence in the form of femicide.

Israeli Criminal Doctrine of Provocation

This chapter was written before a legislative reform regarding homicide was enacted in 2019. Despite the legislative reform, Israel's doctrine of provocation has been left largely intact. Because Israeli femicide case law so far has been dealt with by applying former homicide legislation, this chapter refers to homicide legislation prior to the 2019 reform. However, because the legislative reform regarding the doctrine of provocation is mainly a technical change in the numbering of the relevant section and the insertion of case-law precedent into the current wording of the relevant new section, our critical perspective of the doctrine and its dire implications for intimate-partner femicide is applicable, despite the current legislative reform regarding homicide crime.

Israel's doctrine of provocation is based on 17th century English common law, as absorbed in many countries once governed by the British Empire.[2] Compatible with the English doctrine, Israel's doctrine perceives provocation by the victim as a factor instigating intense anger, which thereby diminishes the moral guilt of the person accused of murder.[3] The doctrine permits mitigation of criminal liability with respect to acts of homicide committed when the killer was provoked that would otherwise be defined as murder.

According to this doctrine, such circumstances negate the existence of the mental element of malice aforethought that is required for a murder conviction, particularly the requirement for premeditation,[4] set forth previously in Section 300 (a)(2) of the Penal Code of Israel (PCI):

1 Similar arguments were made regarding Western doctrines of provocations in Anglophone states. See Berman and Farrell, 2011: p. 1048; Dressler, 1982: pp. 442–444.

2 See Horder, 1992: p. 23, regarding the roots of the doctrine. For comments on the Israeli doctrine of provocation see Dayan, 2014; Kamir, 1997; Kremnitzer and Levanon, 2009; Shachar, 1981, 1984.

3 Similar to other Anglophone versions of the doctrine of provocation; see Pei-Lin, 2000: pp. 205–206. In effect, this places some of the guilt for the act of murder on the victim. See Berman and Farrell, 2011: pp. 1036–1037; Horder, 1992; Kremnitzer and Levanon, 2009; Lee, 2003: p. 28.

4 See Shachar, 1981.

> (a) If a person did one of the following, then he shall be accused of murder and is liable to life imprisonment, and only to that penalty: . . . he caused the death of any person with premeditation.

As in other ex-British colonies,[5] the legal partial defense does not preclude the control, free choice, and awareness of the accused, but regards certain kinds of provocation as severely impairing a person's rational abilities.[6] Accordingly, it attributes less moral guilt to persons accused of murder while losing control, and therefore reduces convictions in such cases from murder to manslaughter, as per former legislation in section 298 of the PCI.[7]

A murder conviction mitigated to manslaughter makes a huge difference in the possible sentence. A person convicted of murder is statutorily and mandatorily sentenced to life imprisonment:

> (a) If a person did one of the following, then he shall be accused of murder and is liable to life imprisonment, and only to that penalty.

Contrary to mandatory life imprisonment, the maximum sentence for a manslaughter conviction as per former section 298 of the PCI was 20 years:

> 298. If a person caused the death of another by a prohibited act or omission, then he is guilty of manslaughter and is liable to twenty years' imprisonment.

The different sentences were based on the Israeli doctrine of homicide offences that statutorily construed murder committed under provocation as manslaughter, as formerly legislated in section 301(a) of the PCI:

> 301. (a) For purposes of section 300, a person who killed a person shall be deemed to have killed him with premeditation, if he resolved to kill him and killed him in cold blood without any provocation immediately before the act, under circumstances in which he was able to think and to understand the result of his actions, and after he prepared himself to kill him or prepared the instrument with which he killed him.

Originally, traditional English law recognized provocation under four categories: Wherein the victim gravely insulted the accused immediately before the killing; the victim seriously injured a family member of the accused; the victim deprived an Englishman of his freedom; or the victim had committed adultery with the wife

5 For example, the British doctrine of provocation still prevails in many U.S. states. See Dayan, 2018.

6 Berman and Farrell, 2011; Lee, 2003; Pei-Lin, 2000.

7 For similar American legal constructions of homicide, see Berman and Farrell, 2011: p. 1048; Dressler, 1982: pp. 442–444; Lee, 2003.

of the accused.[8] The last original British law category meriting the application of the provocation doctrine, wherein the victim had committed adultery with the wife of the accused, is the only category that did not involve violent behavior on the part of the victim toward the defendant.[9] Furthermore, this last category of legally adequate provocation, a husband's observation of his wife having sexual relations with another man, seems to explicitly apply to male defendants. Similar to many other ex-British colonies and Anglophone states, Israeli law also absorbed the socio-legal underpinnings of this provocation category and its 18th-century British-ruling precedent; namely, the *Manning* case.[10] This case constructed the legal causal link between adultery and possessive manly sexual jealousy subsequently applied in common-law countries, Israel included. The English doctrine related to a husband's observation of his wife in the act of adultery as sufficient provocation was in fact rooted in the sociocultural assumption that married women are the property of their husbands. This notion contributed to the gendered social belief that a wife's infidelity is an extraordinary affront to her husband's sense of self and manhood.[11] This British conceptualization of such circumstances interpreted the provocation of adultery and sexual jealousy as related to manly emotion, not to be justified but certainly to be excused.[12]

Israel followed British common law's preconditions and tests aimed at regulating the doctrine's application. First, the doctrine of provocation is only applicable in the context of homicide (murder); it cannot be applied to other criminal offenses.[13] Second, the doctrine of provocation is not a full criminal defense but only a partial defense, reducing the defendant's criminal liability[14] and consequently enabling a conviction for manslaughter as opposed to murder.[15]

Israel also followed English case-law doctrine, which developed general conditions intended to limit the application of the doctrine of provocation and established objective tests that must all be satisfied before the defense can be asserted: The existence of "adequate provocation"; the killing was committed before the perpetrator had "cooled off"; the existence of an element of "immediacy" between the provocation and the act of murder; and the existence of a causal connection among the provocation, the ensuing loss of control, and the fatal act.[16]

In addition to British case-law preconditions and limitations for the doctrine's application, Israel followed British doctrinal developments that introduced the

8 Berman and Farrell, 2011; Horder, 1992; Lee, 2003; Pei-Lin, 2000.
9 Lee, 2003: p. 20.
10 See *Regina v. Mawgridge* (1706) 84 Eng. Rep. 1107 (U.K.) 137; Keling 119.
11 See Lee, 2003: p. 21.
12 "When a man is taken in adultery with another man's wife, if the husband shall stab the adulterer, or knock out his brains, this is bare manslaughter: *for jealousy is the rage of the man, and adultery is the highest invasion of property*" [emphasis added]; see *Regina v. Mawgridge* (1706) 84 Eng. Rep. 1107 (U.K.) 137; Keling 119.
13 Horder, 1992; Kremnitzer and Levanon, 2009.
14 Berman and Farrell, 2011; Kremnitzer and Levanon, 2009.
15 Brown, 1999; Kremnitzer and Levanon, 2009.
16 See Pei-Lin, 2000: p. 205.

concept of the "reasonable man" into the doctrine of provocation.[17] Based on the reasonable-man approach, this latter development in the doctrine of provocation eliminated the rigid categorization of the original English doctrine of provocation, as the concept of the reasonable man employed a reasonableness requirement to determine which types of behavior could be considered legally adequate for the claim of provocation.

Unlike the early common-law approach, which allowed a defendant to claim provocation only if he was responding to something that fell in one of the strictly defined categories of legally adequate provocation, the objective test that conceptualizes the doctrine's application with respect to the reasonable man seemed to adopt a context-sensitive approach that permits more defendants to claim provocation as a defense.[18] The basic premise of this legal contestation to the objective standard embedded in the reasonable-man notion was that criminal liability should be based on the subjective individual, his personal mens rea, and his blameworthiness – given the circumstances of the case. This contestation seems particularly relevant for homicide offences, where upon conviction, a person might lose his freedom and in some places, even his life.

The reasonable-man test in the doctrine of provocation has been interpreted as being strictly objective, in the sense that neither the mental nor physical peculiarities of the individual accused can be considered in determining whether his or her loss of self-control was "reasonable."[19] Hence, the reasonable-man concept was used as a normative, objective social standard to evaluate the defendant's mens rea for his fatal acts.

The concept of reasonableness is central to the modern doctrine of provocation, because instead of applying the rigid original categories, fact finders are requested to decide the concrete culpability of the defendant in said circumstances.[20] According to Donovan and Wildman, the origins of this conceptualization are rooted in the fundamental tenet of Anglo-American criminal jurisprudence that requires the jury to examine the actual state of mind – the mental state (mens rea) – of the individual accused of crime and decide whether the perpetrator indeed possessed the requisite mens rea to be convicted of having performed the criminal act (actus reus).[21]

According to Lee,[22] the question whether reasonableness standards should be objective or subjective is part of a broader debate over whether criminal law should focus on the objective harm caused by the defendant or the defendant's subjective

17 Kamir, 1997; Shachar, 1984.
18 See similar legal approach in the United States. Lee, 2003: p. 25.
19 Allen, 1988; Donovan and Wildman, 1981.
20 Miller, 2010: p. 265.
21 Donovan and Wildman, 1981: p. 449. This request is fundamental to the crime of homicide because the actus reus, the killing of a human being by another, is the same for different intentional killings, and it is the mental state of the actor that distinguishes an intentional murder from a manslaughter (p. 450).
22 Lee, 2003: pp. 206–207.

mental state or culpability. Objectivists believe that the most important factor in determining criminal liability is whether an individual caused social harm, either by engaging in bad conduct or causing bad results. A purely objective standard of reasonableness is one that excludes consideration of any of the defendant's characteristics. Under such a standard, the defendant is allegedly compared to the reasonable person, devoid of gender, race, religion, culture, etc. Subjectivists, in contrast, believe that criminal liability should focus on what was going on in the defendant's mind at the time of his wrongful act. The reasonable-man concept is criticized because, both de facto and de jure, it imposes liability for murder based on a defendant's culpability vis-à-vis a constructed standard, instead of requiring proof of his personal subjective culpability regarding the killing.[23] Indeed, such criticism seems embedded in the incorporation of the reasonable-man socio-legal construct as an objective concept to test the subjective mens rea. As Donovan and Wildman articulated, the reasonable-man test, being objective in nature, is antithetical to the concept of mens rea: "Like all objective standards, it is an external standard of general application that does not focus on an individual accused's mental state. Thus, from the point of view of traditional Anglo-American jurisprudence, a paradox is inherent in the use of the 'reasonable man' standard to test criminal responsibility: the presence or absence of criminal intent is determined by a standard which ignores the mental state of the individual accused."[24]

Israeli courts have pondered this inherent paradox in using the "reasonable-man" test. Indeed, Israeli courts during the state's first ten years debated whether the provocation doctrine should be based on the English-law objective requirement of the reasonable man or whether a more subjective legal standard should be constructed.[25] Israeli criminal case law resolved the debate over the objective and subjective criteria by requiring, as a general matter, both objective criteria in the legal conceptualization of the reasonable man and subjective criteria regarding the defendant's personal and subjective state of mind at the time of the killing.

The Israeli approach favoring the objective test, requiring the defendant to behave as a reasonable, normative man, has led to legal criticism, maintaining that such a prescriptive normative test sets too high a standard for Israelis to meet.[26] Still, in the early years of the state, Supreme Court decisions ruled that the English-law objective test in conceptualizing the Israeli reasonable man should be emulated.[27] In such a legal construction, Israeli courts still had to decide whether the doctrine could be expanded by interpreting the objective standard of the Israeli reasonable man as that of the "typical" or "ordinary" Israeli person, or whether it should aim for a higher objective standard, one that would result in restricting the circumstances to which the doctrine of provocation could be legally applied.

23 Op. cit.
24 Donovan and Wildman, 1981: p. 251.
25 Shachar, 1984: pp. 215–216.
26 Shachar, 1984: pp. 91–93.
27 Criminal Appeal 46/54 *Attorney General v. Baruch Segal* 9(1) PD 393 (1955).

The legal discourse about the proper interpretation of the objective criteria of the Israeli reasonable-man test led to further deliberation by the Supreme Court in 1969.[28] The court ruled that the proper legal interpretation of the Israeli reasonable-man objective test should not be based on a lower threshold, that of descriptive criteria, that would conceptualize the typical or ordinary Israeli as the legal standard of the Israeli reasonable man. Instead, the Supreme Court ruled that a higher legal threshold, that of a normative, prescriptive conceptualization of the reasonable man, should be the standard for the Israeli reasonable-man legal objective test.[29] This legal ruling restricted the circumstances whereby a provocation claim could be successfully claimed. This ruling was reinstated in 2004, when the Supreme Court ruled once again that both tests (subjective and objective) should be required and that the legal interpretation of the objective test should continue to apply the prescriptive legal interpretation of the Israeli reasonable man.[30] Following these Supreme Court rulings, Israeli criminal courts continue to require both a subjective state of provocation and an objective test translated into the requirement that a normative, not an ordinary or typical Israeli person, would be the standard according to which the defendant's actions are evaluated.

Seemingly, the explicitly categorical approach of early common law eventually gave way to the ostensibly gender-neutral approach that permits mitigation if a reasonable person in the defendant's shoes would also have been provoked. However, and as demonstrated by the critical deconstruction of Israeli femicide case law, the descriptive meaning of the term "reasonableness" is in fact given almost entirely to the sole interpretation and discretion of legal fact finders and decision makers and decided based on the concrete circumstances of each case brought to trial. This sole discretion may have dire consequences for defendants and victims alike, because judges may be unaware of the way they incorporate their own personal biases and gender stereotypes into the way they interpret, conceptualize and legally apply their perception of objective, normative and descriptive criteria of the Israeli reasonable man.

Provocation Doctrine in Israeli Femicide Cases

Whereas Israel's de jure approach to provocation seems to have wholeheartedly incorporated the British doctrine with its tests and preconditions, Israel's de facto approach to the doctrine appears to be quite different. Israel seems to have distanced itself from the British doctrine of provocation altogether, as Israeli case law de facto restricted its application to the point of its almost de facto abolition. Israeli criminal courts have been extremely reluctant to accept claims of provocation and have hardly ever applied the doctrine of provocation.[31] The de jure

28 Criminal Appeal 396/69 *Naim Avraham Beno v. The State of Israel* 24(1) PD 561 (1970).

29 Kremnitzer and Levanon, 2009; Kamir, 1997; Shachar, 1984.

30 CFH 1042/04 David Bitton v. The State of Israel.

31 See Shachar, 1984.

objective, prescriptive and normative requirement for accepting a provocation defense led, de facto, to an almost complete rejection by the criminal courts of provocation claims. Except for the fourth category relating to the adulterous wife, the Israeli legal approach rendered the doctrine of provocation as a partial defense for murder practicably inapplicable.[32]

To date, despite endless claims of provocation in almost every murder case, Israeli case law has applied the doctrine in only four cases, two of which resembled a self-defense claim.[33] The very rigid and high normative, legal threshold requirements regarding the objective element imply that the very few criminal cases whereby a provocation claim was accepted are, in and of themselves, exemplars of the prescribed normative Israeli reasonable man. In this respect, case law reflects the way social paradigms, values and norms are perpetually constructed and reconstructed. Furthermore, the precedent legal principle by which prior case-law rulings are imposed on consecutive cases creates a continuous chain of similar case-law rulings that perpetuates norms of behavior or characterizations of personality types. Thus, the precedent legal principle is one of the major mechanisms by which common law exerts its power in constructing social norms and behavior.[34]

Interestingly, and of utmost relevance to our discussion, two of these four cases wherein a provocation claim was accepted were cases of a post-separation murder. In these two cases, the female intimate partners were adamant about terminating their intimate relations with the killer, despite the religious court's refusal to grant them a divorce and the killers' unceasing refusal to accept and respect the women's personal decision to separate.[35] An overall critical examination of the doctrine's application reveals that the development of Israeli case law with respect to this doctrine was hybrid – on one hand, almost de facto abolishing the doctrine by using rigid de jure interpretations that restricted its application, and on the other hand, grossly expanding the interpretation of the fourth category of the 17th-century doctrine of provocation whereby defendants who killed their wives claimed to have done so because they lost control due to the victims' alleged adultery. With respect to this fourth category, instead of the specific and rigid tests for application of the partial defense in circumstances of adultery under

32 Dayan, 2014; Shachar, 1984.

33 Criminal Appeal 50/64 Elgabri v. The State of Israel; Criminal Appeal 95/82 Zelig Lyubov v. The State of Israel; Criminal Appeal 746/14 Yonatan Heilo v. The State of Israel.

34 Similar to all countries that adopted common law judicial methods, Israel relies on prior legal precedent and case analysis. Such legal methods are in practice the way social paradigms, values and norms are perpetually constructed and reconstructed. By using such case law methodology, judges claim to have found a method that enables them to establish the truth about events and therefore, also determine justice. Regarding the case law precedent principle as a potent mechanism for social construction see Smart, 1989: p. 10.

35 Criminal Appeal 30/73 Shmuel Shumlevich v. The State of Israel; Criminal Appeal 3071/92 Morris Azoualus v. The State of Israel 50(2) PD 573 (1996).

British common law, Israel enabled gross expansion of the range of cases permitting the mitigation of criminal liability in circumstances of intimate femicide.

The Provoking, Adulterous Israeli "Chained Wife": Shmulevich Case

Let us examine the Shmulevich case, ruled on in 1973, in which the Supreme Court rejected the state's appeal to reverse the Criminal District Court's mitigation of the defendant's murder conviction of his ex-wife.[36] For the sake of case presentation, we refer to the victim in the manner the court referred to her, i.e., the defendant's wife, although later we discuss such misleading and fatal terminology. According to the facts of the ruling, one night, armed with his military submachine gun, the defendant arrived at midnight in 1972 at the residence of his wife's new partner and saw his wife wearing a nightgown. When the wife's new partner fired a shot, Shmuel Smulevich activated his submachine gun, killing his estranged wife and severely wounding her new partner. Both the district court and Supreme Court ruled that such facts merit the application of the doctrine of provocation to the defendant's claim that he lost control over seeing his estranged wife wearing a nightgown with her new partner.

Substantiating the ruling, the Supreme Court reframed the facts of the case as circumstances whereby a husband sees his wife committing adultery. The court went further, noting that contrary to a 17th-century British man, provocation claims of adultery in 20th-century Israel should be expanded to justly apply to a contemporary Israeli reasonable man. Thus, the court argued in favor of accepting provocation claims, as in this case, even if the defendant did not see the victim having sex with another partner and as in this case, even if the wife had already left the defendant and they lived separately.[37] Furthermore, the Supreme Court judges maintained that the correct legal interpretation of the objective standard of the "reasonable Israeli" man justifies the provocation doctrine's expansion to circumstances wherein the victim was not married to the defendant.[38] How could the court apply mitigation when the wife had left her shared home with the killer and filed for a divorce? How could the court apply mitigation when the perpetrator armed himself with a submachine gun and came to the new partner's residence at midnight? How could the court apply mitigation when the killer fired multiple gunshots at the victims?

Part of the explanation of this very disturbing gross expansion of the objective standard of the Israeli reasonable man in circumstances of adultery has to do with the way the court described Shmulevich's alleged loss of control about his wife's desire and decision to terminate her marriage to the killer:

36 Criminal Appeal 30/73 Shmuel Shumlevich v. The State of Israel.

37 Section 3 Smulevich case.

38 Section 3 Smulevich case.

> The deceased was still married to the appellant, and he was eager to return her back to his home to raise their children – so much so, that he even threatened to shoot himself and to commit suicide. He filed suit for marital reconciliation with the rabbinical court, and refused – according to the district court ruling – to believe that his wife was committing adultery . . . *Objectively such provocation falls within the framework of the boiling blood of the regular Israeli husband who does not believe his wife is being unfaithful, and wants wholeheartedly to get closer to her and get her back, and catches her in the midst of evildoing – leading to his whole world falling apart, instantly.*
>
> [Trans., emphasis added][39]

First, even the killer's deadly violent behavior (by threatening to shoot himself and commit suicide) is sublimated, not to say disregarded and interpreted as a socially legitimate act to make the woman comply with her social and moral role by returning to "his home" (note that the court does not use the phrase "their home," but rather "his home") and raising their children. Second, implied in the defendant's filing of an appeal for "marital conciliation" to the religious court is the fact that he was not willing to grant the victim a divorce. Such refusal is hidden in the Supreme Court's comments, praising the killer for filing for marital conciliation. Use of the Hebrew term for marital conciliation stigmatizes the victim as a disruptive person seeking dispute, while portraying the killer as a peaceful person seeking a "peaceful" reconciliation (*shalom bayit* in Hebrew, which literally means "peaceful conciliation"). Last, the court's terminology in referring to the victim as the killer's wife is incorrect and disrespectful toward her resolute decision to separate: At the time of her alleged provoking immoral behavior, she was not his wife. At most, she was no more than a de jure "chained wife," whose autonomous decisions and wishes to separate were disregarded by the Supreme Court, who continued to frame her as "the defendant's wife" and accordingly, as morally and socio-legally an "adulterous wife."

A crucial legal issue is concealed among the facts of this precedent case and considered legally irrelevant to the application of the doctrine of provocation. These facts relate to the Israeli legal structure whereby both women and men are subjected to Jewish religious law in all personal matters. Indeed, the most fundamental religious legislation in Israel, incorporated into the secular legal system, is personal law, according to which issues of marriage and divorce pertaining to Jews come under the exclusive jurisdiction of the rabbinical courts and are determined according to Jewish religious laws.[40]

Alas, Jewish religious law is nowhere near gender-neutral.[41] For example, as noted by Yuval-Davis, according to religious law, any woman, regardless of how

39 Criminal Appeal 30/73 *Shmuel Shmulevich v. The State of Israel* 27(2) PD 598 (1973), Section 3.

40 Halperin-Kaddari, 2004: p. 227.

41 Halperin-Kaddari, 2000; Kamir, 2014; Lifshitz, 2003; Raday, 1992, 1995, 2003; Shmueli, 2013.

knowledgeable she may be, is unfit to fill the position of judge in the rabbinical court. What's more, religious law prohibits women from even appearing as witnesses in rabbinical courts.[42] Furthermore, the guiding principle of Jewish law states that from her marriage onward, a Jewish woman is forbidden to all except her husband and cannot sever this tie until he dies or divorces her. Although she may ask for a divorce, she can only be its passive recipient.[43]

According to Halperin-Kaddari, Jewish law adopts a double standard with respect to the sexual behavior of men and women in general and of married men and married women in particular.[44] Under this double standard, men's adulterous acts hardly carry any legal consequences, whereas women's adultery bears extremely harsh social and legal outcomes for her and her offspring over an extremely lengthy period.[45] Particularly relevant is Jewish law regarding adultery. An adulterous wife "is to be immediately divorced while losing all her monetary rights otherwise acquired according to the Jewish law. She is prohibited from later marrying either her former husband or the man with whom she had 'committed adultery' and any child that results from the adulterous relationships is considered a 'bastard' who is precluded from marrying within the Jewish community, except for a convert or a 'bastard' like him/herself."[46]

Furthermore, and particularly relevant to the legal case under discussion, according to Jewish abiding law, a woman must receive her husband's official agreement to her divorce request. Moreover, because according to Jewish law, the husband's agreement to divorce must be a voluntary and autonomous decision, courts cannot impose divorce on men in the event they refuse to grant it. In other words, men have absolute power over the divorce, because their voluntary agreement to the divorce is an absolute prerequisite without which the divorce is invalid.[47] According to Halperin-Kaddari, invalidity of the divorce means that the wife is still a married woman and therefore, any sexual relations she may later conduct will still be considered adulterous, with harsh consequences.[48]

Consequently, Jewish women married to husbands that under no circumstances agree to grant them a divorce remain forever formally and legally trapped, caged and chained to them. Furthermore, a gruesome future awaits women who decide to wait no longer for their husband to grant a divorce and begin a new life with a new intimate partner. According to Yuval-Davis, if the rabbinical court learns of the fact that the woman is living with another man while still "officially" married to her husband, such a woman will not be allowed to marry her chosen new intimate

42 Yuval-Davis, 2005: p. 123.
43 Halperin-Kaddari, 2000; Kamir, 2014; Lifshitz, 2003, 2005; Raday, 1992; Yuval-Davis, 2005.
44 Halperin-Kaddari, 2004: p. 236.
45 See Halperin Kaddari, 2004: p. 236.
46 See Halperin Kaddari, 2004: p. 236.
47 Halperin-Kaddari, 2009; Lifshitz, 2003, 2005; Stopler, 2003; Triger, 2005.
48 See Halperin-Kaddari, 2004: p. 237; Yuval-Davis, 2005.

partner, even if and when she is granted a divorce by her first husband, and any child born to such a couple will subsequently and officially be declared a bastard.[49]

Under such circumstances, and in line with their inability to obtain alternative legal remedies, women devoid of their husband's approval for divorce will likely do what the victim did – develop an intimate relationship with a man other than her husband. In despair and having lost faith in the possibility of ever being granted a divorce, and after years of desperation and frustration, women may – as the victim did – begin their intimate life with their new partner, although de jure they are still "married" to the individual refusing to give them a divorce, their former husband. When such "chained" women decide to wait no more for a divorce and begin their new life with a new intimate partner, they are officially, formally, and legally committing adultery. Such a technical legal construction of "adultery" results, lamentably, in ill judgments on the part of the courts, which blame the women and mitigate the murder conviction of their de jure husbands.

Such religion-based criminal mitigation is not a one-time ruling. Nor will it dissipate soon. An alarming recent verdict by a religious court, issued in 2018 with respect to a divorcing couple, ruled that the adulterous wife was not entitled to half the couple's house – which they jointly renovated and shared for 30 years – because according to the supreme religious court, it is improbable that the husband would have granted his wife half the house, legally owned by him, in the event she committed adultery.[50] Despite the legal contradiction between this ruling by a religious court and prior Supreme Court rulings regarding equal division of divorcing couples' assets, even in cases where they are formally solely owned by the husband,[51] the Supreme Court rejected the wife's appeal and reinstated the validity of the religious court's ruling. The implications of such a patriarchal religious ruling regarding adulterous wives, and its adoption by the Supreme Court, are yet to be seen. However, the social power of such a ruling most likely reinforces the negative social attributions toward adulterous wives, according to which they, and only they, should be blamed, whereas their killer should be vindicated.

Even more disturbing is the fact that the "reasonable" Israeli wife killer enjoys a double-edged legal umbrella under which his premediated murder is sublimated under the auspices of the law, both religious personal law and criminal law. Thus, the reasonable Israeli wife killer may first take advantage of religious law that grants

49 Yuval-Davis, 2005: p. 124. According to Yuval-Davis, even when a man is not found, as was the case with many men in the aftermath of the 1973 war, and there is no clear evidence that he died, his wife is prohibited from remarrying. She is at great social risk, even if evidence of his death becomes available. If she subsequently remarries and her first husband reappears, although she acted in good faith, she is forced to divorce from both men and the children of the second marriage are declared, officially, as "bastards" (op. cit). According to Yuval-Davis, a vast network of self-appointed informers ensures that the rabbinical authorities have up-to-date lists of culprits and potential culprits (op. cit).

50 HCJ 4602/13 Anonymous v. Great Rabbinical Court.

51 HCJ 1000/92 Hava Babli v. Great Rabbinical Court.

him patriarchy-based unlimited ability to refuse to grant a divorce, chaining the woman to be his de jure wife forever. Then, he can enjoy yet another patriarchal legal advantage, offered by criminal law, by using the legal construction of mitigation in circumstances of the wife's alleged adultery, to mitigate his murder of his chained de jure wife. How can the legal system serve as the platform, and in fact, the instrument, by which "reasonable" Israeli men chain and kill women, yet receive legal leniency and empathy to the point of mitigating the murders they commit?

Provocation, Loss of Control, and Spree Killings: Azoualus Case

Almost 20 years after the Smulevich case, one night in 1991, Moris Azoualus shot and killed his estranged wife and their neighbor.[52] He did this several months after he had left their shared home, against the backdrop of his demand that she stop all social interactions with the neighbor, with whom he suspected she was having an affair. In response, she decided to file for a divorce. In the religious court, Azoualus claimed she was an adulterous wife and refused to grant her a divorce. The wife, on her part, was unwilling to consider the requests of both her husband and the religious-court judges for reconciliation and was adamant about ending the marriage. During the months before the killing, the wife filed several complaints with the police, reporting Azoualus' violence and threats against her over her alleged intimate relations with the neighbor and her wish to divorce. The wife recounted that during these violent attacks, Azoualus cursed at her, called her a prostitute, beat her, and threatened to kill both her and her alleged lover, the neighbor, to the point of choking her a few times.

One night, Azoualus decided to "put an end to it."[53] Armed with his newly licensed gun, he looked for his wife, who was nowhere to be found. He headed toward his neighbor's house, seeing her in his neighbor's car. When the neighbor got into the car, Azoualus began to scold them, threatening to kill the neighbor. According to Azoualus, it was only then, when his wife and the neighbor admitted to being lovers and kissed, that he realized his long-time suspicions of his wife's love affair were correct. He shot his wife in the head at close range, killing her instantly. He then went on to shoot the neighbor, killing him, too. When the police arrived, he admitted that he had been aware of whom he was shooting, and that he had shot them both at close range, starting with a shot right to his wife's head and then shooting her lover.

The district criminal court ruled that the events prior to the killing could not posit severe provocation because the defendant's knowledge about his wife's love affair was not new. This ruling of the court was based on the defendant's prior knowledge of his wife's affair, as evident from the testimonies given in religious

52 Criminal Action (Nazareth) 195/91 *The State of Israel v. Morris Azoualus.* Hereinafter, the Azoualus criminal case.

53 See Azoualus criminal case, section 2.

court (that dealt with the wife's filing for divorce) and police records containing the wife's accounts of the defendant's battery over this matter. Azoualus appealed to the Supreme Court, which reversed the murder conviction and mitigated the verdict to manslaughter.[54]

It is important to stress at the outset of this discussion that in this case, the court referred to the victim as Azoualus' "wife," despite numerous court hearings about her request for a divorce, which was not granted to her. Thus, the victim, viewed by the court as "his wife," was at most, like Shmulevich's victim, his estranged wife. Had she been lucky to have been granted the divorce by Azoualus or the religious court, at the time of her killing, she would have been his ex-wife. Therefore, and as in Shmulevich's case, she was the defendant's "chained wife" de jure and his estranged wife de facto.

It is also important to emphasize that Israeli criminal courts of appeal do not intervene, as a rule, with the factual elements decided by the court that held the evidence and testimony hearings. Thus, in principle, court of appeal rulings are tied to the facts as decided by the trial court. However, as this case of a court-of-appeal ruling demonstrates, facts can be interpreted differently. The Supreme Court reversed Azoualus' murder conviction because, according to its interpretation, it was only after the wife and neighbor admitted to having a love affair, and more to the point, upon seeing them kissing, that the defendant truly realized his wife's adultery. Based on this account of the events, the Supreme Court accepted Azoualus' appeal and ruled that these circumstances led to a catastrophic collapse of the defendant's entire world.[55] Thus, according to the Supreme Court, Azoualus' killings merit mitigation because his actions satisfied all doctrine demands: Severe provocation that led to loss of control and the ensuing immediate killings.[56]

The Supreme Court stated in this appeal that both the subjective and objective requirements of the doctrine of provocation were met, because according to the Supreme Court judges, any reasonable Israeli man or woman would have lost control under such tormenting circumstances. In the court's words:

> The blood of the regular Israeli man, as well as the blood of a regular Israeli woman, might boil upon the mere sight of an adulterous intimate partner, more so when the adulterous act is conducted for the sole purpose of disclosing the existence of an adulterous affair
>
> [Trans.].[57]

The mitigation granted in this case, based on the killer's claim of provocation, is extremely disturbing. To begin, Azoualus' account of the events should have

54 Criminal Appeal 3071/92 *Morris Azoualus v. The State of Israel* 50(2) PD 573 (1996). Hereinafter, Azoualus criminal appeal.

55 See section 10, Azoualus criminal appeal.

56 See Azoualus case.

57 See section 11, Azoualus criminal appeal.

been, at the very least, taken with a grain of salt.[58] Here, unfortunately and for want of any alternative witnesses or other forensic evidence such as video or audio recordings, the killer's defense narrative becomes the main, if not the sole, basis for establishing the facts and truth about the events that led to his killing of the victims.[59] This lack of alternative evidence leads, very awkwardly, to the killer's defense claims becoming in fact the foundation on which the judges constructed the factual and truthful description of the events that led the defendant to kill his wife and his neighbor. Second and criminologically speaking, this case of provocation mitigation (as in Shmulevich's case) is in fact post-separation femicide. Empirical studies, both global and in Israel, show that estrangement is the greatest risk factor for femicide, because most intimate-partner femicide cases are perpetrated against the backdrop of the woman's decision to terminate an intimate relationship with the killer.[60] Moreover, women are at particularly high risk, and their lives are in danger, if and when they leave someone for a different man.[61] Furthermore, and in direct relevance to the doctrine of provocation, empirical findings show that such post-separation homicides are more often than not premediated, and certainly not the outcome of a "sudden loss of control."[62]

Third, even if we accept the killer's defense narrative as the truthful description of the events that led to the double murder, we cannot help but seriously ponder the merit of such killings as provoked. There are many reasons to question the suitability of applying the provocation defense in the circumstances the defendant himself described. How could the Supreme Court accept his claim of provocation when he had already been living separately from the victim for six months, specifically if considering her declared wish to terminate their relationship? Furthermore, how could the Supreme Court accept his claim of provocation when she had been trying legally to obtain a divorce in the religious court and he had refused to grant a divorce, time and again, for a year and a half prior to the killing? How could his claim of provocation be accepted based on his alleged narrative of seeing his de facto ex-wife (still de jure wife) kissing with their neighbor in his car? How could the Supreme Court accept his claim of provocation when he had armed himself with his newly licensed gun prior to reaching the neighbor's residence? How could the court accept the claim knowing that he had shot his ex-wife in the head, at close range, and had gone on to shoot their neighbor as well? How could the court accept the claim of provocation when the defendant himself admitted to resolving, before heading to the neighbor's residence, "to put an end to this"? How could his claim be accepted when he had threatened to kill his neighbor just minutes before he shot him? How could the court accept his

58 The district criminal court judges indeed stated that the defendant's account of the neighbor's acts prior to the event was not by definition the correct description of the truthful events. See Azoualus criminal case, section 4(b).

59 Morgan, 1997.

60 Campbell et al., 2003, 2007; Howe, 2013; Ramsey, 2010; Rapaport, 1996.

61 Campbell et al., 2003.

62 Ben Ze'ev and Goussinsky, 2008; Dawson and Sutton, 2017; Donovan and Wildman, 1981.

claim while there were numerous police complaints filed by his de facto ex-wife against his ongoing battery over the issue of her alleged love affair, threatening to kill her, beating her, and even choking her? How could they accept his claim when he admitted to the police that at the time of the shooting he was aware of whom he was shooting? Killing under such circumstances seems to be nothing but an intentional and premediated double murder.

Such a ruling by the Supreme Court is possible because, among other noted considerations, Israeli provocation case law has incorporated, alongside the British doctrine, the American "heat-of-passion" conceptualization of the doctrine of provocation. The heat-of-passion conceptualization of the provocation doctrine is embedded in the realm of human weaknesses, in the so-called sudden loss of control that is not to be praised but certainly understood and excused, and as such, represents a "concession to human weakness."[63] Such legal concession means that the law is prepared to partially excuse a defendant by mitigating his killing, and to do so by partially excusing the acts he commits as the result of provocation sufficiently egregious to provoke strong emotions. Under such circumstances, it is assumed that the defendant's capacity for self-control has been reduced to such a degree that it is morally unjust to treat him as a murderer. In other words, as argued by Dressler, the gist of such legal mitigation is that the "heat of passion reduces punishment because the actor is, unfortunately, like most humans."[64]

The combination of provocation and the heat of passion accords the doctrine of provocation an almost exclusively subjective character that, in practice, unrestrictedly extends the range of cases regarding "adulterous wives" to which it can be applied. This expansive approach to provocation in effect removes many acts of homicide from the scope of the offense of murder, because the supposedly "normative" threshold of an "ordinary (passionate) guy" with his human weakness is lower than the normative, prescribed threshold of a reasonable man. Such an intertwined combination of provocation and the heat of passion is even broader than applying the doctrine of provocation to the reasonable-person concept, because it further expands the subjective component according to which the defendant's claim for mitigation can be accepted.[65] In other words, Israel expanded the doctrine of provocation regarding adulterous wives by using both the British reasonable-man approach as an objective standard and the American heat-of-passion approach to expand the subjective standard.

This alleged gender-neutral concession to human weakness, when combined with the patriarchal social underpinnings of the fourth category of the legal doctrine of provocation (the adulterous wife), poses a danger, in that under sexually related circumstances, wife killers might enjoy criminal mitigation. One such example relates to a recent ruling regarding the merits of criminal mitigation in

63 Dressler, 1982: p. 735; Keetley, 2008.
64 Dressler, 1982: p. 756.
65 Berman and Farrell, 2011; Dressler, 1982; Lee, 2003.

yet another post-separation femicide case; in this instance, the killer claimed his wife made personal remarks about the size of his penis, causing him to allegedly lose control and kill her.[66] Although the Supreme Court rejected the defendant's appeal to mitigate his murder conviction, it based its decision on odd grounds.

Notwithstanding the factual evidence showing that the victim had been severely beaten by her brothers and husband for choosing to leave him and start a new life with her lover, and evidence that she had been forced and coerced into leaving her lover and returning to her wedded husband, as the relevant circumstances of her alleged provoking remarks, we would have hoped that the Supreme Court would reject the merit of provocation mitigation because such remarks do not fit the objective, prescriptive, and normative element of the 21st-century Israeli doctrine of provocation. Alas, the Supreme Court judges did not rule that an estranged wife's remarks about the defendant's penis size do not meet the objective legal standard. Instead, they rejected the appeal for provocation mitigation just because the wife's remarks over which the defendant killed her did not satisfy the doctrine's requirement of constituting a "sudden" provocation that led to a loss of control. The Supreme Court concluded that because the victim had made similar remarks during the two-month period during which she was violently forced to return home and prior to being killed, the defendant was acquainted with these remarks, and they were thus not "sudden" for him. Furthermore, the Supreme Court concluded that such remarks could not have led to his sudden provocation and ensuing loss of control – because the defendant did not kill his wife in any of these prior instances. In other words, according to this ruling, had the husband killed his wife after she had made these remarks for the first time, he could have possibly been granted a provocation mitigation over his alleged loss of control over comments regarding the size of his penis by his wife.

Lamentably and by way of discussion, the Supreme Court reinforced once again the Azoualus ruling, stating that although cases of remarks about penis size do not merit criminal mitigation, cases of adulterous wives – as in the Azoualus case – indeed do.[67] Moreover and even more disturbing is the fact that one district-court judge dissented, stating that a wife's remarks over a husband's penis size constitute severe provocation and merit, in and of themselves, criminal mitigation.[68] Such rulings play a formative social role in the sense that they lower the normative objective standard against which post-separation femicide defendants are socially and criminally judged and measured.

This expansive legal concession, based on expansion of the subjective standard in line with the heat-of-passion approach, is further explicitly demonstrated by the extremely lenient sentence accorded to Azoualus. As noted, Azoualus killed both his ex-wife and neighbor, and his double-murder conviction was mitigated upon his appeal to the Supreme Court to a double-manslaughter conviction.

66 Criminal Appeal 1426/12 *Ahmed Muzafer v. The State of Israel*. Hereinafter, Muzafer appeal.
67 Section 9, Muzafer appeal.
68 Judge Drori M., see section 1 in Judge's Solberg opinion, Muzafer appeal.

Consequently, and in line with the mitigated conviction, the district criminal court sentenced Azoualus to 15 years in prison for each victim. However, Azoualus appealed once again to the Supreme Court, this time arguing that the previous Supreme Court's murder mitigation of killing while under loss of control should have also been applied by the district criminal court to his sentencing.[69] Accordingly, he claimed that the district court erred when sentencing him to 15 years in prison for each victim and should have sentenced him for the killing of only one person, for a maximum of 20 years' imprisonment.[70] In 2000, the Supreme Court accepted Azoualus' second appeal (with four judges consenting and three judges dissenting) – ruling that despite killing two victims at close range, shooting consecutive, different shots while admitting to being aware of the identity of the victims he was shooting, he had done all this in a sudden moment of provocation that led to his severe loss of control.[71] Accordingly, his sentence was reduced to 15 years in prison, a sentence that is in fact five years less than the maximum penalty for one count of manslaughter, statutorily set to 20 years of imprisonment.

This gross criminal leniency toward femicide perpetrators is extremely disturbing, because the leniency afforded by the heat-of-passion approach in fact results in overlooking the gravity of the killing; namely, the killing of multiple victims. Such a ruling in fact suggests that under circumstances of alleged adulterous wives, even those de jure chained ones, the number of victims is immaterial. As long as criminal courts award a killer the mitigation of the doctrine of provocation, he can, as a matter of rule, kill as many victims as he wishes and still be sentenced with a penalty equivalent to one count of manslaughter (or even less, as this disturbing ruling shows). This legal result utterly and horrendously discriminates against women's autonomy and, furthermore, perpetrates and instigates violence not only against women, but also against many people. In fact, a blind, indiscriminating "mass spree" killing might be instigated by the provocation-doctrine conceptualization within the heat-of-passion approach.

Conclusion

Law has the power to construct social norms, values and behaviors and as such, the deeply gender-biased legal vision and practices of the reasonable-man approach may serve to produce and perpetuate fixed gendered norms and identities.[72] Indeed, the law has at its disposal one of the most potent mechanisms for defining social reality – the way it constructs "provocation" – and it uses this power in the realm of homicide, with the most dramatic consequences.

69 CFH 3372/98 *Morris Azoualus v. The State of Israel* 54(4) PD 502 (2000). Hereinafter, Azoualus second appeal.

70 As stated in the relevant PCI 298 section.

71 See Azoualus case.

72 Howe, 2004, 2013; Smart, 1989, 1995.

In this realm, the power of the law exerts itself by constructing an objective conceptualization of male sexual jealousy in the framework of human nature and behavior. This conceptualization then serves as a standard against which a defendant's actions are judged and calibrated according to their nearness to or distance from that which is defined as normative, reasonable and meriting mitigation.[73] Although the objective-reasonableness legal standard is presented as a gender-neutral reasonable-person standard, the legal framework is not and cannot be detached from the social system in which it is interpreted and applied when it comes to constructing its version of the course of events.[74] In this respect, judges might rely on their own gender prejudices and stereotypes in applying the standard to criminal defendants,[75] without even being aware of their own deeply ingrained gender biases.[76] Such biased conceptualization engenders and normalizes socially harmful gendering practices, of which femicide is one such possible case.[77]

In post-separation femicide cases, the legal threshold of the reasonable sexually jealous male who loses control defines gendered norms that may border on accepting violent, almost mass-spree killers. In two femicide cases wherein a provocation claim was accepted, the sociocultural underpinnings of the conception of the Jewish Israeli reasonable man entrenched in the legal conceptualization reveal a deeply rooted patriarchal male-chauvinist norm by which violent possessive men are constructed as reasonable and normative, and married women's resolution to terminate their intimate relationships with the would-be killers as adulterous provocation.[78] Accordingly, these women are blamed for inciting their own sometimes gruesome killing. In line with the Israeli legal doctrine requiring a normative, prescriptive and objective standard of reasonableness, and the Supreme Court's rulings mitigating the aforementioned defendants' murder convictions, killers of ex-intimate partners are construed – socio-legally, judicially and morally – as "reasonable wife killers."

Having dealt with a critical crimino-legal analysis of the main femicide subtype in Israel, the following chapter, Chapter 4, focuses on F.H.K., which seems to be a significant component of femicide in Israel.

References

Allen, H. (1988). One law for all reasonable persons? *International Journal of the Sociology of Law*, *16*, 419.

Ben Ze'ev, A., & Goussinsky, R. (2008). *In the name of love: Romantic ideology and its victims.* Oxford University Press.

73 For a similar argument relating to legal norms, see Smart, 1995: p. 49.

74 Coss, 2006; Smart, 1989: p. 11.

75 Miller, 2010: p. 266.

76 Hunter and Tyson, 2017; Miller, 2010; Smart, 1989; Tucker, 2013.

77 Dayan, 2014; Spatz, 1991.

78 Howe, 2004; Miller, 2010.

Berman, M. N., & Farrell, I. P. (2011). Provocation manslaughter as partial justification and partial excuse. *William and Mary Law Review*, *52*(4), 1027.

Brown, H. (1999). Provocation as a defence to murder: To abolish or to reform? *Australian Feminist Law Journal*, *12*, 137.

Campbell, J. C., Glass, N., Sharps, P. W., Laughon, K., & Bloom, T. (2007). Intimate partner homicide: Review and implications of research and policy. *Trauma, Violence, & Abuse*, *8*(3), 246–269.

Campbell, J. C., Webster, D., Koziol-Mclain, J., Block, C., Campbell, D., Curry, M. A., Gary, F., Glass, N., McFarlane, J., Sachs, C., Sharps, P., Ulrich, Y., Wilt, S. A., Manganello, J., Xu, X., Schollenberger, J., Frye, V., & Laughon, K. (2003). Risk factors for femicide in abusive relationships: Results from a multisite case control study. *American Public Health*, *93*(7), 1089–1097.

Coss, G. (2006). The defence of provocation: An acrimonious divorce from reality. *Current Issues in Criminal Justice*, *18*(1), 51.

Dawson, M., & Sutton, D. (2017). Similar sentences, similar crimes? Using deep sample analysis to examine the comparability of homicides and punishments by victim-offender relationship. *International Journal of Law Crime and Justice*, *49*, 58.

Dayan, H. (2014). Mine or dead: Femicide and a bill to amend article 301 of the Israeli penal code. *Hukim: The Hebrew University Law Faculty's Journal on Legislation*, *6*, 205–232 (in Hebrew).

Dayan, H. (2018). *Femicide and the law: American criminal doctrines*. Routledge.

Donovan, D. A., & Wildman, S. M. (1981). Is the reasonable man obsolete: A critical perspective on self-defense and provocation. *Loyola of Los Angeles Law Review*, *14*, 435.

Dressler, J. (1982). Rethinking heat of passion: A defense in search of a rationale. *Journal of Criminal Law and Criminology*, *73*, 421.

Halperin-Kaddari, R. (2000). Gender construction under Halachic marriage and divorce laws. *Talpiot*, *22*, 451–464 (in Hebrew).

Halperin-Kaddari, R. (2004). *Women in Israel: A state of their own*. University of Pennsylvania Press.

Halperin-Kaddari, R. (2009). The missing women's enigma: The scope of the Get refusals predicament in Israel. *Kolech: Being a Jewish Woman*, *5*, 83–95.

Horder, J. (1992). *Provocation and responsibility*. Clarendon Press.

Howe, A. (2004). Provocation in crisis – law's passion at the crossroads? New directions for feminist strategists. *The Australian Feminist Law Journal*, *21*, 53.

Howe, A. (2013). Mastering emotions or still losing control? Seeking public engagement with 'sexual infidelity' homicide. *Feminist Legal Studies*, *21*, 141.

Hunter, R., & Tyson, D. (2017). The implementation of feminist law reforms: The case of post provocation sentencing. *Social and Legal Studies*, *26*, 129.

Kamir, O. (1997). Reasonableness killed the woman. *Plilim*, *6*, 137 (in Hebrew).

Kamir, O. (2014). Be a Jewish woman at home and (a small) Israeli man outdoors: The sources of the deep split in the identity of Jewish Israeli women. In A. Hakohen & A. Maoz (Eds.), *Jewish Israeli identities* (pp. 325–335). Tel Aviv University (in Hebrew).

Keetley, D. (2008). From anger to jealousy: Explaining domestic homicide in antebellum America. *Journal of Social History*, *42*(2), 269–297.

Kremnitzer, M., & Levanon, L. (2009). Lack of provocation in premeditation: Following CrimFH 1042/04 Biton v. State of Israel. In *David Weiner volume on criminal law and ethics* (pp. 549–584). Israel Bar Publishing House (in Hebrew).

Lee, C. (2003). *Murder and the reasonable man: Passion and fear in the criminal courtroom*. New York University Press.

Lifshitz, S. (2003). Equality in marriage, the right to divorce and autonomy of communities. *Tel-Aviv University Law Review, 27*, 139 (in Hebrew).

Lifshitz, S. (2005). I want to get a divorce now! On civil regulation of divorce law. *Tel-Aviv University Law Review, 28*(3), 671 (in Hebrew).

Miller, A. E. (2010). Inherent (gender) unreasonableness of the concept of reasonableness in the context of manslaughter committed in the heat of passion. *William & Mary Journal of Women and the Law, 17*, 249.

Morgan, J. (1997). Provocation law and facts: Dead women tell no tales; tales are told about them. *Melbourne University Law Review, 21*, 237.

Pei-Lin, C. C. (2000). Provocation's privileged desire: The provocation doctrine, "homosexual panic," and non-violent unwanted sexual advance defense. *Cornell Journal of Law and Public Policy, 10*(1), 195.

Raday, F. (1992). Israel – the incorporation of religious patriarchy in a modern state. *International Review of Comparative Public Policy, 4*, 209.

Raday, F. (1995). Religion, multiculturalism and equality: The Israeli case. *Israel Yearbook on Human Rights, 25*, 193.

Raday, F. (2003). Culture, religion and gender. *International Journal of Constitutional Law, 1*(4), 663–715.

Ramsey, C. B. (2010). Provoking change: Comparative insights on feminist homicide law reform. *Journal of Criminal Law and Criminology, 100*(1), 33.

Rapaport, E. (1996). Capital murder and the domestic discount: A study of capital murder in the post-Furman era. *SMU Law Review, 49*(5), 1507.

Shachar, Y. (1981). Premeditation and legislative intent. *Mehkarei Mishpat, 2*, 204 (in Hebrew).

Shachar, Y. (1984). The reasonable person in criminal law. *Hapraklit, 38*, 78 (in Hebrew).

Shmueli, B. (2013). Civil actions for acts that are valid according to religious family law but harm women's rights: Legal pluralism in cases of collision between two sets of laws. *Vanderbilt Journal of Transnational Law, 46*, 823.

Smart, C. (1989). *Feminism and the power of law*. Routledge.

Smart, C. (1995). *Law, crime and sexuality: Essays in feminism*. London.

Spatz, M. (1991). A 'lesser' crime: A comparative study of legal defenses for men who kill their wives. *Columbia Journal of Law and Social Problems, 24*, 597.

Stopler, G. (2003). Countenancing the oppression of women: How liberals tolerate religious and cultural practices that discriminate against women. *Columbia Journal of Gender & Law, 12*, 154.

Triger, Z. (2005). Love's dominion: Marriage and divorce between Jews in Israel. In O. Ben-Naftali & H. Naveh (Eds.), *Trials of love*. Ramot (in Hebrew).

Tucker, J. (2013). Taming the green-eyed monster: On the need to rethink our cultural conception of jealousy. *Yale Journal of Law and Feminism, 25*, 217.

Yuval-Davis N. (2005). Bearers of the collective women and religious legislations in Israel. In F. Esther (Ed.), *Israeli women's studies* (pp. 121–132). Rutgers University Press.

4 (Dis)“honor” Femicide

Introduction

F.H.K. has been a long-standing phenomenon among Arab societies in the Middle East and is also a rising phenomenon among the Middle Eastern diasporic communities in Western societies, increasingly identified in Europe and the Anglophone world.[1] Alarming figures of F.H.K. have been noted in the past few years in Israel. Arab women, who belong to the largest non-Jewish minority in Israel, composed mainly of Palestinians, are grossly overrepresented.[2] Epidemiological characteristics of F.H.K. in Israel show that at least ten Arab women are killed each year. As we noted in Chapter 2, the Arab population in Israel represents only 20% of the total population, yet 30% to 40% of women killed every year are Israeli Arab women, and in 2015–2016, they accounted for more than 50% of all femicide victims in Israel.

In the literature, femicide of Arab women is usually termed *“honor” killing* and is regarded as a particular form of “honor” violence against women, wherein the killing of a woman is perpetrated by a member or members of her family who do not approve of her social behavior in general and her sexual behavior in particular.[3] This definition has been criticized for being overly broad because it includes a wide host of family murders, including spousal murders, and for ignoring the fact that “honor” and perceptions of women’s sexuality may serve as motives for femicide in the West as well.[4] The criminological critique of the term “honor” killing has been exacerbated by scholars repudiating such labeling as a racist and xenophobic term that discriminates and dehumanizes cultural religious and national social groups of Muslim, Middle Eastern, and South Asian origin.[5]

Notwithstanding the controversies over the term “honor” killing, which led us to term it “(dis)-honor,” scholars agree that key characteristics of F.H.K. relate

1 Payton, 2014.
2 Dayan, 2021; Edelstein, 2011; Landau and Hattis-Rolef, 1998; Sela-Shayovitz, 2010.
3 Abu-Rabia, 2011; Shalhoub-Kevorkian, 1999, 2002.
4 Shier and Shor, 2016: p. 1165.
5 Shier and Shor, 2016: 1164, p. 1180.

DOI: 10.4324/9781003333272-6

to its familial, collective, and “honor”-related nature.[6] Although “honor” killings may be the outcome of notions of “honor” and target men as well as women, the gender-specific notion of “honor,” *ʿird*, mainly refers to women and seems to intersect with the larger phenomenon of femicide. Though intersected, “honor” killings cannot be equated with femicide. The most prevalent form of femicide is intimate-partner homicide that is most often perpetrated by the male intimate partner and linked to the victim’s desire to terminate the relationship, whereas “honor” killings are usually of an agnatic collective nature,[7] encompassing a wider range of family killings, male killings included,[8] ingrained in the power of collective cultural notions of “honor.”[9] The phenomenon of F.H.K. should not be equated with “honor” killings, because such killings are not by definition exclusively related to conceptions of “honor” crimes. The killing of an Arab woman may be linked to an “honor” crime, yet it may also be related to intimate-partner femicide or domestic violence.

Gender, “Honor” Violence, and Femicide

The family is the foundation of Middle Eastern society,[10] and the Arab community in much of the Middle East, including Israel. The Arab community is structured among super-extended family clan lines called *hamula*, creating in each Arab village and town a mosaic of large and small hamula groups[11] wherein literally everybody knows everybody – and in many cases, are related to them either directly or indirectly.[12] The Arab sociocultural orientation puts its emphasis on collective identity as opposed to individual identity, wherein the societal base is one’s group origins going back generations.[13] The family structure is based on values of an agnatic society and is predominantly patrilineal in nature.[14]

According to Kulwicky,[15] in the traditional patrilineal family context, a woman belongs to her agnatic group and male relatives are morally, legally and economically responsible for the woman. Men are favored over women, and according to Hasan,[16] women’s subordination is perpetuated by the Arab custom to deny women their share in inheritance (an economic situation that fosters their dependent and submissive status vis-à-vis their male relatives). In a patriarchal system, men have authority and power over women due to their dominance of

6 Abu-Odeh, 1997; Chesler, 2010.
7 Payton, 2014: p. 2871.
8 Kressel et al., 1981: pp. 145–146.
9 Dogan, 2014: p. 379; Dogan, 2016: p. 54.
10 Ruggi, 1998.
11 Al-Haj, 1989: pp. 179–186; Pely, 2011: p. 211.
12 Pely, 2011: p. 214.
13 Abu-Rabia, 2011: p. 37.
14 Kulwicky, 2002: p. 84.
15 Op. cit.
16 Hasan, 2002: p. 7.

material and social resources. Consequently, men are often responsible for supporting their wife financially, in exchange for her fidelity and domestic services.[17] Women have rights in circumscribed spheres, but when compared to men, they are considered subordinates and treated as individuals who should be protected by men.[18] Contrary to the Arab patrilineal system, the wife in a patriarchal system takes the name of her husband and is associated with her husband's lineage rather than her father's.[19]

Scholars agree that the social status of families in Arab societies is linked to the notion of "honor."[20] Family "honor" in Arab society refers to a concern for the reputation of one's family[21] and is expressed through the generosity and honesty of its members, the manliness (courage, bravery) of its men, and the sexual purity and chastity of a sister or daughter and fidelity of a wife and mother, as embedded in the Arab term 'ird.[22] In Arab families, the "honor" of men and their households, the political and social status of the family, and their reputation – particularly of women – are all interdependent.[23] "Honor" is bestowed on families at large, rather than exclusively on male members, although men are held more accountable for their family's "honor."[24] Although masculine "honor" (toughness, strength, protecting one's reputation) refers to a concern for being able to live up to the standards set for men, family "honor" refers to a concern for the reputation of one's family.[25]

Norms related to concepts of "honor" give meaning to family and female behavior, and control the social and sexual behavior of all group members.[26] According to Baxter, holding "honor" brings economical, psychological, political, social and emotional rewards: For example, respect in the community, ability to arrange reputable marriages, eligibility for career advancement and economical rewards in business since people choose to do business with those of "honor"able repute. On the other hand, for those who do not live up to the

17 Kulwicky, 2002: p. 84.
18 Op. cit.; Al-Haj, 1989: p. 189.
19 Baker et al., 1999: p. 166.
20 Awwad, 2001: p. 39. Among Turks, the concept is termed ***namus*** (van Osch et al., 2013: p. 335); among Bedouin, the concept is termed *'ar* (Abu-Rabia, 2011: p. 34); and in Sudan, it is termed *fadiiha* (Dodd, 1973: p. 43).
21 Baxter, 2007; van Osch et al., 2013.
22 Abu Rabia, 2011; Kulwicky, 2002.
23 Abu-Rabia, 2011: p. 37.
24 Baxter, 2007: p. 747.
25 Van Osch et al., 2013: p. 335. Although masculine "honor" seems to play an essential role in explaining men's violent reactions (van Osch et al., 2013: p. 334) and is linked empirically to femicide in Western cultures, the "honor" related to homicidal acts in Arab societies is probably not linked to masculine "honor," but rather family "honor." According to van Osch et al. (2013: p. 335), one's "honor" in Mediterranean "honor" cultures is intertwined with family "honor"; hence, the concern for family "honor" might be just as or even more important than concerns for masculine "honor."
26 Kulwicky, 2002: p. 85.

"honor" principles, "psychological consequences may be enormous: feelings of embarrassment, humiliation, shame, and guilt."[27]

The concept of family "honor" in Arab society includes two notions of "honor": Gender-neutral and gender-specific.[28] The gender-neutral notion of "honor" refers to family "honor," and the gender-specific interpretation relates to the sexual behavior of women as encapsulated in the Arab term 'ird. Family "honor" as embedded in the concept of 'ird refers to "honor" specifically related to women.[29] 'Ird's historical roots are pre-Islamic and appear to be secular; thus, it can exist in communities that place little or no emphasis on orthodox Islam, such as nomadic pastoralists, the Druze, and even Christians.[30] Although 'ird notions are most evident in the tribal and peasant sectors of society,[31] 'ird appears to be a fundamental organizing component of the contemporary urban sector as well, "in all but the most 'modernized' families."[32] 'Ird's controlling value is overarching and present among various Arab groups, encompassing traditional and modern cultures. Although forces of change (such as urbanization and education) may have an impact on 'ird and its associated norms, the value of 'ird and its correlative norms "resist the processes of change."[33] Moreover, Hasan contends that today, the concept of 'ird' has become more inclusive, encompassing other forms of behavior perceived as a threat to male domination.[34]

'Ird refers to a notion that combines a dual-gender aspect: Men's reputation for their "honor"able deeds, ability and willingness to defend themselves, and women's sexual purity and chastity.[35] However, its major meaning is in connection with "honor," particularly the sexual "honor" of women in the family. Taken together with the central social importance of the family unit to the organization of the Arab

27 Baxter, 2007: p. 746.
28 Dogan, 2014: p. 367.
29 Abu Rabia, 2011: p. 34.
30 Dodd, 1973: p. 44.
31 According to Awwad (2001: p. 40), the historical roots of "honor" killing are anchored in the loose organization of pre-Islamic Arab communities along the absence of a centralized state control. These sociopolitical circumstances enforced the family as the main social unit and led to each family to strive to protect its resources and improve its chances to access more resources. The more resources a family owned, the higher its social status in the community. To keep resources in the family, inheritances were passed along the male lineage in the family and important political and economic decisions were made at the sole discretion of the men in the family. Women were endowed with the responsibility of bearing healthy, strong male children for the family (p. 41). Sociologically speaking, the link to the female family members' sexual organs lies, according to Awwad, in the fact that it is of great interest for the Middle Eastern family to be large and at the same time, protect its lineage. The code of "honor" thus acts as boundary maintenance for the family: It allows it to define, protect, and maintain its boundary in a confusing and loosely organized structure and encourages feelings of unity and loyalty to the family as the central social group (p. 45).
32 Dodd, 1973: p. 40.
33 Op. cit.
34 Hasan, 2002: p. 3.
35 Awwad, 2001: p. 41.

society, ʻird can be seen as a major controlling value in the social norms, behavior, and structure of the Arab society.[36] ʻIrd differs from the notion of male "honor," termed *sharaf.* Whereas male "honor" (sharaf) can be acquired and augmented through the right behavior and great achievements, female "honor" (ʻird) is an ascribed passive status[37] that can only be lost by the misconduct of an individual woman, staining the collective identity and social status of the family.[38] Once ʻird is lost, it can hardly be regained.[39] Though ʻird is a collective possession that affects the "honor" of the whole family unit,[40] it appears to be a personal possession, and each woman is responsible for her "honor"able corresponding behavior, affecting the total family "honor."[41]

The network of norms surrounding ʻird extends to many actions that are only remotely connected with sex and may include loud speech, bearing, appearance in public places and even being single or divorced.[42] According to Baker et al., in addition to physical symbols of separation, such as the veil or restrictive and segregated quarters, "honor" demands that women in the home behave in narrowly prescribed submissive ways that are considered equivalent to sexual purity.[43] Therefore "a woman can bring disʻhonor' by conversing with a strange man, talking back to her husband, criticizing her in-laws, laughing a lot, or otherwise failing to fulfill expectations of appropriate feminine behavior."[44] Kevorkian argued that requiring virginity in women as a regulatory practice of gender exceeds the physical and biological body and is reproduced onto the gendered political body; thus, a crime of "honor" occurs when a woman crosses any of the bodily, physical or social borders. Thus, women are killed along this regulatory gendered practice "not only because they fail to bleed on their wedding night, but also if they disʻhonor' and shame the family by, for example, conversing with a man, smoking, coming home late, or engaging in a romantic relationship."[45]

36 Dodd, 1973: p. 40.
37 Hasan, 2002: p. 6.
38 Hasan (2002) pointed to the absurdity of a social power matrix where "the passive woman, thought to be inferior in status, holds within her body the public worth of all her male relatives, worth which she can directly damage and diminish, but which she cannot augment" (p. 7). Baxter (2007) argued that the fact that a woman can cause great damage to the family "honor" is itself an expression of her powerful abilities, even if destructive in nature (p. 747), and therefore, women are both supported and restrained by men, and men are deemed authorities but also vulnerable to women's dominant power on family "honor" (p. 764).
39 See Abu-Zeid in Dodd, 1973: p. 42; Baker et al., 1999: p. 170.
40 Which includes in the Arab social structure not only the nuclear and extended family, but the super-extended family clan lines called hamula; see Pely, 2011: p. 211.
41 Dodd, 1973: pp. 40–41.
42 Abu-Rabia, 2011: p. 36; Dodd, 1973: p. 45; van Osch et al., 2013: p. 335.
43 Baker et al., 1999: p. 167.
44 Op. Cit.
45 Shalhoub-Kevorkian, 2002: p. 579.

A corollary of the issue of "honor" is shame.[46] In Arab society, "honor" and shame are familial, rather than male: Women are subject to "honor" and shame, which they may gain, maintain or lose based on local norms and beliefs. Abu-Rabia argued that the fact that individuals are controlled by public threats to their personal reputation and "honor" is what transforms rural Arab societies into "shame cultures."[47] Lately, the emotion of shame has been recognized as linked to domestic violence, and Baker et al. argued that "honor" as a belief system can generate a shame response when the sense of "honor" has been violated.[48] According to Cooney, typical challenges to "honor" that may lead to loss of social status may be directed either to contest dominance (and usually involves men) or contest sexual norms (and usually involves women).[49] In "honor" patterns of femicide, the aggressor's sense of identity is based on the behavior of another, and such dependence on another person's behavior is a powerless role that might heighten the felt need to maintain control, regardless the cost.[50]

Another social aspect of the notion of shame and ʻird relates to the fact that ʻird may be a matter of reputation even more than fact: What other people think becomes as important as what takes place, and thus, offenses against ʻird become very serious when public notice is taken of the offenses.[51] The loss of ʻird may sometimes occur due to men's actions, independently of the women's precipitation and collaboration. Even though women may have done nothing to encourage the event (and even may have been raped), the dis"honor" brought on the family by the event is attributed to the women.[52] An additional gender aspect of ʻird relates to the social fact that although ʻird is primarily a possession of men, women of the family take responsibility for the observance and enforcement of the code.[53] Women watch for infringements of the code on the part of the family, and when a violation goes unpunished, they may urge the father or brother to do his duty to protect the family's ʻird. Thus, although ʻird is primarily a value aligned with the individual behavior of each woman, the patrilineal family collaborates in its construction and maintenance: Older patrilineal women (mothers, aunts) watch over it and enforce it daily, and men protect it.[54]

46 Baker et al., 1999: p. 169. Shame from the viewpoint of the Bedouin society, for example, is not the act itself, but public knowledge that someone's daughter has had illicit sexual relations (Abu-Rabia, 2011: p. 34).

47 Abu Rabia, 2011.

48 Baker et al., 1999: p. 176.

49 Cooney, 2014: p. 407.

50 Baker et al., 1999: p. 177. According to Baker et al. (1999), "the conception of 'honor' used to rationalize killing is founded on the notion that a person's 'honor' depends on the behavior of others and that behavior, therefore, must be controlled. Thus the behavior of another becomes an essential component in one's self esteem and community regard" (p. 165).

51 Dodd, 1973: p. 45.

52 Op. cit.

53 Dodd, 1973: p. 46.

54 Op. cit.

Family "honor" is controlled through the implementation of norms chiefly binding women and determining their behavior, actions, desires and even thoughts.[55] The rules of "honor," coupled with the threat of violent enforcement, guide female behavior and serve as a mechanism of social control.[56] "Honor" violence may be conceptualized variously as a crime, gendered violence, violation of human rights or social-construction discourse, but its best understanding can be gained through looking at it as a form of social control,[57] as a social call for renewed obedience of all women and girls to patriarchal norms.[58] In this respect, scholars argue that "honor" concepts are but another way of understanding the operation of patriarchy, which in the case of "honor" killings, refers to a sub-category of male dominance stemming from the authority of the father or male household head.[59] In this respect, Hasan, for example, contended that "honor" killings should be seen as part of the social structure wherein the family is a patriarchal unit and "honor" refers chiefly to the "honor" of men in the family.[60] Thus, the maintenance of "honor" is the perpetuation of male control, and an assault on that "honor" undermines the patriarchal system of domination.

Social control through "honor" violence is a form of group-on-individual, or collective, violence, whereby the group inflicting violence is not the community at large but the social unit on which the community is based – in this case, the family.[61] "Honor" violence can be conceptualized as a collective rather than an individual framework, wherein "honor" codes are not solely about individual men controlling the lives of individual women, but rather about community norms, social policing and acts of punishment.[62] Its collective nature leads to family and the wider community being united against the "misbehaving" woman, to address

55 Hasan, 2002: p. 3. According to Hasan (2002), in such systems, the cultural norms reinforce the power structure between the superior men and subordinate women by cultural norms that allow men to sexually and financially control their wives.

56 Baker et al., 1999: p. 167.

57 Cooney, 2014: p. 407. Cooney (2014) conceptualized violence as a response to deviant social behavior on the part of the victim that was punished and corrected by the family: "to the parties themselves (as distinct from external observers), 'honor' violence is inflicted by the family to punish wrongful conduct, actual or alleged, against the family" (p. 407).

58 Abu Rabia (2011) argued that Bedouin society obliges each family to begin the moral education of chastity codes among girls at an early age, with the expectation that such social indoctrination will make them chaste wives. Should a girl or a woman behave in an immoral way, the shame is attributed to all tribal men of her father for having betrayed their social trust (p. 35). Murder of kin for the sake of family "honor" can be seen as an indication of a weakening of morality that calls for renewed obedience to norms using external means.

59 Baker et al., 1999: p. 166.

60 Hasan, 2002: p. 3.

61 Cooney, 2014.

62 Johnson, 2008: p. 128; Pely (2011) argued that the community is often supportive of severe punishment acts against the individual that damaged family "honor," and in most cases, both male and female relatives see the act of punishment as unavoidable (p. 214). The severe punishment aims both to restore lost "honor" and deter other women in the family from similar behavior (p. 214).

and prevent such serious social deviations on her behalf, "leaving punishment, rather than prevention, as the only remedy."[63] Although "honor" violence is of a collective nature, the violent act itself is typically perpetrated by an individual acting alone, as an agent of the family, vindicating and reinforcing the verdict and the punishment called for by the family for breaching its norms.[64]

Along with the collective notion of "honor," individuals are intimately affiliated with their hamula, and when an individual commits an infraction of social norms, the entire hamula is held responsible for the act and its consequences.[65] Such an interweaved social structure intensifies the magnitude of public knowledge of the loss of "honor," because each community member knows that kin and neighbors will spread the story throughout the community.[66]

In line with the patrilineal social structure of the Arab society, wherein marriage ties are less important than blood (agnatic) ties, the loss of "honor" based on sexual or social misconduct does not affect the family "honor" of the husband's lineage, but rather the family "honor" of women's lineage.[67] Consequently, the responsibility for retaliation in cases of sexual misconduct of women falls primarily on the agnates: Fathers, brothers, fathers' brothers, and agnatic cousins.[68] Hence, those who murder for the sake of family "honor" are the agnates (paternal kinsmen) of the woman, not her husband or in-laws, should she be married.[69]

63 Johnson, 2008: p. 125.
64 Cooney, 2014: p. 411.
65 Cooney, 2014: p. 411.
66 Pely, 2011: p. 214. In such communities, "an ideology, idiom, and imagery of 'honor' binds individuals and groups together with shared moral standards, but it also drives them apart when accusations of breaching those standards are voiced" (Cooney, 2014: p. 408).
67 Dodd, 1973: p. 45. According to Hasan (2002), women in patriarchal families are sacrificed on the altar of "honor" because that has a cheaper social price tag for the family, because any vengeance against the man who had sexual misconduct with a woman would trigger the traditional vicious cycle of a blood feud (p. 2, 14). She added: "Even though tribal law states that the male bears responsibility, it is clear that if the law were actually applied, the principles of blood vengeance would unleash unending tribal warfare. By contrast, the elimination of a woman by her own kin is an internal private event. . . . It is possible to say that the apparatus of maintenance of the tribe or lineage found a way to avoid its weakening or destruction by constructing scapegoat, a surrogate victim for execution of judgment" (p. 14). This introduces, according to Hasan, an additional aspect of the substitution of the man's life for the woman's life: the sacrificial victim. The woman is sacrificed by the agnatic family, thus releasing itself from the obligation to murder the man who dis"honor"ed the family (p. 14).
68 Dodd, 1973: p. 44.
69 Hasan, 2002: p. 9. Hasan suggested that instances of murder by their husbands in Arab society are the result of "excessive beating" by their husbands: "the 'right' to beat one's wife is given to the husband, and if he 'goes too far' and causes her death, then his act of killing is by conjugal entitlement – and nothing more" (p. 10). According to Hasan, the male agnatic relatives of the woman are her brothers, father, uncles, cousins, and adult sons. The relation between the husband is weaker and can be terminated. According to Hasan (2002), if a woman breaks the code of "honor," her husband is exempted from killing her because his "honor" and his family's "honor" is not sullied if there is no blood relation between them.

Although most family-"honor" violence is not lethal, a substantial number of people, women more often than not, are killed in its name.[70] According to Standish, legal structures in the Arab world widely consider "honor" killings to be "private issues," and many Arab countries excuse murder for reasons of family "honor."[71] Cases of "honor" femicide represent a small portion of the total cases of 'ird. Generally, when there is a possibility of hiding the 'ird loss, the woman is not murdered. According to Abu-Rabia, only if information about a woman's promiscuity becomes common knowledge does such behavior become an open scandal, and many premarital and extramarital affairs are settled quietly and without fuss. Although many become public knowledge, most are settled with alternative sanctions, and only a small proportion end in a killing.[72] The preferable solutions for 'ird loss are elopement, marriage, hushing up of violations, compensation and banishment, seclusion, verbal abuse, physical abuse or any combination thereof.[73] Killing for the loss of 'ird is rare and would be the last resort in cases where other solutions fail.[74]

Arab Women in Israel

As noted in Chapter 2, despite myriad social, economic and urbanization changes in Arab society, its patriarchal culture and clan social structure retain their powerful roles. Similar to all Arab societies, the Arab population in Israel retains its collective society in terms of individuals' private and public life and its social harmony by culturally preserving family ties, social interdependence, mutual responsibility between individuals and placing community interests ahead of individual interests.[75] Traditional patterns of marriage are maintained (with women required to obtain the blessing and consent of their family), and early marriage is common. Older family members are generally consulted when family problems arise, and they provide concrete and immediate solutions.

According to Shalhoub-Kevorkian, the minority social position of Arabs in the Israeli hegemonic context reinforces internal social interaction and informal structures, including kinship, patriarchy, and the traditional tribal system.[76] Such strengthening of informal structures contributes to the regulation of social behavior, roles, responsibilities and relations among members of Arab society in

70 Cooney, 2014: p. 407.

71 Standish, 2014: 114.

72 Abu Rabia, 2011: pp. 35–36; Baxter, 2007: p. 753; Cooney, 2014: p. 412. Abu Rabia (2011) contended that "there is a host of statistics about women who were killed in the name of family 'honor,' but there are no statistics regarding women who were not killed even though they engaged in illicit sexual relations . . . 'honor' killings are the exception to the rule, not the rule in Arab society, despite social norms in the Arab sector that mandate female modesty" (p. 43).

73 Abu Rabia, 2011: p. 36; Dodd, 1973: p. 43; Hasan, 2002: p. 4; Kulwicky, 2002: p. 85.

74 Kulwicky, 2002: p. 85.

75 Shalhoub-Kevorkian, 1999: p. 193, 197, 200.

76 Shalhoub-Kevorkian, 1999: p. 192.

general, which is achieved through the reinforcement of traditional social norms and codes of "honor" that define and delimit mobility, choice of spouse, type and level of education, dress, profession and sexual behavior.[77] Women are controlled, monitored, sanctioned and constrained by the men in their family (fathers, brothers and husbands).[78] Divorce or violence against a woman is seen as reflecting her failure and inability to competently manage her private life.[79] Women are exposed to domestic violence that is exacerbated by sociocultural conditions.[80]

Epidemiological Characteristics of FHK in Israel

As noted in Chapter 2, Arab women, who belong to the largest non-Jewish minority in Israel, are grossly overrepresented in femicide cases.[81] Epidemiological characteristics of F.H.K., based on femicide cases from 2010 to 2015, show that at least ten Arab women are killed each year. In fact, 30% to 40% of women killed every year are Israeli Arab women, and in 2015–2016, they accounted for more than 50% of all femicide victims in Israel.

The majority of F.H.K. incidents, 49%, occurs in the most densely populated region of Israel, the central region, and more than half of these killings are perpetrated in mixed cities composed of a mixed Jewish and Arab population, such as Jaffa, Ramla and Lod. Among the killings in this central region, about a third are carried out in an area known as the Triangle: A concentration of Israeli Arab towns and villages adjacent to the Green Line.[82] The second geographic area with substantial F.H.K. (39%), is the northern part of Israel known as Galilee, a relatively non-populated region with a large Arab, mostly Muslim, population. The third geographic area, where about 12% of F.H.K. takes place, is the desert and semidesert southern region of Israel known as Negev.[83]

Regarding the sociodemographic characteristics of the victims, more than half (59%) are married, but 41% are unmarried (such as never married, estranged or divorced). Similar to international findings, a noteworthy characteristic of F.H.K. killings in Israel is the victim's young age, with a mean of 33 years ($SD = 13.88$) among all victims. Indeed, studies on "honor" killings worldwide noted that many victims are young women, primarily the perpetrator's daughter or sister, and sometimes his wife or girlfriend.[84]

77 Shalhoub-Kevorkian and Daher-Nashif, 2013: pp. 300–302.
78 Hasan, 2002.
79 Shalhoub-Kevorkian, 1999: p. 194.
80 Op. cit.
81 Dayan, 2021; Edelstein, 2011; Landau and Hattis-Rolef, 1998; Sela-Shayovitz, 2010.
82 In the eastern Sharon plain among the Samarian foothills, with Umm al-Fahem and Tayibe as the main sociocultural and economic centers for Arab residents of the region.
83 With several Jewish development towns and small Bedouin cities: Rahat, Tel as-Sabi, and Lakyah.
84 Chesler, 2010: pp. 3–4; Kulwicky, 2002: p. 80; Shalhoub-Kevorkian, 2002: pp. 594–595.

Additional empirical observations relate to the intersection of F.H.K. and domestic violence, because prior complaints of and indictments or convictions for gender-based domestic violence were noted in at least 37% of F.H.K. cases. This observation was either not found in earlier studies of F.H.K.[85] or reported as a much lower rate; for example, Touma-Sliman estimated that domestic violence occurs in only 4% of F.H.K. cases in Israel.[86] The actual incidence of domestic violence against victims may be even higher, given that Arab women rarely report domestic violence or abuse. Gal, for example, reported that 30% of Arab women and 90% of Bedouin women experience unreported domestic violence.[87]

Scholars maintain that domestic violence is more often than not targeted at women and over time, results in a greater likelihood of the women being killed.[88] Indeed, gender-based domestic violence has been linked to two different femicide phenomena.[89] Wallace found that in more than a quarter of femicide–suicide cases with a conflictual characteristic, the offender had physically or verbally abused and threatened to kill the victim on previous occasions, and that severe and usually prolonged interpersonal conflict, often combined with serious domestic violence or threats of violence, was common.[90] Similarly, Dobash et al. stated that "Men often kill wives after lengthy periods of prolonged physical violence."[91]

F.H.K. sometimes involves several female members of the same family unit; multiple female victims were noted in 24% of cases, with two cases in which two related female family members were killed (two sisters and a mother and daughter). Also, the number of fatalities in such killings tends to be higher than the number of women killed, and multiple victims (other than the main targeted woman) are found in at least 20% of all F.H.K. cases.

The profile of the perpetrators in terms of gender seems similar to other femicide subtypes; namely, perpetrators of femicide against Arab women are men. However, F.H.K. seems to be a collective agnatic matter, and most killers are members of the victim's nuclear or extended family (brothers, cousins, uncles, sons or fathers). This familial notion in the killing is further reinforced by the fact that in about a quarter of all F.H.K. cases, multiple perpetrators are involved as criminal accomplices, most of them men from the victim's extended family (cousins and uncles).

Thus, in terms of the agnatic, collective pattern of this femicide subtype, F.H.K. in Israel closely resembles empirical patterns found in Arab societies worldwide and in previous studies conducted in Israel. The perpetrator's identity in F.H.K. cases is

85 Edelstein, 2011; Kressel et al., 1981.
86 Touma-Sliman, 2005: pp. 185–186.
87 Gal, 2004: p. 102.
88 Siegel, 1996: p. 2172.
89 Brewer and Smith, 1995: p. 176; Wallace, 1986: pp. 184–186.
90 Wallace, 1986: p. 184.
91 Dobash et al., 1992: p. 81.

often linked to the victim's patrilineal family.[92] Our observations do not differ from previous international studies on female "honor" killing, pointing to the victim's brother as the most common perpetrator, followed by her father and cousins.[93]

Yet along the high rate of extended-family perpetrators, we observed a significant share of current or ex-intimate partners as perpetrators. This trend was also identified in earlier empirical data on femicide in Israel.[94] However, a conclusion regarding a change in the pattern of the perpetrators' identity toward a higher rate of current or former intimate partners should be made cautiously. Marriage among relatives (mostly patrilineal endogamous patterns) is still very common in Arab society in Israel[95] and constitutes 45% of all marriages.[96] According to Vardi-Saliternik et al., there are high consanguinity rates in the Arab population, noting that rates of first-cousin-and-closer pairings were stable over time, in contrast to a significant decrease in the rates of distant consanguineous pairings.[97] Hence, husbands who participate in killing their wife may be related to her in a patrilineal sense.[98] This observation was echoed by Kressel et al., who argued that "only in rare cases are there fiancés or husbands among the perpetrators, and a second glance at them reveals that these are also patrilineal cousins."[99] In any case, as Kulzycki and Windel argued, our observations imply that the boundaries between the two domains, intimate-partner femicide (sometimes called "crimes of passion" by scholars) and "honor" killing, are unclear: "lack of information about the circumstances surrounding the murder and the inability to draw firm conclusions about the motive of the perpetrator make it impossible to be certain about the degree of similarity or dissimilarity between crimes of 'honor' and crimes of passion."[100]

Empirical observations relate to the fact that although previous international studies[101] as well as earlier studies conducted in Israel[102] report that most motives for F.H.K. are traditionally related to interpretations of female dis"honor." However, we would like to note a much more expansive and versatile interpretation of "honor." The breach of family "honor" interpreted as a motive for killing[103]

92 Edelstein, 2011: pp. 120–127; Johnson, 2008: p. 124; Kressel et al., 1981: p. 146; Shalhoub-Kevorkian, 2002: p. 585; Touma-Sliman, 2005: pp. 185–186.
93 Chesler, 2010: pp. 3–4; Edelstein, 2011: p. 122; Kressel et al., 1981: pp. 145–146; Touma-Sliman, 2005: pp. 184–185.
94 Sela-Shayovitz, 2010: p. 1431.
95 Al-Haj, 1989: pp. 183–184.
96 Hasan, 2002: p. 22.
97 Vardi-Saliternik et al., 2002: p. 422.
98 Hasan, 2002: p. 22; Kressel et al., 1981: p. 147.
99 Kressel et al., 1981: p. 151.
100 Kulczycki and Windle, 2011: p. 1448.
101 Kulwicky, 2002: p. 81.
102 Kressel et al., 1981: pp. 145–146.
103 Numerous terms, with different meanings, are used interchangeably in the literature to indicate the motive for F.H.K., among them intent, reason, motive, cause, justification, excuse, and explanation (Landau and Hattis-Rolef, 1998: p. 84; Sela-Shayovitz, 2010: p. 1428). This study followed Landau and Hattis-Rolef (1998) definition of motive, focusing on the immediate interactional reason for the fatal attack (p. 85).

actually features numerous and various motives. In other words, whereas sexual allegations were noted in a small share of the cases (16%), the most common motives for killings were related to gender-based violence and social or financial disputes among extended-family members (27% and 24%, respectively). Among motives, we observed disputes over a future groom and allegations of the victim being "too Western" in her mode of behavior (14% and 8%, respectively).[104] Thus, when exploring F.H.K., we note that social constructions of dis"honor" may include not only sexual behavior but additional social spheres, which may in turn legitimize a much wider phenomenon of gender-based violence.[105]

In this regard, F.H.K. seems to only partially coincide with "honor" crimes, whereas a much wider phenomenon of gender-based domestic violence perpetrated not only in nuclear families but also by extended families might be misinterpreted as "honor" killings. The fact that as in other types of femicide, the most common killing scene in F.H.K. is the victim's home (61%) further illustrates the domestic nature of these gendered killings. Our view is supported by Dogan, who argued that domestic violence and "honor" killings are two distinct phenomena: Although prevalent domestic-violence motives and victims suggest that this is a strategy targeted at controlling both women and children, "honor" killings are embedded in collective concepts of "honor" and identity[106] that result in the planned killing of women in the family, mostly teenagers and young women.[107] We, thus, believe that lack of empirical and theoretical conceptualization regarding the boundaries and intersections of "honor" killings with gender-based domestic violence clouds our understanding of F.H.K. Indeed, Payton suggested that to better understand the boundaries between the two domains, perhaps we need to reframe our understanding of domestic violence.[108] Payton went on to say that the understanding of scholars studying gender-based domestic violence is grounded mainly in Western familial patterns of dyadic interpersonal relationships and nuclear families, whereas a comprehensive full grasp of the ways it manifests in extended-family relationships and collective societies is lacking.[109] Thus, the collective and agnatic nature of F.H.K. may be related not only to notions of "honor," but also to patterns of domestic violence in extended families, a phenomenon that requires further identification and research.

Conclusion

Some of the patterns ingrained in F.H.K., namely the perpetrator's identity, wider interpretation of "honor," and existence of prior domestic violence, seem to indicate possible intricate intersections of this femicide subtype, not only with "honor"

104 An observation also made by Edelstein, 2011: pp. 122–123; and Touma-Sliman, 2005: p. 186.
105 Shalhoub-Kevorkian, 2002: pp. 579–580.
106 Dogan, 2014: p. 379, 382.
107 Chesler, 2009: p. 63.
108 Payton, 2014.
109 Payton, 2014: p. 2867.

violence but also with intimate-partner femicide and gender-based domestic violence. Further research is needed to gain a better understanding of the boundaries of the intersections between F.H.K. and the four domains: Intimate-partner femicide, gender-based violence, domestic violence, and "honor" violence.

Having explored various sociocultural and criminological aspects of F.H.K., the next chapter focuses on an additional social group in Israel, with high rates of femicide: Ethiopian immigrant Jews. In doing so, the chapter focuses on the most prevalent femicide subtype in this group: Femicide–suicide.

References

Abu-Odeh, L. (1997). Comparatively speaking: The 'honour' of the 'east' and the 'passion' of the 'West'. *Utah Law Review*, 287–307.

Abu-Rabia, A. (2011). Family "honor" killings: Between custom and state law. *The Open Psychology Journal*, *4*, 34–44.

Abu Rabia, R. (2011). Redefining polygamy among the Palestinian Bedouins in Israel: Colonialism, patriarchy, and resistance. *Journal of Gender, Social Policy and the Law*, *19*(2), 459–493.

Al-Haj, M. (1989). Social research on family lifestyles among Arabs in Israel. *Journal of Comparative Family Studies*, *20*(2), 175–195.

Awwad, A. M. (2001). Gossip, scandal, shame and "honor" killings: A case for social constructionism and hegemonic discourse. *Social Thought and Research*, *24*, 39–52.

Baker, N. V., Gregware, P. R., & Cassidy, M. A. (1999). Family killing fields: "honor" rationales in the murder of woman. *Violence against Women*, *5*(2), 164–184.

Baxter, D. (2007). "honor" thy sister: Selfhood, gender and agency in Palestinian culture. *Anthropological Quarterly*, *80*(3), 737–775.

Brewer, V. E., & Smith, M. D. (1995). Gender inequality and rates of female homicide victimization across U.S. cities. *Journal of Research in Crime and Delinquency*, *32*(2), 175–190.

Chesler, P. (2009). Are "honor" killings simply domestic violence. *Middle East Quarterly*, 61–69.

Chesler, P. (2010). Worldwide trends in "honor" killings. *Middle East Quarterly*, 3–11.

Cooney, M. (2014). Death by family: "honor" violence as punishment. *Punishment and Society*, *16*(4), 406–427.

Dayan, H. (2021). Female honour killing: The role of low economic status and rapid modernization. *Journal of Interpersonal Violence*. https://doi-org.ezproxy.haifa.ac.il/10.1177/0886260519872984

Dobash, R. P., Dobash, R. E., Wilson, M., & Daly, M. (1992). The myth of sexual symmetry in marital violence. *Social Problems*, *39*(1), 71–91.

Dodd, P. C. (1973). Family "honor" and the forces of change in Arab society. *International Journal of Middle East Studies*, *4*, 40–54.

Dogan, R. (2014). Different cultural understandings of "honor" that inspire killing: An inquiry into the defendant's perspective. *Homicide Studies*, *18*, 363–338.

Dogan, R. (2016). The dynamics of "honor" killings and the perpetrators' experiences. *Homicide Studies*, *20*(1), 53–79.

Edelstein, A. (2011). *Intimate homicide in Israel: Theoretical and empirical aspects.* Bialik (in Hebrew).

Gal, N. (2004). *Violence against women: Norm or deviation?* Hakibutz-Hameuhad (Hebrew).

Hasan, M. (2002). The politics of "honor": Patriarchy, the state and the murder of women in the name of family "honor". *Journal of Israel History, 21*, 1–37.

Johnson, P. (2008). Violence all around us: Dilemmas of global and local agendas addressing violence against Palestinian women, an initial intervention. *Cultural Dynamics, 20*(2), 119–132.

Kressel, G. M., Bausani, A., Ginat, J., Joseph, R., Khazanov, A. M., Landau, S. F., & Shokeid, M. (1981). Sororicide/filiacide: Homicide for family honour. *Current Anthropology, 22*(2), 141–158.

Kulczycki, A. and Windle, S. (2011). Honour killings in the Middle East and North Africa: A systematic review of the literature. *Violence against Women, 17*(11), 1442–1464.

Kulwicky, A. D. (2002). The practice of "honor" crimes: A glimpse of domestic violence in the Arab world. *Issues in Mental Health Nursing, 23*, 77–87.

Landau, S., & Hattis-Rolef, S. (1998). Intimate femicide in Israel: Temporal, social and motivational patterns. *European Journal on Criminal Policy and Research, 6*, 75–90.

Payton, J. (2014). "honor" collectivity and agnation: Emerging risk factors in "honor" based violence. *Journal of Interpersonal Violence, 29*(16), 2863–2883.

Pely, D. (2011). When "honor" trumps basic needs: The role of "honor" in deadly disputes within Israel's Arab community. *Negotiation Journal, 27*(2), 205–225.

Ruggi, S. (1998). Commodifying honour in female sexuality: Honour killings in Palestine. *Middle East Report, 28*(1), 12–15

Sela-Shayovitz, R. (2010). The role of ethnicity and context: Intimate femicide rates among social groups in Israeli society. *Violence against Women, 16*, 1424–1436.

Shalhoub-Kevorkian, N. (1999). Law, politics, and violence against women: A case study of Palestinians in Israel. *Law and Policy, 21*(2), 189–211.

Shalhoub-Kevorkian, N. (2002). Femicide and the Palestinian criminal justice system: Seeds of change in the context of state building? *Law and Society Review, 36*(3), 577–606.

Shalhoub-Kevorkian, N., & Daher-Nashif, S. (2013). Femicide and colonization: Between the politics of exclusion and the culture of control. *Violence against Women, 19*(3), 295–315.

Shier, A., & Shor, E. (2016). Shades of foreign evil: "honor" killings and family murders in the Canadian press. *Violence against Women, 22*(10), 1163–1188.

Siegel, R. B. (1996). The rule of love: Wife beating as prerogative and privacy. *Yale Law Journal, 105*, 2117–2207.

Standish, K. (2014). Understanding cultural violence and gender: Honour killings; dowry murder; and Zina ordinance and blood-feuds. *Journal of Gender Studies, 23*(2), 111–124.

Touma-Sliman, A. (2005). Culture, national minority and the state: Working against the "crime of family "honor"" within the Palestinian community in Israel. In L. Welchman & S. Hossain (Eds.), *"honor": Crimes, paradigms, and violence against women* (pp. 181–198). Zed Books.

van Osch, Y., Breugelmans, S. M., Zeelenberg, M., & Boluk, P. (2013). A different kind of "honor" culture: Family "honor" and aggression in Turks. *Group Processes and Intergroup Relation, 16*(3), 334–344.

Vardi-Saliternik, R., Friedlander, Y., & Cohen, T. (2002). Consanguinity in a population sample of Israeli Muslim Arabs, Christian Arabs and Druze. *Annals of Human Biology, 29*, 422–341.

Wallace, A. (1986). *Homicide: The social reality*. Bureau of Crimes Statistics and Research, Attorney General's Department.

5 Femicide–Suicide

Introduction

Among people who kill, a certain percentage also commit suicide soon after, in a phenomenon known as homicide–suicide. Previous studies indicate that femicide–suicide (female-intimate-partner homicide–suicides) accounts for the vast majority of homicide–suicide occurrences. Though the femicide–suicide phenomenon cuts across regions and societies, there is a dearth of studies on patterns, motives and characteristics of femicide–suicide in non-Western populations. Most empirical observations are based on studies conducted in Western societies and are questionable in relation to different cultural settings. As Adinkrah indicated, very few studies have been conducted in non-Western societies, and our understanding of sociocultural patterns and variations of homicide–suicide is still in dire need of research.[1] We, therefore, believe that it is imperative to further explore the overlap of the phenomenon with sociocultural circumstances and ethnic minorities, including immigrant ethnic minorities. In line with the need to understand sociocultural relativity in this femicide subtype, this chapter endeavors to explore femicide–suicide in non-Western societies, taking Israel as a case study. Following this framework of analysis, the chapter addresses the occurrence of femicide–suicide and its modus operandi.

Homicide–Suicide

Homicide–suicide is a generic term that refers to an event in which an individual commits homicide and immediately or shortly thereafter commits suicide.[2] It is sometimes termed *murder–suicide*, although the term *homicide–suicide* is more applicable because it encompasses both intentional homicide and manslaughter.[3] Some scholars argue that homicide–suicides resemble suicide more than they do cases that only involve homicide,

1 Adinkrah, 2014: p. 365.
2 Adinkrah, 2014: p. 365; Harper and Voigt, 2007: p. 295; Marzuk et al., 1992: p. 3179; Panczak et al., 2013: p. 28; Saleva et al., 2007: p. 205.
3 Large et al., 2009: p. 294; Liem, 2010: p. 154.

DOI: 10.4324/9781003333272-7

viewing them as a kind of "extended suicide,"[4] whereas others associate homicide–suicide with homicide.[5] Still others argue that homicide–suicide appears to be a distinct phenomenon "occupying a distinct epidemiological domain that displays similarities and differences from both types of violence."[6]

There are wide variations in operational characteristics of the homicide–suicide act: For example, the time between the homicide and the perpetrator's suicide that has been found to range from 24 hours to three months[7] to an indefinite period of time.[8] The data show that the incidence of homicide–suicide across developed countries tends to be between 0.2 and 0.3 per 100,000 persons, with a relatively constant occurrence rate unrelated to the overall rate of homicides or suicides.[9] Although homicide–suicides account for a relatively small share of total homicides, they are likely to result in injury to people other than the primary victim, have multiple victims in addition to the perpetrator and primary victim, and have devastating effects on families and communities.[10]

Several typologies have been suggested to classify various subtypes of homicide–suicide. Proposing a classification that categorizes homicide–suicide by type of victim–offender relationship and common motives, Marzuk et al. argued that the four most common subtypes are spousal homicide–suicide due to jealousy, spousal homicide–suicide as a result of declining health, filicide (the killing of children by their parents), and familicide (the killing of the family by the perpetrator).[11] Wallace proposed four types of homicide–suicide classified by motive: Interpersonal conflict, altruism (merciful action), extreme mental abnormality, and miscellaneous (accidental killings and others).[12] Harper and Voigt differentiated between the following homicide–suicide subtypes: intimate or domestic lethal violence–suicide, family annihilation–suicide (heads of households who think they can no longer care for their family), mercy killing–suicide, and public killing spree–suicide.[13]

Femicide–Suicide

Although termed slightly differently (spousal homicide–suicide due to jealousy, interpersonal conflict, or intimate or domestic lethal violence–suicide), all typologies include the category of intimate partner homicide–suicide as the

4 Rosenbaum, 1990: pp. 1036–1039; Van Wormer and Odiah, 1999: pp. 361, 364–365.
5 Cooper and Eaves, 1996: pp. 100–101, 105; Large et al., 2009: pp. 294, 306; Milroy, 1995: p. 64.
6 Marzuk et al., 1992: p. 3181; Saleva et al., 2007: p. 209.
7 Marzuk et al., 1992: p. 3179.
8 Liem, 2010: p. 155; Van Wormer and Odiah, 1999: p. 364.
9 Scott, 2009: pp. 371, 375; Large et al., 2009: p. 294; Liem, 2010: p. 158.
10 Flynn et al., 2009: p. 309; Liem et al., 2011: p. 75; Lund and Smorodinsky, 2001: p. 452; Marzuk et al., 1992: p. 3179; Panczak et al., 2013: p. 29.
11 Marzuk et al., 1992: p. 3180.
12 Wallace, 1986: pp. 183–184.
13 Harper and Voigt, 2007: p. 307.

phenomenon's primary subtype, accounting for most homicide–suicide events. Indeed, empirical studies show that homicide–suicide incidents involving current or former intimate partners are the most prevalent and account for the vast majority of homicide–suicide occurrences.[14]

The term *intimate partner homicide–suicide* disregards the gendered nature of the phenomenon, although homicide–suicides are largely committed by the male intimate partner against his female partner.[15] In fact, international empirical findings note the gendered characteristics of the phenomenon, whereby intimate partner homicide–suicides are perpetrated by men against female victims.[16] Because it is extremely rare for women to commit homicide–suicide against their intimate partner, and considering the fact that the primary victims of this subtype of homicide–suicide are women, the term *femicide–suicide* would be preferable from the gender-sensitive perspective.[17]

From a gender-based-violence perspective, for example, scholars found that in more than a quarter of homicide–suicide cases characterized by conflict, the offender had physically or verbally abused and threatened to kill the victim on previous occasions, and that severe and usually prolonged interpersonal conflict, often combined with serious domestic violence or threats of violence, was common.[18] In addition, studies pointed to high levels of brutality, as demonstrated by intimate or domestic lethal violence–suicide cases with multiple face and head wounds. In more than two-thirds of a sample of intimate or domestic cases, the perpetrators seemed bent on not just taking a life but also obliterating the victim by destroying her face or defacing her with multiple facial gunshot wounds.[19]

Although the femicide–suicide phenomenon cuts across geography and societies, there is a dearth of studies on patterns, motives and characteristics of femicide–suicide in non-Western societies.[20] Furthermore, most studies conducted in non-Western societies examined the overall phenomenon of homicide–suicide (filicide and pack suicides included) – increasing the difficulty of comparing the particular phenomenon of femicide–suicide. A comparison of the few findings about femicide–suicide in non-Western societies with international findings to Western societies (United States, Australia and European Union countries) raises

14 Banks et al., 2008: pp. 1070, 1075; Berman, 1996: p. 343; Flynn et al., 2009: p. 313; Harper and Voigt, 2007: p. 312; Liem, 2010: p. 158; Liem et al., 2011: p. 72; Milroy, 1995: p. 119; Saleva et al., 2007: p. 206; Scott, 2009: pp. 372–373; Wallace, 1986: pp. 180, 182; Warren-Gordon et al., 2010: p. 1595.

15 Stack, 1997: pp. 442, 445; Wallace, 1986: p. 191.

16 Flynn et al., 2009: p. 315; Harper and Voigt, 2007: p. 312; Liem, 2010: p. 156; Liem et al., 2011: p. 72; Milroy, 1995: p. 120; Scott, 2009: p. 374; Warren-Gordon et al., 2010: p. 1595.

17 Flynn et al., 2009; Harper and Voigt, 2007; Panczak et al., 2013: p. 28; Marzuk et al., 1992: p. 3180; Saleva et al., 2007; Wallace, 1986: p. 186.

18 Cooper and Eaves, 1996: p. 107; Harper and Voigt, 2007: pp. 302–303; Morton et al., 1998: p. 95; Scott, 2009: p. 375; Wallace, 1986: p. 184.

19 Harper and Voigt, 2007: pp. 302, 311.

20 Adinkrah, 2014: p. 365.

questions that need to be examined regarding similarities and dissimilarities of the phenomenon.

Cultural Relativity in Femicide–Suicide

Few shared sociodemographic and criminological characteristics of femicide–suicide have been found in both Western and non-Western societies. Among the shared characteristics are the perpetrator's (male) and the victim's (female, most often the perpetrator's intimate partner) gender.[21] Similarities were noted also regarding the perpetrator's and victim's mean age, the former between 30 and 45 years of age and the latter slightly younger,[22] although ages of perpetrators and victims found in South Africa were slightly younger.[23] Similarities were also found regarding the domestic setting of the crime scene[24] and the killing motive, typically related to the women's desire to end the relationship with the intimate partner.[25] Studies of both Western and non-Western societies also noted the perpetrator's state of depression at the time of the killing.[26]

Additional empirical findings noted in studies of the phenomenon in Western societies are still in question because they have yet to be validated with respect to non-Western societies. First, the empirical finding regarding the perpetrator's ethnic background as white Caucasian[27] obviously is not applicable to non-Western societies and therefore should be examined and compared between these societies. The Western findings regarding the Caucasian ethnic background of the perpetrator may be understood as the social dominant ethnic profile in the

21 Adinkrah, 2003: pp. 68–70; Adinkrah, 2014: pp. 375–377; Chan et al., 2003: pp. 262–266; Cooper and Eaves, 1996: p. 10; Dogan et al., 2010: p. 113; Flynn et al., 2009: pp., 313, 315; Harper and Voigt, 2007: p. 312; Liem, 2010: p. 156; Liem et al., 2011: pp. 72, 76; Lund and Smorodinsky, 2001: p. 454; Milroy, 1995: p. 120; Saleva et al., 2007: p. 208; Scott, 2009: p. 373; Van Wormer and Odiah, 1999: p. 362; Warren-Gordon et al., 2010: p. 1595.

22 Banks et al., 2008: p. 1070; Chan et al., 2003: p. 262; Cooper and Eaves, 1996: p. 103; Flynn et al., 2009: p. 313; Sakuta, 1995: p. 145.

23 Mathews et al., 2008: p. 555; Roberts et al., 2010: p. 886.

24 Adinkrah, 2003: pp. 68–70; Adinkrah, 2014: pp. 375–377; Chan et al., 2003: pp. 262–266; Dogan et al., 2010: p. 113; Harper and Voigt, 2007: p. 302; Liem et al., 2011: p. 76; Sakuta, 1995: p. 142; Warren-Gordon et al., 2010: p. 1595.

25 Adinkrah, 2003: pp. 68–70; Adinkrah, 2014: pp. 375–377; Chan et al., 2003: pp. 262–266; Cooper and Eaves, 1996: p. 106; Dogan et al., 2010: p. 113; Harper and Voigt, 2007: pp. 303, 304, 310; Liem et al., 2011: p. 76; Mathews et al., 2008: p. 556; Milroy, 1995: p. 119; Morton et al., 1998: p. 96; Sakuta, 1995: p. 142; Saleva et al., 2007: p. 208; Scott, 2009: p. 374; Stack, 1997: p. 439; Wallace, 1986: p. 172.

26 Byard et al., 1999: p. 326; Chan et al., 2003: p. 266; Cooper and Eaves, 1996: p. 106; Harper and Voigt, 2007: p. 308; Flynn et al., 2009: p. 315; Milroy, 1995: p. 121; Morton et al., 1998: p. 96; Sakuta, 1995: p. 146; Saleva et al., 2007: p. 208; Scott, 2009: p. 374; Starzomski and Nussbaum, 2000: pp. 470–471; Van Wormer and Odiah, 1999: p. 362.

27 Flynn et al., 2009: p. 313; Morton et al., 1988: p. 93; Stack, 1997.

population group of the society being studied. Seen as such, Roberts et al.'s finding[28] that the ethnic profile of the common perpetrator in South Africa belonged to the ethnic-majority black Africans corresponds with the Western studies' findings on the Caucasian profile of perpetrators. Still, research is required to understand contradicting patterns in non-Western societies, such as South Africa and Fiji, where opposite patterns emerged, i.e., overrepresentation of minority populations in the phenomenon: Whites in South Africa[29] and Indians in Fiji.[30] This highlights the need for further study and validation of the distribution and characteristics of femicide–suicide across ethnic groups in societies with different ethnic compositions.

Among the findings that still await empirical validation in non-Western societies, for example, is how the suicide outcome was found to be most common when the perpetrator was the victim's intimate partner at the time of the killing and less common when the intimate partners were already separated.[31] Findings in Western society still in need of validation are the perpetrators' (low) alcohol and drug-consumption profile[32] and the low incidence of prior criminal behavior.[33] Finally, the link between femicide–suicide and the criminological characteristic of prior gender-based domestic violence found in Western studies requires comparison and validation in non-Western societies.[34]

Particularly noteworthy is the fact that studies in non-Western societies seem to contradict the main criminological findings in Western societies. For example, in Western studies, the firearm was found to be the primary weapon.[35] The use of a firearm as the overwhelming weapon of choice is particularly characteristic of homicide–suicide in the United States, and Panczak et al. found that the use of firearms was substantially less frequent in the European Union countries (such as the Netherlands and England) and other non-European countries (such as Australia and Canada), compared to the United States.[36] In non-Western societies, contradicting findings were noted: In Fiji, the knife was the primary weapon, used to stab the victim,[37] whereas in Hong Kong and Japan, the perpetrator often used his

28 Roberts et al., 2010: p. 891.
29 Mathews et al., 2008: p. 556; Roberts et al., 2010: p. 881.
30 Adinkrah, 2003: pp. 69, 71.
31 Lund and Smorodinsky, 2001: p. 454; Saleva et al., 2007: p. 208.
32 Cooper and Eaves, 1996: p. 107; Harper and Voigt, 2007: p. 311; Morton et al., 1998: p. 93; Panczak et al., 2013: p. 32; Starzomski and Nussbaum, 2000: p., 471.
33 Cooper and Eaves, 1996: p. 107: Flynn et al., 2009: p. 309; Morton et al., 1998: p. 95; Scott, 2009: p. 374.
34 Harper and Voigt, 2007: p. 303; Wallace, 1986: pp. 184–186.
35 Byard et al., 1999: p. 324; Cooper and Eaves, 1996: p. 106; Harper and Voigt, 2007: p. 311; Liem, 2010: p. 156; Liem et al., 2011: p. 76; Lund and Smorodinsky, 2001: p. 454; Morton et al., 1998: p. 95; Saleva et al., 2007: p. 206; Scott, 2009: p. 374; Warren-Gordon et al., 2010: p. 1595.
36 Panczak et al., 2013: p. 32.
37 Adinkrah, 2003: pp. 68–70.

hands to strangulate the victim.[38] Additional criminological patterns that contradict prior Western studies were also noted regarding the method of femicide–suicide. Whereas findings in Western societies indicated the use of the same method for both killing and committing suicide,[39] femicide–suicides in Fiji, Hong Kong and Japan were characterized by separate methods for the killing and the suicide: Stabbing for killing and hanging to commit suicide in Fiji;[40] strangulation for killing and jumping from heights to commit suicide in Hong Kong;[41] and strangulation for homicide and gas or drug poisoning to commit suicide in Japan.[42] Contradicting sociodemographic characteristics were also found regarding the perpetrators' socioeconomic statuses. Whereas studies in Western societies noted that perpetrators are most often fully employed,[43] perpetrators in Hong Kong, Japan, Ghana and Fiji were most often unemployed, not permanently employed or came from low socioeconomic backgrounds.[44]

These contradicting findings imply that variations in sociodemographic and criminological characteristics of femicide–suicide are sociocultural in nature, and that as a phenomenon, it is socioculturally relative. Thus, this chapter highlights the scholarly need to further our understanding of the possible sociocultural variations in femicide manifestation.

For the sake of this chapter, the femicide–suicide cases that we refer to were identified as such, wherein a suicide appears to have been intrinsically linked to a prior femicide. Our operational definition of the interval between the femicide event and the suicide event follows Marzuk et al.'s[45] definition in the sense that the perpetrator's suicide occurred within one week of the femicide incident, with the exclusion of cases wherein the femicide–suicide was not confirmed, the homicide occurred during a terror attack, only a multiple murder occurred, only multiple suicides occurred, the perpetrator failed to die from his suicide attempt or the suicide took place one week or more after the killing.

Similar to sociodemographic findings in Western studies, when observing empirical characteristics of femicide–suicide in Israel, we find that all perpetrators are male and most often the victim's current or former intimate partner (divorced or physically separated). Further, similar to Western studies, no major observations of perpetrator depression and substance abuse are noted.[46]

However, unique sociodemographic characteristics are found in Israel regarding perpetrator ethnic and socioeconomic status: Whereas Western study findings

38 Chan et al., 2003: pp. 262–263; Sakuta, 1995: p. 144.
39 Flynn et al., 2009: p. 309; Warren-Gordon et al., 2010: p. 1596.
40 Adinkrah, 2003: p. 71.
41 Chan et al., 2003: pp. 262–263.
42 Sakuta, 1995: p. 144.
43 Morton et al., 1998: p. 93; Scott, 2009: p. 374.
44 Adinkrah, 2003: p. 69; Adinkrah, 2014: pp. 375–377; Chan et al., 2003: p. 266; Sakuta, 1995: p. 142.
45 Marzuk et al., 1992: p. 3179.
46 Dayan, 2021.

point to predominantly White Caucasian perpetrators, representing their distribution in these societies,[47] a different ethnic distribution is noted in Israel, with underrepresentation of the Arab population and about a third of the perpetrators belonging to the minority of Ethiopian immigrant Jews that is overrepresented compared to its 2% share in the total Jewish population.[48]

The overrepresentation of immigrant Ethiopian Jews in fatal gender-based violence corroborates previous findings regarding their overrepresentation in femicide in general, in Israel.[49] This cultural pattern of femicide–suicide corroborates patterns noted in non-Western societies, such as Fiji and South Africa, with reported overrepresentation of ethnic-minority populations.[50] However, the fact that former SSRR immigrant Jews and Arabs are underrepresented among femicide–suicide cases suggests, in our opinion, that variations in the femicide–suicide frequency are not by definition intrinsically related to belonging to an ethnic minority. Indeed, the Arab population, the biggest ethnic minority in Israel, constituting 20% of the total population, is virtually absent in femicide–suicide cases in Israel.

Given the absence of femicide–suicide cases among other Israeli minorities, we believe that other sociocultural factors contribute to overrepresentation of a certain ethnic minority in femicide–suicide: In this case, Ethiopian immigrant Jews. Indeed, Geiger,[51] Sela-Shayovitz[52] and Weil[53] linked the overrepresentation of the Ethiopian immigrant minority regarding femicide in general and femicide–suicide in particular to strain theories related to immigration. In this respect, it is noteworthy that overrepresentation of immigrant populations in femicide–suicide was also noted by Wallace in her study in New South Wales.[54]

In attempting to explain the strains that Ethiopian immigrants Jews faced and continue to face, scholars refer to the major cultural gap they had to bridge to assimilate into Israeli society.[55] According to Geiger, the disintegration of traditional norms and social mechanisms that followed the Ethiopian Jews' efforts to become part of the dominant Israeli culture may have contributed to the high rates of lethal domestic violence in the Ethiopian community in Israel.[56] This can be viewed as an anomic response to the social disintegration with which these immigrants contended, referring to the social phenomenon of anomy observed by Durkheim.[57] Durkheim predicted that times of rapid social disorganization

47 Flynn et al., 2009: p. 313; Lund and Smorodinsky, 2001: p. 455; Morton et al., 1998: p. 93.
48 Dayan, 2021.
49 Edelstein, 2011; Sela-Shayovitz, 2010; Weil, 2016.
50 Adinkrah, 2003; Mathews et al., 2008; Roberts et al., 2010.
51 Geiger, 2013.
52 Sela-Shayovitz, 2010.
53 Weil, 2016.
54 Wallace, 1986: p. 182.
55 Geiger, 2013; Landau and Hattis-Rolef, 1998; Sela-Shayovitz, 2010; Weil, 2016.
56 Geiger, 2013: pp. 234–239.
57 Durkeim, 1897/1951.

and social change, when traditional norms and constraints break down, deprive individuals of social regulation and norms that are vitally needed to regulate their behavior. For Durkheim, such deprivation of social regulation is an irritating "source of torment" that may consequently create a social condition that increases the human tendency to commit anomic suicide or homicide.[58] Still, this theory does not explain femicide–suicide as a form of the anomie phenomenon. Although Durkheim predicted higher rates of suicide or homicide, anomie theory does not offer a suitable explanation of homicide followed by suicide, particularly the killing of a female intimate partner followed by the perpetrator's suicide among Ethiopian immigrant Jews in Israel.

Furthermore, immigration alone cannot explain higher rates of femicide–suicide, because immigrant Jews from the former USSR are underrepresented in intimate-partner homicide–suicide cases in Israel.[59] Perhaps specific interacting cultural ethnic notions, in addition to social strains and immigration-related anomy, interact to increase or decrease femicide–suicide tendencies. One plausible interacting factor working in conjunction with the social strain and influencing the increase in such tendencies relates to the rural characteristics of the communities from which Ethiopian immigrants came. According to Geiger, "the collectivist orientation of the Ethiopian community regards individual members' identity as inseparable from the extended family and community."[60] Such collective patriarchal notions by which men see the whole family (children included) as one integral, inseparable nuclear unit may contribute to the tendency to see them undivided even when facing strain followed by collective death.

When looking on the criminological manifestations of femicide–suicide in Israel, similar criminological characteristics compared to Western findings are noted. Similar to Western manifestations, femicide–suicide in Israel has a greater likelihood to result in multiple victims, mainly the victim's children (in addition to the victim)[61] and involve the victim's home as the main crime scene,[62] although the suicide is often committed in a different room than the homicide. We note further similarities to Western findings with respect to the immediate motive triggering the homicide – the intimate female partner's desire to terminate the relationship.[63] Indeed, in line with our previous observations presented in Chapter 3, noting that the most common motive for intimate-partner femicide refers to the victim's wish to end the intimate relationship, a similar pattern is noted in this

58 Durkeim, 1897/1951: p. 257.
59 Dayan, 2021.
60 Geiger, 2013: p. 236.
61 Liem et al., 2011: p. 75; Morton et al., 1998: p. 95.
62 Flynn et al., 2009: p. 309; Harper and Voigt, 2007: p. 302; Liem et al., 2011: p. 76; Warren-Gordon et al., 2010: p. 1595.
63 Cooper and Eaves, 1996: p. 106; Harper and Voigt, 2007: pp. 303–304, 310; Liem et al., 2011: p. 76; Milroy, 1995: p. 119; Morton et al., 1998: p. 96; Saleva et al., 2007: p. 208; Scott, 2009: p. 374.

femicide subtype as well. In femicide–suicide, the most common motive was also the victim's desire to terminate her intimate relationship with the perpetrator.[64]

The killing motive related to the victim's wish to separate from her intimate partner seems to be entangled, in this femicide subtype, with domestic violence. In this respect, we note that the percentage of all cases involving known prior domestic violence (with prior complaints filed by the victim, victim's family, welfare agencies, or police or a restraining order issued against the perpetrator) is about 35%, with half of the cases involving domestic violence toward the victim, perpetrated by their former intimate partners (divorced or physically separated), and half involving domestic violence toward the victim, from their current intimate partner.[65] The link between domestic violence and femicide–suicide has been noted in Western studies, reporting relationships between the perpetrator and victims as often characterized by domestic violence,[66] control[67] and obsession on the part of the male partner.[68] Indeed, this thematic link echoes Starzomski and Nussbaum's observation that perpetrators of homicide–suicide are often immersed in long-standing domestic relationships marred by chronic (e.g., wife-battering or stalking) or acute (e.g., separation or divorce) types of problems.[69]

In line with our endeavor to explore the cultural relativity of femicide–suicide, notable are unique criminological characteristics of femicide–suicide modus operandi among various ethnic and sociocultural groups in Israel. Whereas veteran Jews, Russian immigrant Jews and Arabs tend to use a firearm as their preferred weapon,[70] a knife is the weapon of choice among Ethiopian immigrant Jews. This criminological characteristic of femicide–suicide among Ethiopian immigrant Jews resonates with patterns of homicide–suicide reported in several non-Western society studies: That is, the use of primary weapons other than a firearm (such as machetes in Fiji and strangulation in Japan and Hong Kong).

We would also like to note additional cultural relativity in femicide–suicide modus operandi: Although veteran Israeli Jews, Russian immigrant Jews, and Arabs are most likely to use the same method for the killing and suicide,[71] Ethiopian immigrant Jews tend to use different methods for killing (stabbing) and suicide (hanging). In other words, whereas criminological characteristics among veteran Jews and Russian immigrant Jews resemble those reported in Western societies in the sense of administering the same method for killing and committing suicide,

64 Dayan, 2021.
65 Dayan, 2021.
66 Cooper and Eaves, 1996: p. 107; Harper and Voigt, 2007: pp. 302–303; Morton et al., 1998: p. 95; Scott, 2009: p. 375; Starzomski and Nussbaum, 2000: pp. 471–472.
67 Harper and Voigt, 2007: p. 303; Starzomski and Nussbaum, 2000: p. 471.
68 Cooper and Eaves, 1996: p. 110; Saleva et al., 2007: p. 206.
69 Starzomski and Nussbaum, 2000: pp. 471–472.
70 Byard et al., 1999: p. 324; Cooper and Eaves, 1996: p. 106; Harper and Voigt, 2007: p. 311; Liem, 2010: p. 156; Liem et al., 2011: p. 76; Lund and Smorodinsky, 2001: pp. 454–455; Morton et al., 1998: p. 95; Panczak et al., 2013: p. 32; Saleva et al., 2007: p. 206; Scott, 2009: p. 374; Warren-Gordon et al., 2010: p. 1595.
71 Flynn et al., 2009: p. 309; Warren-Gordon et al., 2010: p. 1596.

Ethiopian immigrant Jews' modus operandi seems to resemble reports from homicide–suicide in non-Western societies, which use different methods for killing and suicide (strangulation for killing and jumping from heights for suicide in Hong Kong; strangulation for killing and gas or drug poisoning for suicide in Japan).[72]

Overall, empirical findings of femicide–suicide in Israel show variations in the distribution of femicide–suicide and the criminological patterns of this femicide subtype across different ethnic and sociocultural groups in Israel. Except for variations in their distribution among ethnic and social groups in Israel, characteristics of femicide–suicide in Israel seem to resemble patterns observed in studies of Western societies, in the sense of the close proximity of this homicidal type of intimate-partner femicide. However, with respect to criminological characteristics, femicide–suicide in Israel manifests with variations among various ethnic and social groups in Israel: Although veteran Jews are underrepresented and Arabs virtually absent, this femicide subtype seems to be intrinsically linked in Israel to a particular Jewish social minority: Ethiopian immigrant Jews. This social group exhibits femicide–suicide characteristics that echo findings in non-Western societies, both in terms of the choice of weapon and the killing and suicide method.

Our empirical findings stress the importance of cultural relativity in femicide in general and femicide–suicide in particular. Indeed, in line with our empirical observations of femicide–suicide in Israel, we embrace Harper and Voigt's call to continue to contribute quantitative and qualitative data from different geographic locations so that we can better understand the homicide–suicide phenomenon.[73] Indeed, future comparative research is needed to gain a better understanding of the possible mediating role of various sociocultural factors on the manifestations of femicide–suicide, and how policy recommendations sensitive to cultural diversity could be outlined.

Having used a nation-based framework of analysis to explore theoretical and empirical aspects of femicide–suicide, a phenomenon accounting for the vast majority of homicide–suicides, we offer in the last chapter of this part of the book, Chapter 6, a perspective on yet another subtype of femicide – concealed femicide – composed of cases that bear more elusive and inconclusive characteristics. Examining cases in which women died in circumstances identified as "proxies to crime," the chapter discusses femicide methods usually overlooked by both the criminal system and scholars researching the field.

References

Adinkrah, M. (2003). Homicide-suicide in Fiji: Offense patterns, situational factors and sociocultural contexts. *Suicide and Life-Threatening Behavior*, *33*, 65–73.

Adinkrah, M. (2014). Homicide-suicide in Ghana: Perpetrators, victims, and incidence characteristics. *International Journal of Offender Therapy and Comparative Criminology*, *58*(3), 364–387.

72 Dayan, 2021.

73 Harper and Voigt, 2007: p. 312.

Banks, L., Crandall C., Sklar, D., & Bauer, M. (2008). A comparison of intimate partner homicide to intimate partner homicide-suicide: One hundred and twenty-four New Mexico cases. *Violence Against Women, 14*(9), 1065–1078.

Berman, A. (1996). Dyadic death: A typology. *Suicide and Life-Threatening Behavior, 26*, 342–350.

Byard, R., Knight, D., James, R. A., & Gilbert, J. (1999). Murder-suicides involving children: A 29-year study. *American Journal of Forensic Medicine and Pathology, 20*, 323–327.

Chan, A. Y., Beh, S. L., & Broadhurst, R. G. (2003). Homicide-suicide in Hong Kong 1989–1998. *Forensic Science International, 137*, 165–171.

Cooper, M., & Eaves, D. (1996). Suicide following homicide in the family. *Violence and Victims, 11*(2), 99–112.

Dayan, H. (2021). Sociocultural aspects of femicide-suicide: The case of Israel. *Journal of Interpersonal Violence*. Advance online publication. https://doi.org/10.1177/0886260518792983

Dogan, K., Demirci, S., Gunaydin, G., & Buken, B. (2010). Homicide-suicide in Konya, Turkey between 2000–2007. *Journal of Forensic Sciences, 17*, 110–115.

Durkeim, E. (1897/1951). *Suicide: A study in sociology* (J. A. Spaulding & G. Simpson, Trans.). Free Press.

Edelstein, A. (2011). *Intimate homicide in Israel: Theoretical and empirical aspects.* Bialik (in Hebrew).

Flynn, S., Swinson, N., While, D., Hunt, I., Roscoe, A., Rodway, C., Windfuhr, K., Kapur, N., Appleby, L., & Shaw, J. (2009). Homicide followed by suicide: A cross-sectional study. *The Journal of Forensic Psychiatry & Psychology, 20*(2), 306–321.

Geiger, B. (2013). Ethiopian males account for the double acts of murder and suicide committed by males in Ethiopian families' post-migration to Israel. *International Criminal Justice Review, 23*(3), 233–252.

Harper, D. W., & Voigt, L. (2007). Homicide followed by suicide: An integrated theoretical perspective. *Homicide Studies, 11*(4), 295–318.

Landau, S., & Hattis-Rolef, S. (1998). Intimate femicide in Israel: Temporal, social and motivational patterns. *European Journal on Criminal Policy and Research, 6*, 75–90.

Large, M., Smith, G., & Nielssen, O. (2009). The epidemiology of homicide followed by suicide: A systematic and quantitative review. *Suicide and Life-Threatening Behavior, 39*(3), 294–308.

Liem, M. (2010). Homicide followed by suicide: A review. *Aggression and Violent Behavior, 15*, 153–161.

Liem, M., Barber, C., Markwalder, N., Killias, M., & Nieuwbeerta, P. (2011). Homicide-suicide and other violent deaths: An international comparison. *Forensic Science International, 207*, 70–76.

Lund, L., & Smorodinsky, L. (2001). Violent death among intimate partners: A comparison of homicide followed by suicide in California. *Suicide and Life-Threatening Behavior, 31*(4), 451–459.

Marzuk, P. M., Tardiff, K., & Hirsch, C. S. (1992). The epidemiology of murder-suicide. *Journal of American Medical Association, 267*, 3179–3183.

Mathews, S., Abrahams, N., Jewkes, R., Martin, L. J., Lombard, C., & Vetten, L. (2008). Intimate femicide-suicide in South Africa: A cross-sectional study. *Bulletin of the World Health Organization, 86*(7), 552–558.

Milroy, C. M. (1995). The epidemiology of homicide-suicide (dyadic death). *Forensic Science International, 71*, 117–122.

Morton, E. C., Runyan, K. W., Moracco, E., & Butts, J. (1998). Partner homicide-suicide involving female homicide victims: A population-based study in North Carolina, 1988–1992. *Violence and Victims*, *13*(2), 91–106.

Panczak, R., Geissbühler, M., Zwahlen, M., Killias, M., Tal, K., & Egger, M. (2013). Homicide-suicides compared to homicides and suicides: Systematic review and meta-analysis. *Forensic Science International*, *233*, 28–36.

Roberts, K., Wassenaar, D., Canetto, S. S., & Pillay, A. (2010). Homicide-suicide in Durban, South Africa. *Journal of Interpersonal Violence*, *25*, 877–899.

Rosenbaum, M. (1990). The role of depression in couples involved in murder-suicide and homicide. *American Journal of Psychiatry*, *147*, 1036–1039.

Sakuta, T. (1995). A study of murder followed by suicide. *Medicine Law*, *14*(1–2), 141–153.

Saleva, O., Putkonen, H., Kiviruusu, O., & Lonnqvist, J. (2007). Homicide-suicide – An event hard to prevent and separate from homicide or suicide. *Forensic Science International*, *166*, 204–208.

Scott, E. (2009). Murder-suicide: A review of the recent literature. *The Journal of the American Academy of Psychiatry and the Law*, *37*, 371–376.

Sela-Shayovitz, R. (2010). The role of ethnicity and context: Intimate femicide rates among social groups in Israeli society. *Violence against Women*, *16*, 1424–1436.

Stack, S. (1997). Homicide followed by suicide: An analysis of Chicago data. *Criminology*, *35*(3), 435–453.

Starzomski, D., & Nussbaum D. (2000). The self and the psychology of domestic homicide-suicide. *International Journal of Offender Therapy and Comparative Criminology*, *44*(4), 468–479.

Van Wormer, K., & Odiah, C. (1999). The psychology of suicide-murder and the death penalty. *Journal of Criminal Justice*, *27*(4), 361–370.

Wallace, A. (1986). *Homicide: The social reality*. New South Wales Bureau of Crimes Statistics and Research, Attorney General's Department.

Warren-Gordon, K., Byers, D. B., Brodt, S. J., Watak, M., & Biskupski, B. (2010). Murder followed by suicide: A newspaper surveillance study using the New York Times Index. *Journal of Forensic Science*, *55*(6), 1592–1597.

Weil, S. (2016). Failed femicides among migrant survivors. *Qualitative Sociology Review*, *7*(4), 6–21.

6 Concealed Femicide

Feminist Theory and Circumstantial Evidence

Introduction

Having conducted theoretical and empirical analyses of three femicide subtypes – intimate-partner femicide, F.H.K., and femicide–suicide – this chapter, the last chapter in Part II of the book, offers a crimino-legal analysis of yet another subtype of femicide, concealed femicide, composed of cases that bear more elusive and inconclusive characteristics.

The traditional methodological approach to studying femicide relies heavily on empirical data extracted from clear-cut and conclusive cases of homicide, missing a hidden bulk of femicide cases not recognized as such and identified as concealed-femicide cases. Examining cases in which women died in circumstances identified as "proxies to crime," we recently argued that concealed-femicide cases are normally overlooked by both the criminal system and scholars researching the field.[1] In this chapter, we delve into the phenomenon of concealed femicide from two additional viewpoints. First, we entrench it in theoretical feminist premises. Second, we define the different processes in which concealed cases are revealed and the ingrained circumstantial nature their forensic evidences bare, which render the women's victimhood susceptible to doubt.

This chapter proceeds in three parts. The first and theoretical part reintroduces the notion of concealed femicide, focusing on its gendered peculiarity and the underlying feminist theory. Drawing on dominance-based feminist theory and feminist analysis of the vulnerability the private-public dichotomy assumes for women, the article presents the "why," "how," and "where" questions of femicide. Pointing to the domestic nature of the criminological traits of H.S.S. types, we define concealed femicide as a gendered phenomenon. Upon linking the domestic environment of H.S.S. with the typical absence of direct evidence to prove femicide, the theoretical part of our analysis culminates with an introduction of the differences between circumstantial and direct evidence and how their hierarchical disposition vis-à-vis each other is harmful to femicide victims.

1 Bitton and Dayan, 2019.

DOI: 10.4324/9781003333272-8

The second and more methodological part uses the descriptive and criminological analysis of four Israeli decisions regarding at-home deaths of women. These cases demonstrate common patterns of domesticity-related murders and their distinctive features as shaping the different processes in which they were revealed. Classification of these processes is as follows: (a) Cases revealed by the criminal legal system, (b) cases revealed by the civil legal system, and (c) cases left suspected as concealed femicide, with no formal recognition as such.

In its concluding third part, the chapter reveals the harms of the nearly inevitable use of circumstantial evidence as a basis for conviction in concealed femicide. Invoking this evidentiary tool bears ramifications that disadvantages femicide victims, even in the legal process established to identify them as victims.

Concealed Femicide

Reports of lethal violence perpetrated against women are identified as cases of femicide, i.e., cases in which women were identified as having been murdered, mostly by men, based on data provided by prosecutorial authorities.[2] This has resulted in a systemic failure to explore a wider range of femicide cases that fall outside the scope of the authorities' categorical identification of femicide.[3] In a recent research study, we proposed another factor supporting the claim of conservative femicide-rate estimates overlooked by femicide researchers: The prevalence of concealed femicide. According to our analysis, the following three cumulative conditions following a woman's death are useful in identifying a concealed femicide: (a) A woman was found dead; (b) the woman was buried pursuant to an official determination of her death as natural or noncriminal; and (c) the real reason for her death was femicide.[4]

Importance of Uncovering the Prevalence of Concealed Femicide

Although the horror of femicide is blatantly clear, the ramifications of concealed femicide warrant some elaboration. Acknowledging the reality of concealed femicide highlights the distorted representation of the prevalence of femicide as a social phenomenon, not only quantitatively but also qualitatively. This distortion produces a triangular harmful effect, in the public, private and social-change spheres, all engendered by the concealment of femicide.

2 Campbell et al., 2003.

3 This could be a result of varied distortions in data collection, such as misidentifying data regarding the nature of the relationship between some female victims and their male perpetrators (Corradi and Stöckl, 2014) and not including cases of women who kill themselves to avoid further abuse by their partners, women who die of homelessness while escaping violence (O'Neil, 2016; Zorza, 1991), etc.

4 Bitton and Dayan, 2019.

The most easily identifiable harmful effect is that caused to the public interest. Treated differently than in the past, ostensibly private violence perpetuated against a private woman by a private man is no longer viewed as a private matter, but rather as a public and even global concern.[5] Harm caused by concealed femicide to the public interest stems from the basic fact that a crime perpetrator can escape the due process of the law. The second harmful effect of concealed femicide lies in the private sphere and emanates from a woman's rudimentary right to autonomy, her right to "write" her own life story. The right to autonomy usually refers to a person's ability to shape the course of their life, an element abruptly and violently seized from victims of femicide.[6] Yet even in the face of such a rightless reality for the murdered woman, enabling her murderer to lie about her cause of death turns her rightless life into a rightless death. A harmful effect in the private sphere involves rights to the woman's estate and her survivors' right to inherit her estate. In case of a murder, for example, some legal systems deny guardianship or inheritance rights to murderers, transferring them to the victim's relatives.[7] Furthermore, in criminal-death cases in these systems, the victim's rights conferred on the victim's relatives are de facto nullified and withheld due to the noncriminal façade of such murders.[8] The third harmful effect of femicide concealment relates to social change. Identifying the realistic prevalence of femicide as a social phenomenon would enable researchers to extract the common modus operandi employed by perpetrators against their female victims. This information is required primarily to design prevention measures against future femicide.[9]

How is it possible that even in the face of these imperative reasons, the murder of women can still go unnoticed? To answer this question, this chapter lays the theoretical feminist foundations to women's vulnerability, the "why"; continues with a criminological analysis of the murder staging, the "how"; and concludes with the synthesis of both, the "where."

Why? Feminist Analysis of Women and Deadly Violence

Women die, as all people eventually do. This seemingly neutral fact of life, however, warrants specific attention, because women's existence – and hence, death – is more susceptible to an unnatural ending at the hands of men than vice versa.[10]

5 Corradi et al., 2016.

6 Benton, 1993; Dan-Cohen, 2000.

7 See, for example, Tennessee's Tenn. Code Ann. § 36–1–113(g)(7), providing that a parent or guardian's parental rights are terminated if they are convicted of or found civilly liable for the intentional and wrongful death of the child's other parent or legal guardian. Also, under Israeli inheritance law, a murderer cannot inherit his murder victim; see Act of Succession, 1965, clause 5(a)(1).

8 A murdered woman's estate is also entitled to bring a civil suit against the man who murdered her, an entitlement that is nullified when the murder is concealed as a natural death.

9 Corradi and Stöckl, 2014.

10 Jordan et al., 2010.

More to our point, a recent study on the worldwide prevalence of intimate-partner homicide showed that these homicides constitute a large portion of all homicides, with gender-based statistical significance.[11] This unequal reality has led feminist theorists to concentrate heavily on analyzing the violence that gender relations entail for women, as part of the patriarchal order. The notion of patriarchy, symbolizing the dominance of men over women, fosters the coercive and hierarchical nature of femicide, which is defined along gender lines: Men (mostly) kill women because they are women.[12] Femicide, according to this reasoning, is the embodiment of patriarchy's most violent manifestations.

Catherine MacKinnon's dominance-based theory of gender violence offers a sophisticated perspective on the inextricability of femicide and its concealment.[13] MacKinnon drew on Marxist theory, adapting its basic ideas to the gender-relations experience. Arguing that "sex is for women what work is for the Marxist theory," she conceptualized women's sexuality and autonomy as capital belonging to women, confiscated from them by men, who use it to gain control over women for their own enjoyment.[14] These exploitative relations persist through the coerced and violent commodification of women's sexuality and the subjugation of their autonomy to men's desires.[15] This theory is particularly illuminating with regard to femicide committed by men against their intimate female partners, acting on the notion of their right to dominate and control their female spouse. Femicide enables the male perpetrator to express his dominance in the ultimate manner, according to which the pure existence of his female partner is dependent on his decision, allowing her no sense of agency whatsoever.[16] More to the point, intimate-partner femicides usually occur when the man suspects he is losing his power to dominate and control the woman, whom he sees as his possession.[17]

Alongside other prominent feminist theories,[18] MacKinnon's monumental work serves to warn us against evaluating our gendered lives as neutral. She points to how women are subjugated by male dominance, thereby becoming more prone, susceptible and vulnerable to harm induced by gender-based violence. This vulnerability to unnatural and wrongful death merits extreme caution from a criminological perspective that seeks to ensure that a woman's allegedly random death is not, in fact, a femicide, concealed by staging the murder scene.

11 Stöckl et al., 2013.
12 Messerschmidt, 2017.
13 MacKinnon, 1987, 2005.
14 MacKinnon, 1983.
15 MacKinnon, 1979; MacKinnon and Dworkin, 1997.
16 Adams, 2007; Goussinsky and Yassour-Borochowitz, 2012.
17 Farr, 2002: p. 268; Messerschmidt, 2017.
18 For other feminist works underpinning the feminist approach to femicide, see Corradi et al., 2016: p. 5–6.

How? Lethal Violence against Women and Its Concealment: Homicide-Scene Staging (H.S.S.)

Research identifies three main types of H.S.S.: Primary staging, which is either ad hoc or preplanned and aims to misdirect the criminal investigation by manipulating physical or verbal evidence; secondary staging that manipulates the crime scene devoid of the intention to misdirect the investigation; and tertiary scene alterations aimed at protecting the dignity of the deceased victim.[19] In this chapter, we focus mainly on primary staging, which bears substantial implications for society's ability to identify femicide and secure its perpetrators' due criminal conviction.[20]

According to Douglas and Munn, staging materializes when someone purposefully alters the crime scene prior to the arrival of the police. They identified two reasons why someone would engage in staging: To redirect the investigation away from the most logical suspect or to protect the victim or the victim's family.[21] Staging is accomplished by altering physical evidence at the scene after the murder, and sometimes even beforehand, to present a misleading appearance of the crime scene. It imitates a crime during which the victim was hurt, a "legitimate death" scenario, or the disappearance of the victim.[22] Staging is thus a primary means of purposefully obstructing the criminal-justice process by concealing the true nature of the crime.[23]

Pettler[24] offered a typology of six major types of behavioral profiles associated with H.S.S., presented according to their frequency:

1) The fabricator: Does not substantially alter the scene's physical evidence, but instead relies heavily on his verbal ability to persuade investigators about what happened, often by spreading his lies even before the victim is reported missing.
2) The cleanser: Hides or destroys any evidence related to the crime he thinks might reveal his guilt, using extreme measures such as fire or water.
3) The Creator: Tactically adds physical articles to the crime scene rather than removing them from the scene. The creator typically moves the body and the weapon, then adds something to the scene so that it appears to look as if resulting from an accident, suicide, sexual-assault homicide or robbery homicide.
4) The cleaner: Attempts to strip the scene of evidence of the crime, typically using household cleaners to wash the scene, the body of the victim, or his own clothes and car.

19 Chancellor and Graham, 2014; Douglas and Douglas, 2006.
20 Pettler, 2016.
21 Douglas and Munn, 1992.
22 Pettler, 2016.
23 Cobin, 2009: p. 1; Hazelwood and Napier, 2004: p. 745.
24 Pettler, 2016.

5) The planner: Organizes and plans the murder in advance down to the smallest foreseeable detail, including taking measures before the murder and after its execution.
6) The inflictor: The last and least common behavioral profile in this typology. This type inflicts wounds and bruises on himself to stage evidence of an attack allegedly befalling him as well during the event.

Epidemiological Aspects and the Importance of Studying H.S.S.

The current literature is divided as to the prevalence of murder staging, with some estimating it to be as high as 8% of murder scenes,[25] whereas others set it as low as 0.1%.[26] These numbers, even the lowest estimation, should be questioned in light of the fact that they pertain to crimes that were eventually solved, and thus relevant only to the "formerly concealed, then revealed" category of cases. Our research, however, highlights the intrinsic nature of femicide as particularly susceptible to manipulative H.S.S. acts by the perpetrator. This implies that some femicide cases will most likely not be solved unless the legal system changes its approach to femicide. Furthermore, concealed femicide is expected to increase, given the public's access to homicide-investigation strategies through news, true-crime books, television series and detailed movies.[27]

Gendered Nature of H.S.S.

What makes femicide particularly susceptible to H.S.S.? First and foremost, a relationship or acquaintance with the victim is associated with murder-staging cases.[28] More to the point, the most common victim–offender relationship involving H.S.S. is an intimate-partner relationship, and most staged homicide scenes involve the killing of an intimate partner.[29] These H.S.S. characteristics comfortably align with the fact that in most H.S.S. cases, the perpetrator knows the victim and was the last person to have seen the victim alive. Added to this typicality are other gendered H.S.S. features: Stagers are more often men rather than women,[30] and women comprise the majority of victims of crimes in which H.S.S. took place.[31] These findings suggest that men employ H.S.S. to effectively conceal the femicide of their intimate partners.[32]

25 Schlesinger et al., 2012.
26 Hazelwood and Napier, 2004: p. 1308.
27 Ferguson, 2015; Geberth, 1996.
28 Douglas and Douglas, 2006.
29 Pettler, 2016.
30 Keppel and Weis, 2004; Hazelwood and Napier, 2004.
31 Pettler, 2016.
32 Douglas and Douglas, 2006.

Additional distinctive characteristics of H.S.S. are significant domestic elements closely related to femicide. To name a few: Most scenes are staged in the home, availing the perpetrator unobstructed time alone on the murder premises;[33] in most H.S.S. cases, the victim had previous relations with the offender and it was the offender who discovered the victim's body; most murder scenes were in the victim's home, etc.[34] From a socio-criminological perspective, these characteristics resemble those of femicide, whereby offenders usually act alone,[35] most are male,[36] and their killing mostly involves one victim, most often a woman between the ages of 19 and 44. The association between femicide and H.S.S. is further supported by the fact that men who kill their intimate partners usually have a more "ordinary" and "conventional" personal appearance,[37] which naturally helps sustain the noncriminal façade of their murder scene.

Where? Liberal Dichotomies and the Desertion of Women at Home

This chapter's analysis focuses on the home as the template of an unsafe space for women, where most femicide acts occur away from the public eye.[38] Additionally, this chapter focuses on women's intimate partners or former partners, because most commonly, women die at the hands of an intimate partner.[39] Despite this gender-uneven reality, bound by the underpinnings of liberal thought, the law still struggles when applied to the person's most private sphere, traditionally perceived as a sacred – however masculine – haven.[40] This failure to identify women's needs and redress their hurts was identified in feminist theory as a state of lawlessness, wherein the lack of legal intervention, particularly inside the home, accounted for lack of proper protection of women, who needed it.[41] The public-private dichotomy delineated the state's legitimate regulatory function regarding the public, while ordering its refrainment from interfering with private matters. This dichotomy was used throughout the patriarchal tradition as a tool for preserving the inferior status of women in society.[42] This liberal proposition led legislatures and courts to promulgate statutes and doctrines that were blind to women's needs and suffering.[43] One such statute identified "rape" as only occur-

33 Dobash and Dobash, 2015; Eke, 2007: p. 92; Pettler, 2016: pp. 18, 20.
34 Ferguson, 2015; Pettler, 2016.
35 Ferguson, 2015.
36 Ferguson, 2016; Pettler, 2016: p. 39.
37 Dobash et al., 2004.
38 Marcuello-Servós et al., 2016: p. 968. More support for this proposition is the fact that most sexual assaults on women take place at home. Interestingly, the home is still perceived by women as safer than public spaces. See Bitton and Shavit, 2015.
39 Bloom, 2008.
40 Landes, 1998.
41 MacKinnon, 1987: pp. 106–109.
42 Landes, 1998.
43 Gavison, 1992.

ring if the woman was not the rapist's lawfully married wife.[44] The court's refusal to apply rules of fairness or to enforce intermarriage contractual relations embodied such desertion.[45]

Protected from the law's invasion, the home became for women a territory of lawlessness. In extreme circumstances, this lawlessness paved the way to criminality, as represented by the concept of crime as "self-help" social control. The theory underpinning this concept maintains that the state drives people to take matters into their own hands. This is done to restore the social order these people perceive as having been violated by their victim. Domestic relationships are a template of such experience, particularly for women,[46] even today, when the law no longer immunizes the home from social interference and invasion.[47]

Though it still forms and facilitates the inferiority of women to men, liberal law has progressed to include women and continues to foster more rights designed to elevate their status.[48] In this new functionality, where the law is present in many aspects of women's lives and protects them against discrimination, even at home, perceiving women's unnatural death as a neutral phenomenon is a new means for preserving their vulnerable and inferior position, particularly because even nowadays, most assaults on women occur domestically.[49] The law's leniency toward men's domestic violence is reflected in its willingness to admit the accountability-diminishing relevance of spousal domesticity, privileging men with "domestic discounts."[50] Allowing intimate partners to invoke claims of jealousy-driven provocation, for example, extends this favoritism to femicide

44 Estrich, 1987.

45 Thus, for example, the First Restatement of the Law of Contracts (1932), § 587 states: "[B]argain between married persons or persons contemplating marriage to change the essential incidents of marriage is illegal." See Restatement (First) of Contracts § 587 (Am. Law Inst. 1932); also see Singer, 1989 (suggests treating marriage as an investment partnership for divorce financial settlements) and Hunter, 1991 (for a further discussion of this issue in the American context).

46 Gauthier and Bankston, 2004. Interestingly, the authors indicate that most of the cases of men killing women are motivated by control and dominance of the men, whereas many instances when women kill men are motivated by their despair emanating from being caught in abusive relationships with their victim. Also, when men kill women, the murder is an escalated part of normally long-lasting abuse and violence inflicted upon the woman (see pp. 99–100). Another theoretical theme explaining the differences in motivation assigns sexual-proprietariness theory to men killing their partners and self-defense theory for women killing their partners: Serrana and Firestone, 2004 (the authors challenge the conclusive role of these theories, but not their validity) and Hannawa et al., 2006.

47 For the less tolerant approach of current law to the private sphere of the home, see Marcuello-Servós et al., 2016: p. 968.

48 Frug, 1992.

49 See Walby and Myhill, 2001. Also see Corradi et al., 2016: pp. 6–7; a greater rate of women die at the hands of man and in domestic settings, rendering this phenomenon socially gendered, not neutral.

50 The term "domestic discounts" was coined by Rapaport, 1996.

cases.[51] From this vantage point, this leniency toward domesticity allows the persistence of concealed femicide. The domestic nature of concealed femicide renders it susceptible to staging and concealment. Consequently, refrainment from strict scrutiny of every woman's death at home is yet another "domestic discount" given to men at the expense of women's safety. Largely successful law reforms have been adopted to ameliorate its gendered favoritism in the field of homicide, and the law should remain responsive to further changes in this direction.[52]

To sum up, the feminist perspective on the association of H.S.S. and femicide mandates that considerable legal and forensic attention should be assigned to the latter. In some cases, only meticulous forensic autopsies can detect the primary reason of death and prior related injuries.[53] Suspicion should be established for at-home deaths of women to overcome what might be the offender's elaborate lies shaped to conceal a femicide.[54] Moreover, concealed femicide is expected to grow, because crime-scene staging is correlated with increased public access to homicide investigations through news and detailed true-crime books and documentary media.[55] The feminist emphasis on domesticity as warranting the reconsideration of women's unsuspected deaths as suspicious illustrates not just its physical harmfulness but also domesticity's devastating legal effect on these dead women.

Direct Evidence vs. Circumstantial Evidence and Their Hierarchical Order

From a legal standpoint, concealed-femicide cases are more likely to be decided based on the invocation of circumstantial evidence rather than direct evidence, due to the domestic nature of the underlying gendered violence. Domesticity allows concealment; the privacy it provides avails the application of sophisticated concealment measurements; affords control over the body of the women; secures

51 For more about the prevalence of jealousy as an accountability-diminishing factor for men, see Ballinger, 2016: "Condoning female-spouse killings through the provocation defense demonstrates that 'patriarchal narratives of provocation have been incorporated into law and recognized by its hierarchy.'" Other systematic forms of "domestic discounts" were identified in Canada's differential treatment of "regular" homicide perpetrators and intimate partner femicide perpetrators. See Dawson, 2004. In a recent publication, though, Dawson reversed some of her previous findings, claiming that "there have been positive changes in the punishment of femicide over time, paralleling legislative and policy responses to violence against women in Canada" (see Dawson, 2016). Simultaneous to this leniency, and outrageously, the law rigidly declines women's self-help claims if they are the ones to exert domestic violence against violent and abusive men (Bitton and Dayan, 2019).

52 For some of these law reforms, instigated primarily by feminists, see Rapaport, 1996: p. 1510.

53 Bitton and Dayan, 2019.

54 Bitton and Dayan, 2019.

55 Ferguson, 2014; Geberth, 1996: p. 37.

isolation from outsiders in the "safe" home; suggests that the home is typically not a crime scene; and fails to invoke suspicion that regularly warrants diligent investigative means. Combined with the death of the victims, these traits lead to want of eyewitnesses and lower the motivation of defendants to provide confessions. Absent such direct evidence, prosecutors – and consequently, the court – resort to indirect evidence to prove the perpetrator's guilt. Invoking indirect evidence to decide these cases, especially for the purpose of establishing criminal conviction, further burdens the victim and her family with adverse consequences due to the difference between the evidence rules and their hierarchical order.

Direct evidence pertains to the type of evidence that "proves a fact without an inference or presumption and which in itself, if true, establishes that fact. . . . The category of direct evidence thus includes eyewitness identifications and confessions, the ideal examples of which prove the defendant's guilt without the need for inference."[56] Conversely, with circumstantial evidence, the evidence type is one "from which the fact-finder can infer whether the facts in dispute existed or did not exist. . . . [It] thus includes all forensic evidence, such as blood or fingerprints, as well as non-forensic evidence that does not by it."[57]

Circumstantial evidence relates to circumstances whereby culpability is inferred from the factual evidence, as opposed to being inferred from mere presumptions. In other words: "When one or more things are proved from which one can reasonably make an inference that another must have happened, although not proved, it is legitimate to presume that it did happen."[58] To make the inference, the court applies a twofold analysis. First, it establishes the finding, identifying the accused's behavior, other people's testimonies, and his own unconvincing testimony. It then proceeds to the second stage of making the proper and only reasonable inference from the proven finding. Here, the inference must be consistent with all proven facts. Consequently, any other reasonable inference should be ruled out, because only the convicting inference must be reasonably plausible. If another reasonable inference can be deducted from the evidence, doubt is cast on the inferred conclusion, rendering a conviction unviable.[59] If the presumption of guilt is duly inferred, it stands, unless refuted by the accused. Given this structured inference process, circumstantial evidence is seen as no less credible and legally persuasive than direct evidence. Some legal scholars even treat it as superior to direct evidence, more heavily relying on testimonies rather than sheer facts represented by circumstantial evidence.[60]

Though formally enjoying similar legal status and despite their strictly structured nature, circumstantial evidence-based convictions are more rare than direct evidence-based convictions and are perceived as imperfect from a moral point

56 Heller, 2006: p. 248.
57 Heller, 2006: pp. 250–251.
58 Rwelamira, 1992: p. 136.
59 Rwelamira, 1992: p. 138.
60 Heller, 2006: p. 244.

of view, raising doubts about their strength and definiteness.[61] Informally, conviction beyond a reasonable doubt is frequently interpreted as the requirement for direct evidence of criminality. Though empirical research indicated the contrary, circumstantial evidence decisions are reputed as more prone to erroneous judgements and wrongful convictions and are therefore far less trusted. Empirical research revealed this distrust in the legal system itself, by showcasing that although circumstantial evidence is far less likely to lead to false convictions than direct evidence, American jurors were reluctant to use it to convict. Ironically, their fear of false convictions renders circumstantial cases susceptible to the less acknowledged problem of false acquittal.[62] More specifically, in circumstantial-evidence-based cases, the probabilities of acquittal are much higher than in direct-evidence cases, even when they share similar sufficiency of proven guilt.[63]

This dissonance, whereby circumstantial evidence is commonly seen as an inferior judgement tool, emanates from a psychological rather than cognitive flaw. Research indicates that people perceive convictions based on circumstantial evidence as less credible than direct-evidence-convictions. The reason for that, identified as the Wells effect, is the cognitive tendency when faced with circumstantial evidence to imagine alternative exculpatory scenarios – that could not otherwise establish reasonable doubt regarding the defendant's guilt – but are nevertheless imaginable.[64] This effect creates a reality of uncertainty and disbelief, whereby women murdered and having their scene staged do not enjoy the determinative-guilt effect bestowed by criminal convictions on murderers. More to the point, circumstantial evidence is identified as a nonnarrative tool. Rather, it is perceived as a rhetorical tool, aimed at igniting a cognitive process that leads to establishing a probable proof. Direct evidence, on the other hand, works as narratives do: It builds a story formed through the process of revealing the historical account of what has "happened." While the former appeals to procedural abilities, the latter appeals to the ability to recognize and validate the truth.[65] In other words, using circumstantial evidence rather than direct evidence resembles preferring imagination to vividness, a much stronger humanistic and appealing trait for construction of "the truth."[66]

Concealed Femicide: Qualitative Explorative Review

Classifying Concealed Femicide

Following the description of the feminine life experience of death as warranting special crimino-legal attention and a more nuanced analysis, cases of women's sudden and unnatural deaths at home come to mind as potential arenas of concealed

61 Heller, 2006: p. 243.
62 Heller, 2006: pp. 244–245.
63 Heller, 2006: p. 258.
64 Heller, 2006: pp. 258, 264–280.
65 Heller, 2006: pp. 265–266.
66 Heller, 2006: pp. 278–280.

femicide,[67] yet methodological analysis of concealed-femicide cases presents a paradox: How can femicide be identified if it is not recognized as such by the authorities? Hypothetically, given the fact that these cases manage to escape legal scrutiny due to their elusiveness, an attempt to critically review them from a legal outlook is doomed to fail. This hypothesis is true, however, only to a certain extent. Occasionally, some concealed-femicide cases are later suspected or revealed as femicides, either by criminal or civil legal procedures, in a manner that allows us a rare opportunity to classify the process of uncovering them. To this end, we identify and introduce three differently fashioned processes in which femicide cases were uncovered after being concealed and analyze their feminist characteristics and the resulting evidentiary effect they endured. Revealing an unsuspected death as concealed femicide occurs for different reasons. The revealing itself does not annul the initial failed identification of the case. Rather, the scarcity of such cases provides us a rare opportunity to develop our understanding of the field more critically. The test cases demonstrate how on account of their domestic nature and the indirect evidence available to prove them, femicide cases can go unidentified.

In presenting the test cases, we classify them according to the processes that facilitated their uncovering. The first class pertains to cases that were concealed and later officially revealed as femicide by criminal conviction, despite initially being identified as falling outside the scope of criminal suspicion. This process, whereby the murderer was eventually brought to justice and has been criminally convicted for his crime, corrects the initial injustice embedded in escaping the reach of justice, providing the ultimate corrective measure for both society and the victim's loved ones. The second class consists of cases in which no criminal charges are brought against the murderer and/or the H.S.S. perpetrator, but an alternative formal legal venue of civil prosecution is utilized to prove the woman's death was, in fact, a murder. Here, the process only partially corrects the injustice embedded in escaping moral and criminal blame, and yet it allows formal legal recognition of the wrongdoing, voicing the victim's story of death. Additionally, it provides compensation for the hurt induced by the murder. Third is the much more problematic and yet important class of concealed and later unofficially suspected cases. As part of our radical yet established notion of concealed femicide, we recognize that some women's death cases do not reach the point of being later revealed as concealed femicide. Nevertheless, their socio-criminological similarities to cases that were identified as femicide raise substantial concerns about their true nature. Although they lack conclusive answers as to the real reason for the women's death, such cases warrant academic scrutiny. They demonstrate the danger in treating women's at-home-deaths as noncriminal, thereby illuminating the potential that these deaths, if investigated upon occurrence as suspicious, could have been identified as femicides. This class of concealed-femicide cases is more challenging as an analytic tool for the obvious reason of not being formally identified as a murder. However, it bears significance as a means of establishing suspicion instead of ignoring suspicious deaths of women altogether.

67 Ferguson, 2015; Geberth, 1996.

Method of Exploration

This part uses a qualitative analysis method to explore four cases of women's at-home deaths. At first glance, the methodology of analyzing such few cases might seem too meager to enable meaningful discussion. Yet qualitative methodology of this kind is acceptable in exploring femicide for different reasons; inter alia, by hearing the victim's story, which cannot otherwise be heard. Here, added to the intrinsic difficulty of "voicing" dead victims in general is the fact of concealment, rendering these cases even harder to trace and learn from. Therefore, we suggest that the generalizability of these cases' analysis is solid.

The scarcity of sample cases stems from the paradox by which it is improbable – at times, impossible – to identify as femicide what was not suspected and investigated as such by the authorities in the first place. Successful murder-scene staging is what enables the concealment and hence, the alleged meagerness of officially identified court decisions regarding concealed and later revealed femicide in Israel. Despite this backdrop, upon thorough exploration, we identified the following cases. The first case involves a man who was criminally convicted of killing his wife after he was initially exonerated of suspicion. The second case is based on a criminal-court decision convicting the same man of two counts of murder of two of his wives after successfully staging their murder scenes. Though this case had been thoroughly analyzed by us recently,[68] it is important to present it here again, because the concealment of the two murders classically demonstrates the close affinity of concealed femicide to feminist theoretical framing and the dire legal consequences vis-à-vis the nature of their forensic evidence. The third case emanates from a noncriminal-court decision in a civil action and involves a staging done by the murderer's brother. Last, we will present a fourth case, based on a feminist organization's lawyer's experience, which shows similarity to other concealed and then legally revealed femicide cases. Analyzing the test cases allows a close inquiry into the susceptibility of femicide to concealment, utilizing H.S.S. tactics, which consequentially leads to crucial loss of incriminating direst forensic evidence.

Findings: Classification of the Test Cases

Concealed and Later Officially Revealed Femicide by Criminal Conviction

In this process of classification, we introduce three murder cases documented in two legal decisions. All cases involved the intimate-partner murder of women by their spouses, availed by gendered power relations and concealed by domesticity, which led to indirect evidence alone that the men left behind.

68 Bitton and Dayan, 2019.

The Siboni *Case*[69]

Siboni was married to his wife, Mendy, for 15 years. One day, in September 1999, upon deciding it was time for him to move out to live with his young lover, he shot her in their bedroom. Mendy was "found" dead by Siboni after being shot in her head once. Upon "finding" his wife, Siboni called the emergency authorities and asked them to instruct him as to how to revive his wife. Upon arrival at the couple's house, the rescue team was let in by a neighbor, because Siboni was still in the bedroom, holding his wife's bleeding head with a towel. A physician with the rescue team determined Mendy's death. Police investigators at the murder scene documented Siboni's claim that his wife shot herself mistakenly. His version of the events was that he took out the gun he legally owned from the bathroom, left it on their bed, and went downstairs. When he got back to their room, he found Mendy holding the gun in her direction, stating that she was looking for "dirt" in the barrel. Realizing the danger of the situation, he reached out for the gun, trying to get it out of her hand, when it discharged and she was shot in her head.

Siboni's staging of the murder scene was enabled due to, yet again, the domesticity of Mendy's death. She was shot in their house, where they were isolated from others. Conveniently, though the killing happened early in the morning, Siboni made sure he took their young kids to kindergarten before Mendy's death occurred. Additionally, he notified the housemaid that she was exempt from showing up for her cleaning chores that day, because Mendy, as he described it, was not feeling well.[70] In his "efforts" to revive Mendy after the shooting, Siboni moved the gun away from her and explained his fingerprints on it as part of his attempt to prevent her from pulling the trigger. He was, therefore, the only person with her and the last to have seen her alive. Fully and uninterruptedly dominating the household space, he was able to communicate his narrative – that Mendy shot herself – to the rescue team and the neighbors who gathered in the house in the immediate aftermath. At the time, he also described their relationship to the police as ideal, despite being on the verge of divorce given the couple had made a divorce settlement he hid from the police,[71] and despite having a lover for more than a year. Moreover, later it was revealed that Siboni was supposed to leave the house that day, but he had no alternative accommodation arrangements set in advance. Siboni's complete dominance over the couple's domestic premises enabled him to preplan its evacuation, by sending the kids away and releasing the cleaning lady,[72] and to position the gun next to Mendy's body to make it appear as if her death resulted from an accident. This, in return, facilitated the lack of any witnesses supplying direct evidence as to what had happened, which made his narrative persuasive to the police. He was arrested only a year and a half later, with only circumstantial evidence available to prove his guilt.[73]

69 PH 3002/00 People v. Siboni (29.11.2001).
70 Siboni: para. 9.
71 Siboni: para. 14.
72 Pettler, 2016: p. 95.
73 Siboni: para. 8.

The Cooper *Case*[74]

Almost 20 years after murdering his first wife and two years after murdering his second wife, Shimon Cooper's concealed-femicide acts were exposed and he was indicted and convicted of murdering the two women. The elaborate decision delivered by the trial court, spanning hundreds of pages, provides an unusual opportunity to identify, in detail, the different stages of concealment carried out by Cooper's utilization of his gender-based power relations with these women. Analyzing this case elsewhere,[75] we have showed how Cooper embodied the classic and most prominent perpetrator characteristics: A male who (a) kills his female spouse, who died in the typical age range for intimate-partner killing; (b) commits the crime at home; (c) was alone with the victim; (d) had time alone on the premises to stage the crime scene; (e) was the first person to find the victim and the last to have seen her alive; (f) engaged in the primary staging type – ad hoc preplanning aimed at misleading the criminal investigation by manipulating physical evidence; (g) spread rumors about her physical and mental condition prior to her death; (h) staged a legitimate death scenario, whether natural as in sickness-induced death or unnatural yet noncriminal-like suicide; and (i) influenced the impression of the police and the general public by making the homicide appear as a suicide, the most prevalent H.S.S. scheme.

The details of Cooper's two murder convictions illustrate how he was able to stage the femicide scenes due to classic dominance features: He had obtained complete control over the women, mentally abused and financially exploited them, separated them from family and friends' support, interfered in their medical condition, and so on.[76] This controlling posture lingered after their death, as he tried to prevent conducting an autopsy to the women. The fact that the concealment measures were so effective led here, too, to the inevitable lack of any direct evidence as to how these women died.

Concealed and Later Officially Revealed Femicide by Civil Decision

The Elimelech *Case*[77]

Anat Elimelech was a beautiful, successful, rising Israeli model and actress. On December 2, 1997, she was found dead in her estranged spouse's apartment, where he was found dead, too. Both had gunshot wounds from a gun found at the scene.

74 TPH 47934–11–12 People v. Cooper (28.6.2016). This case has been discussed in length and depth in Bitton and Dayan, 2019. Hence, it is presented here only briefly. Copper himself appealed his conviction. The Supreme Court upheld the decision on SC 6922/16 Cooper v. People (19.5.2022).

75 Bitton and Dayan, 2019.

76 Bitton and Dayan, 2019.

77 TMS 29170/05 The Late Elimelech v. The Late Afuta (20.2.2011 – Part I) (8.8.2011 – Part II).

The investigative authority determined at first that it was Anat who murdered her spouse, due to the fact that the gun was found near her hand, coupled with the fact that she sustained one shot wound, whereas her estranged spouse sustained two.[78] The pathologist adopted this initial narrative and confirmed that Anat had murdered her spouse and committed suicide.[79] Anat's family refused to accept the police's conviction and its resulting inclination to close the case, and they exerted pressure through the public media for the police to further investigate the case. Invoking statistics regarding the gendered nature of domestic violence and the couple's past experiences, they demanded that the police run the investigation under the assumption of suspicion that Anat had been the victim of femicide and that the murder scene had been staged to look as if she was the perpetrator of murder rather than the innocent victim. The family also pointed to the spouse's brother, who entered the crime scene before police had entered it, as having the possibility and motivation to stage the murder scene in favor of his murderous brother.

Only three weeks after the murder, and after the narrative of Anat's guilt had spread throughout the nation, the police decided to change the initial conviction and determined that Anat had been murdered and that her spouse committed suicide after murdering her. At this stage, the announcement ignored the H.S.S. that was done by the brother. Furthermore, the police investigated the brother, who denied moving the gun while alone at the murder scene, and the case against him was closed pursuant to a decision not to charge him.[80] It was only 15 years later that a civil court determined the scene had been staged by the murderer's brother to present Anat as the murderer rather than the victim of a murder.

Anat was murdered by a gunshot to her heart. After murdering her, her estranged spouse committed suicide by shooting himself twice. He had done this early in the morning, after Anat succumbed once again to his endless pleas to her to come support him, because he felt deeply upset by her recent separation from him. Worried about his inability to contact his beloved daughter over the phone and realizing she did not show up to her university class later that morning, Anat's father went looking for her at her spouse's residence. There, he found the apartment locked and Anat's car parked outside. Terrified, the father called the spouse's brother, who informed his other brother and called the police. The police's behavior upon arrival relied on classic gendered biases, and the dispatched officers refused to break open the door to the apartment, approaching the case as a domestic-dispute scene rather than a potential crime scene. While everyone, including the police officers, waited outside the building for a professional to unlock the door, the spouse's brothers climbed up to the roof and entered the apartment, breaking through the living room's glass door; one brother moved the gun away from the murderer's hand, positioning it nearby Anat's hand.[81]

78 Elimelech: part II, para. 80–100.
79 Elimelech: part II, para. 120, 141.
80 Elimelech: part I, para. 74.
81 Elimelech: part I, para. 60–75; part II, para 263–275 (made to exonerate his brother of all guilt).

Through this behavior, the murderer's brother demonstrated the unique and less frequent type of staging executed by someone other than the murderer. Having the brother do the staging is still consistent with the primary staging motivation, which is to redirect the investigation away from the most logical suspect, the man.[82] The unusual and extremely wrongful result of the staging was that it turned Anat into the person suspected to have committed suicide, rendering her, synchronically, the murderer. The brother took advantage of fact that the murder scene was domestic, leading the police to apply a discriminatory view of the scene as a domestic dispute scene, rather than a crime scene. Leaving Anat at the mercy of a jealous, obsessed, possessive spouse, alongside the gender-biased police, allowed this fabrication. The fabricator, in return, exploited the time alone at the scene required for staging, without any outsiders' obstruction, again leaving no direct evidence behind.

It was only 15 years after the murder that an Israeli court legally formalized the assertion that Anat had been murdered, that her former spouse murdered her, and that his brother staged the scene to look as if the opposite had happened. The family, who had been going through the agony of having people doubt Anat's innocence, realized and sought the conclusive effect of a formal court decision regarding her death. Although the court concluded 30 days after the murder that Anat was the victim of intimate-partner femicide, it was only upon releasing the court's decision that the concealment of her murder was ultimately acknowledged.

Concealed and Later Unofficially Suspected

Mira's *Case*

In January 2012, Mira, a healthy 37-year-old mother of seven, was found dead in her home. Around a month after her sudden death, her parents approached an Israeli nongovernmental organization (NGO), seeking its lawyers' assistance in getting visitation rights for their grandkids. Specializing in femicide litigation and puzzled with the young woman's sudden death, the NGO's lawyers interrogated the deceased woman's parents as to the cause of her death. The parents' answer startled them: Their daughter was simply found dead, on her house's porch, with no apparent cause that would explain her sudden death and without any police investigation of her death. Motivated by these suspicious facts, the lawyers decided to look for background information about Mira and her husband's relationship. Their investigation was as short as it was telling: An outreach to the district's police station revealed that a formal domestic-violence complaint was filed by Mira six months prior to her mysterious yet uninvestigated death.

The factual picture became clearer as the lawyers further probed Mira's death: Her minor child had found her dead, her husband slept in a locked room, the

82 Douglas and Munn, 1992.

child urged him to call an ambulance, and the ambulance's physician determined Mira's death, which warranted police involvement as mandated by Israeli law in cases of death determined outside medical institutions.[83] The dispatched police officers began the process of moving Mira's body from the scene to the pathology institute; synchronically, the husband, via local politicians, managed to obtain an exemption from police investigation and a religious ban on a postmortem autopsy, and Mira was soon buried, with her parents barely making it in time to attend her burial ceremony.

The question of whether Mira died through authentic yet surprising sudden fatal bodily malfunction or as a result of being subjected to (yet more) fatal domestic violence by her husband remained unsolved and uninvestigated. The compilation of facts renders Mira another potential victim of what we identify as "concealed femicide."

The reason for this potential concealment of femicide was the systemic violence perpetrated against women, endorsed by another privilege provided to men, to have their dead women exempted from a postmortem autopsy, due to Israeli authorities' reluctance to interfere with what it has deemed the "internal affairs" of the ultra-religious Hareidi community. Despite comprising only 10% of Israel's Jewish population, the Hareidi minority in Israel enjoys substantial influence over Israeli politics, notwithstanding its separatist ideology.[84]

The political upper-handedness of the Hareidi community works primarily to the benefit of men and the detriment of women, who fulfill traditional gender roles, assigning women to the household alone.[85] The intersectionality of gender, religion and culture, therefore, makes Hareidi women even more exposed, compared to secular women, to the vulnerability of having their domesticity-related femicide concealed as merely unexpected death.[86]

Mira's case demonstrates how its details, when viewed as a collective context of potential femicide by her partner, comports with many typologies associated with scene staging. The perpetrator not only knew the victim, but also had previous relations with her and she was last seen alive by him. As in many staging cases, here too, the perpetrator discovered the victim. Though Mira's minor child found her, her husband was the first adult to "discover" her death. Staging requires time alone for the perpetrator at the murder premises, because stagers usually act

83 Citing the law: Death inquiry law (1958).

84 Ben-Rafael, 2008. Some depict ultra-Orthodox society as a "society of institutions" that maintains an independent and wide-ranging array of services designed to address almost all individual, familial, and community needs. See also Shilav and Friedman, 1985.

85 Parush and Sternberg, 2004: p. 38. "Being patriarchal, traditional Jewish society – in official outlook at least – relegated women to the domestic sphere. The ideal of the women it held in view was that of a wife who 'looketh to the ways of her household' (Proverbs 31:27), and the passage from the Psalms, 'the full glory of the king's daughter lies within' (Psalms 45:14), was often approvingly cited as an apt expression of this ideal femininity."

86 Parush and Sternberg, 2004.

alone,[87] without any outsiders' obstruction. And indeed, Mira was determined to have been dead for a few hours prior to being found in the morning, when the couple's minor children were asleep, according to the death report as determined by the ambulance physician. The scene was staged at the couple's residence, as normally occurs with staging,[88] which implies that the husband had no verifiable alibi previously established before the alleged murder occurred.[89] From a socio-criminological perspective, these characteristics render Mira's unnatural death, at the age of 37, in her home, as potentially concealed femicide. Her death epitomizes the difficulty in proving a murder when it is staged and concealed – namely, the difficulty in turning a case officially identified as a noncriminal yet unexpected death into a potential femicide. Using the most basic forensic tools scientifically identified by criminologists to analyze Mira's case, such as executing an autopsy and launching a police investigation, was thus mandatory. Given that the latter would have exposed the fact that Mira experienced domestic violence, alongside the feminist perspective on her life's experience as a Hareidi woman, reasonably allows us to reconsider her death as a potential femicide – namely, concealed femicide – in a scientifically persuasive manner.[90]

Discussion: Femicide, Feminist Analysis, and the Ramifications of Circumstantial-Evidence-Based Convictions

To the feminist notion of unsafe domesticity as enabling concealed femicide, another feminist notion of women's powerless voice should be added. Feminist theory attributes key importance to the voice in the development of personality and as a condition for a life of autonomy, freedom and equality. According to Catherine MacKinnon, women's voices are persistently overridden by those of men. Using a harsh metaphor, MacKinnon demands from men: "Take your foot from our neck"[91] as a precondition to identifying women's authentic voices. Silencing or disguising women's hurt is a pervasive phenomenon feminists have long warned against.[92] By the concept "voice," the intention is to refer to its physical sense; its content, the narrative; and its ability to influence. The loss of a femicide victim's ability to bring her narrative to the court reflects this patriarchal

87 Ferguson, 2014.

88 Pettler, 2016: pp. 18–20. Intimate-partner femicides are almost always immediately preceded by a major confrontation in the privatized setting of the home that they usually both share (Dobash and Dobash, 2015).

89 Pettler, 2016: p. 27.

90 Eager to bring justice to Mira, the NGO lawyer decided to approach the national coroner, Dr. Chen Kugel. Dr. Kugel addressed her inquiry, stating that more than 3 years after her burial, Mira's corpse would allow testing only a limited range of potential death reasons. Mira's parents, who also feared being alienated by her children if they asked to dig her out of her grave, decided not to ask for a late autopsy.

91 MacKinnon, 1987: p. 390.

92 MacKinnon, 1993.

flaw not only from a symbolic standpoint, wherein the woman is not even able to tell that she has been murdered, but also regarding its very materialistic harmful consequences. It stresses the prosecution and the court to use circumstantial evidence to prove her death to be a homicide, which decreases her ability to have her assassin adequately convicted or even if he is convicted, to have her narrative gain credibility in and outside the court. To put it in more legal terms, the devastating ramifications of a circumstantial-evidence-based conviction in concealed femicide can be identified as the following:

1) Authoritativeness: The meager reliability attributed to circumstantial evidence renders the conviction vulnerable to social denial, regardless of its legal endurance.
2) Irrevocability: The openness that courts exhibit when contemplating the indirect nature of circumstantial evidence as ostensibly warranting special diligence, combined with their over-justification for using such evidence, render the convictions more susceptible to appeal.
3) Decisiveness: The general reluctance to rely on circumstantial evidences alone as a basis for criminal conviction might encourage legal stakeholders – such as prosecutors and judges – to advocate conviction for a lesser crime, such as manslaughter, rather than murder, as often happens in femicide cases.

All these harmful implications can be easily traced in the cases of Siboni, Cooper, and Elimelech, wherein the courts seem to have adopted the predisposition that circumstantial evidence is indeed inferior to direct evidence. Though entertaining a rhetoric adhering to the formal equal status of these two types of evidence, judges also engaged in an apologetic discourse, emphasizing the need to be particularly diligent and cautious in establishing a conviction based on circumstantial evidence. In Siboni, the dissenting judge used this line of reasoning to refrain from a murder conviction of the accused spouse and to settle for unintended manslaughter.[93] In Cooper, the court explained its lengthy and ultra-detailed decision as resulting from the nature of its conviction as based on circumstantial evidence.[94] It further brought to the fore the concern that this type of conviction is more prone to abridgement of the accused's right to enjoy the presumption of innocence due to a "practical fear" overshadowing the conceptual and professional justification for using this evidentiary rule.[95] Eventually, the court emphasized the excess of circumstances in the case in a somewhat apologetic manner, seeking reaffirmation of its potentially controversial decision.[96] As for the strength of presenting a narrative compared to the weakness of using imagination for conviction, it is worth noting that to date, in all cases, there still exists

93 Siboni: dissent opinion.
94 Cooper: p. 9.
95 Cooper: pp. 204–208.
96 Cooper: p. 219.

a certain degree of doubt as to whether the convicts were indeed responsible for the women's deaths. In Siboni, for instance, the murdered mother's children declared they believe their father's narrative of their mother's death as resulting from an accident. Both Cooper and Siboni have filed an appeal, and in Siboni, the dissenting judge resorted to a lesser felony charge, due to lack of direct evidence for conviction. In Elimelech, Anat's family constantly struggles to clear her name, which has been tainted as belonging to a murderer.

On a positive note and countering Mira's case, the three cases were legally recognized, and the male partners were eventually prosecuted and brought to justice. Through the eventual identification of their deaths as murders, however late and open to controversy, the murdered women were able to gain agency by virtue of turning from passively deceased women into women who were forced to die. The murder conviction of their perpetrator allowed them to tell, from their grave, the story of their concealed femicide. Notwithstanding this local comfort, the ultimate goal is to pave a path that would allow all at-home deaths of women to be investigated properly, given their propensity to H.S.S.

Conclusion

The cases presented in this chapter teach us that not only is concealed femicide present in women's lives and deaths, but it has consistencies. Our analysis indicates that concealment can materialize in many forms by different types of murder-scene stagers and can be exposed through distinctive classification of venues.

The Cooper, Siboni and Elimelech cases exemplify how murder and murderers nearly escaped being brought to justice. It took the prosecution system 16 years to indict Cooper for his first wife's death and two years for the second. In Siboni, it took a year and a half, and in Elimelech, only the civil-court decision, issued 14 years after her murder, legally confirmed that Anat was murdered. Mira's uninvestigated case is particularly alarming, because the legal system's formal tools haven't even been affected. More to the point and even worse, revealing the disguise of these women's deaths would not have been possible but for the insistence, persistence and resource exhaustion of private bodies – the wives' relatives and journalists[97] – who refused to accept the prevailing narrative regarding the deaths of their loved ones. It was not the systemic application of state means that led to eventually exposing these women's deaths as premeditated femicide. Rather, the state failed to do them justice in this respect.

Acknowledging femicide concealment as an abuse of women's inferiority in the domestic sphere and as a creation of a secluded and private killing scene also allows greater understanding of the role of circumstantial-evidence-based convictions in these cases. Concealed-femicide cases are systematically more inclined to

97 Cooper: para. 164–165. In Siboni's case, her relatives were highly concerned about Siboni's behavior during the grief ceremonies and period of mourning, which they perceived as suspiciously displaying no mourning (Siboni: para. 15–16).

result in such convictions, burdening murdered women with yet another set of challenges that emanate from the distrust attributed to circumstantial-evidence-based convictions. This newly presented association among femicide, feminist theory and circumstantial evidence paves a path to restructuring court decisions in a manner more empowering to the women victims and more attentive to their right to finally "tell" their story, even if for the last time and from their graves.

Epilogue

While writing this chapter, during the summer of 2019, two cases of femicide occurred in Israel. Michal Sela and Maria Tal were reported by their husbands and by the press to have committed suicide at home, in the presence of their husbands. A well-organized yet spontaneous protest of individuals and women's organizations forced the police to investigate the cases relentlessly, eventually turning both husbands from witnesses into murder suspects. Our analysis and the set of tools offered in this book are a systemic mechanism aimed at replacing feminist outrage in similar future cases with a structured way for revealing their true nature.

Having explored crimino-legal theoretical and empirical aspects of four various femicide subtypes (intimate-partner femicide, F.H.K., femicide–suicide, and concealed femicide), the next part of the book, Part III, concentrates on femicide's secondary tier, offering an analysis of various victim-legal aspects relating to issues positioned at the penumbra, rather than the core of femicide – namely, matters pertaining to the secondary devastating effects of femicide.

References

Adams, D. (2007). *Why do they kill? Men who murder their intimate partners*. Vanderbilt University Press.

Ballinger, A. (2016). Provocation or responsibility? In K. Fitz-Gibbon & S. Walklate (Eds.), *Homicide, gender and responsibility: An international perspective*. Routledge.

Ben-Rafael, E. (2008). The faces of religiosity in Israel: Cleavages or continuum? *Israel Studies*, *13*(3), 89–113.

Benton, A. (1993). Personal autonomy and physician-assisted suicide: The appropriate response to a modern ethical dilemma. *Ohio NUL Review*, *20*(3), 769–791.

Bitton, Y., & Dayan, H. (2019). The perfect murder: An exploratory study of stage murder scenes and concealed femicide. *British Journal of Criminology*, *59*(5), 1054–1075.

Bitton, Y., & Shavit, T. (2015). Differences between men's and women's monetary valuation of crime avoidance behavior. *Feminist Criminology*, *10*(2), 115–139.

Bloom, S. S. (2008). *Violence against women and girls: A compendium of monitoring and evaluation indicators*. USIAD.

Campbell, J. C., Webster, D., Koziol-McLain, J., Block, C., Campbell, D., Curry, M. A., & Sharps, P. (2003). Risk factors for femicide in abusive relationships: Results from a multisite case control study. *American Journal of Public Health*, *93*(7), 1089–1097.

Chancellor, A. S., & Graham, G. D. (2014). Staged crime scenes: Crime scene clues to suspect misdirection of the investigation. *Investigative Sciences Journal, 6*(1), 19–35.

Cobin S. B. (2009). *Staged hunting mishaps and criminal homicide*. Center for Homicide Research.

Corradi, C., Marcuello-Servós, C., Boira, S., & Weil, S. (2016). Theories of femicide and their significance for social research. *Current Sociology, 64*(7), 975–995.

Corradi, C., & Stöckl, H. (2014). Intimate partner homicide in 10 European countries: Statistical data and policy development in a cross-national perspective. *European Journal of Criminology, 11*(5), 601–618.

Dan-Cohen, M. (2000). Basic values and the victim's state of mind. *California Law Review, 88*, 759–778.

Dawson, M. (2004). *Criminal justice outcomes in intimate and non-intimate partner homicide cases*. Department of Justice.

Dawson, M. (2016). Punishing femicide: Criminal justice responses to the killing of women over four decades. *Current Sociology, 64*(7), 996–1016.

Dobash, R. E., & Dobash, R. (2015). *When men murder women (interpersonal violence)*. Oxford University Press.

Dobash, R. E., Dobash, R. P., Cavanagh, K., & Lewis, R. (2004). Not an ordinary killer – Just an ordinary guy: When men murder an intimate woman partner. *Violence against women, 10*(6), 577–605.

Douglas, J., & Douglas, L. (2006). The detection of staging, undoing and personation at the crime scene. In J. E. Douglas, A. W. Burgess, A. G. Burgess, & R. K. Ressler (Eds.), *Crime classification manual: A standard system for investigating and classifying violent crime* (pp. 31–44). Wiley.

Douglas, J. E., & Munn, C. (1992). The detection of staging and personation at the crime scene. In A. Burgess, J. Douglas, & R. Ressler (Eds.), *Crime classification manual* (pp. 249–458). Jossey-Bass.

Eke, A. (2007). *Staging in cases of homicide: Offender, victim and offence characteristics* [unpublished doctoral dissertation, Toronto University].

Estrich, S. (1987). *Real rape*. Harvard University Press.

Farr, K. A. (2002). Battered women who were" being killed and survived it": Straight talk from survivors. *Violence and Victims, 17*(3), 267–281.

Ferguson, C. (2014). Staged crime scenes: Literature and types. In W. Petherick (Ed.), *Serial crime: Theoretical and practical issues in behavioral profiling* (3rd ed., pp. 141–164). Andersen Publishing.

Ferguson, C. (2015). Staged homicides: An examination of common features of faked burglaries, suicides, accidents and car accidents. *Journal of Police and Criminal Psychology, 30*(3), 139–157.

Ferguson, C., & Petherick, W. (2016). Getting away with murder: An examination of detected homicides staged as suicides. *Homicide Studies, 20*(1), 3–24.

Frug, M. J. (1992). *Postmodern legal feminism*. Routledge.

Gauthier, D. K., & Bankston, W. B. (2004). "Who kills whom" revisited: A sociological study of variation in the sex ratio of spouse killings. *Homicide Studies, 8*(2), 96–122.

Gavison, R. (1992). Feminism and the public/private distinction. *Stanford Law Review, 45*(1), 1–45.

Geberth, V. J. (1996). The staged crime scene. *Law and Order, 44*(2), 89–93.

Goussinsky, R., & Yassour-Borochowitz, D. (2012). "I killed her, but I never laid a finger on her" – A phenomenological difference between wife-killing and wife-battering. *Aggression and Violent Behavior*, *17*(6), 553–564.

Hannawa, A. F., Spitzberg, B. H., Watering, L., & Teranishi, C. (2006). "If I can't have you, no one can": Development of a Relational Entitlement and Proprietariness Scale (REPS). *Violence and Victims*, *21*(5), 539–560.

Hazelwood, R. R., & Napier, M. R. (2004). Crime scene staging and its detection. *International Journal of Offender Therapy and Comparative Criminology*, *48*(6), 744–759.

Heller, K. J. (2006). The cognitive psychology of circumstantial evidence. *Michigan Law Review*, *105*(2), 241–305.

Hunter, N. D. (1991). Marriage, law, and gender: A feminist inquiry. *Law and Sexuality: Review of Lesbian and Gay Legal Issues*, *1*, 9–30.

Jordan, C. E., Pritchard, A. J., Duckett, D., Wilcox, P., Corey, T., & Combest, M. (2010). Relationship and injury trends in the homicide of women across the life span: A research note. *Homicide Studies*, *14*(2), 181–192.

Keppel, R. D., & Weis, J. G. (2004). The rarity of "unusual" dispositions of victim bodies: Staging and posing. *Journal of Forensic Science*, *49*(6), 1308–1312.

Landes, J. B. (1998). *Feminism, the public and the private*. Oxford University Press.

MacKinnon, C. A. (1979). *Sexual harassment of working women: A case of sex discrimination*. Yale University Press.

MacKinnon, C. A. (1983). Feminism, marxism, method, and the state: Toward feminist jurisprudence. *Signs: Journal of Women in Culture and Society*, *8*(4), 635–658.

MacKinnon, C. A. (1987). *Feminism unmodified: Discourses on law and life*. Harvard University Press.

MacKinnon, C. A. (1993). *Only words*. Harvard University Press.

MacKinnon, C. A. (2005). *Difference and dominance: On sex discrimination*. Harvard University Press.

MacKinnon, C. A., & Dworkin, A. (Eds.). (1997). *In harm's way: The pornography civil rights hearings*. Harvard University Press.

Marcuello-Servós, C., Corradi, C., Weil, S., & Boira, S. (2016). Femicide: A social challenge. *Current Sociology*, *64*(7), 967–974.

Messerschmidt, J. W. (2017). Masculinities and Femicide. *Qualitative Sociology Review*, *13*(3) 70–79

O'Neil, B. L. (2016). *Domestic homicide and homicide-suicide in the older population*. Electronic Thesis and Dissertation Repository, Publication No. 3509.

Parush, I., & Sternberg, S. (2004). *Reading Jewish women: Marginality and modernization in nineteenth-century Eastern European Jewish society*. Brandeis University Press.

Pettler, L. G. (2016). *Crime scene staging dynamics in homicide cases*. CRC Press.

Rapaport, E. (1996). Capital murder and the domestic discount: A study of capital domestic murder in the post-Furman era. *SMU Law Review*, *49*, 1507–1548.

Rwelamira, M. R. (1992). Murder without corpus delicti: A brief excursus on circumstantial evidence. *Journal of African Law*, *36*(2), 132–139.

Schlesinger, L. B., Gardenier, A., Jarvis, J., & Sheehan-Cook, J. (2012). Crime scene staging in homicide. *Journal of Police and Criminal Psychology*, *29*(1), 44–51.

Serrana, G., & Firestone, P. (2004). Intimate partner homicide: A review of the male proprietariness and the self-defense theories. *Aggression and Violent Behavior*, *9*(1), 1–15.

Shilav, Y., & Friedman, M. (1985). *Growth and segregation: The Haredi community of Jerusalem*. The Jerusalem Institute for Israel Studies.
Singer, J. B. (1989). Divorce reform and gender justice. *North Carolina Law Review*, *67*, 1103–1121.
Stöckl, H., Devries, K., Rotstein, A., Abrahams, N., Campbell, J., Watts, C., & Moreno, C. G. (2013). The global prevalence of intimate partner homicide: A systematic review. *The Lancet*, *382*, 859–865.
Walby, S., & Myhill, A. (2001). New survey methodologies in researching violence against women. *British Journal of Criminology*, *41*(3), 502–522.
Zorza, J. (1991). Woman battering: A major cause of homelessness. *Clearinghouse Review*, *25*, 421–430.

Part III

Femicide's Secondary-Tier Effects

7 Secondary Victims and the Implications of Femicide

Introduction

This part of the book, Part III, offers critical crimino-legal analysis of various victim-related aspects dealing with issues positioned at the penumbra, rather than the core, of femicide. First, the personas of these secondary victims are introduced in the current chapter. Victims who were not the main killer's target are barely considered as subjects of femicide research. Although secondary victims might not have been physically injured during the crime, these people nevertheless sustain a great deal of agonizing mental, emotional, economic, and social detrimental harms and difficulties as a result of femicide.

Secondary victims, unlike direct-homicide victims, remain largely unknown to the public, and there are few recorded statistics about them.[1] Additionally, for the most part, the legal system was blind to these victims' needs or considered them substitutes of the deceased person, at best. Until recent decades, criminologists were also occupied with the idea that crime had its perpetrators and direct victims alone. With the development of the victimological vantage point as a subfield of criminology as early as the mid-1960s, policy makers began addressing victims and their needs in a move that ignited the 1980s American spree of national recognition of victims' rights – frequently related to as the "victims'-revolution" era. This revolution recognized, first and foremost, direct victims of crime, to whom compensation and support programs were provided. As the field advanced, the notion of victimhood has expanded, and with it the recognition that a crime's reach goes beyond direct and immediate victims and that its ramifications are of great relevance to the victims' relatives as well. This realization permeated the legal system only recently, and it still provides secondary victims a very dull set of legal tools to address their grievances, support their needs and solve their difficulties.

In this chapter, we delve into this newly recognized group of victims and discuss some of the most prominent legal ramifications of their unfortunate status. We do so in three main legal domains that outline our overview. The first part

1 Costa et al., 2017: p. 3088.

DOI: 10.4324/9781003333272-10

discusses the family implications of femicide for secondary victims, primarily in issues of guardianship and inheritance. The second part discusses the criminal law's treatment of secondary victims as having a standing in its proceedings and as eligible for compensation for their injuries. In the third part and given the limited legal comfort and recourse the criminal system allows these victims, we analyze tort law's treatment of secondary victims and their harm, indicating that biases rooted in common-law traditions demarcate this field, too, as carrying little hope for secondary victims to draw remedies from.

Family Implications for Secondary Victims

Guardianship Rights

Little research has been conducted regarding the traumatic impact of femicide on children who lose their parents, often alongside losing their home and routine.[2] In the aftermath of femicide, many legal issues arise that directly affect secondary victims. The matter of guardianship and custody must be decided regarding the children of the woman who was murdered in cases in which the father or male guardian was the perpetrator. Affected children are often taken in by their grandparents or the siblings of their parents (uncles and aunts), who suddenly find themselves responsible for raising the deserted offspring. Israeli law mandates that grandparents are allowed to have connection with their grandchildren, especially when one of the parents is dead.[3] Given that there's no a priori preference to the mother's parents, alongside the challenge of singlehandedly raising their grandchildren, grandparents face legal struggles following femicide, like long custody battles vis-à-vis the husband's family or in attempts to limit the incarcerated father's guardianship over his children.[4]

When grandparents from both sides compete for custody of their grandchildren and there is no legal right of a parent against a nonparent, the only consideration is the child's best interest.[5] According to Israel's family courts, a child's best interest is determined not only by financial ability to raise the child but, first and foremost, by who can provide best for the child's mental and emotional well-being.[6] Family courts are aided in making these difficult custody decisions by the expert professional opinions of child psychologists, social workers and other welfare professionals. The court determines which set of grandparents will be granted custody based on a wide range of considerations that affect the children, including living conditions, stability, continuity, security, feeling of belonging, warmth and love, and stimuli and values appropriate for the child's

2 Jaffe and Juodis, 2006; Dawson et al., 2018.
3 The Legal Capacity and Guardianship Law 1962: art. 28a.
4 Sahar, 2011: p. 33.
5 AM 464/03 Palmoni v. Almoni (08.08.2004).
6 AM 464/03 Palmoni v. Almoni (08.08.2004).

development.[7] These considerations do not necessarily comport with the interest of the deceased mother's family to raise her orphans under any circumstances. Moreover, to some extent, the right of the father's side of the family might be valued independently, rendering their right equal in its weight to that of the mother's family.[8]

Israel's family courts tread carefully when deciding issues of guardianship and are extremely careful about negating or limiting a biological parent's guardianship over their child, even in cases in which the parent was convicted of harming his children or wife.[9] According to Israeli law, parents are the natural guardians of their minor children,[10] by virtue of their natural biological parenthood. The family unit in Israel is protected from state intervention because it is constructively assumed that the child's parents know their child better than anyone and will make the best decisions for them.[11] Parental obligations as guardians include the right to take care of the minor's needs, including his or her education, training for work, and employment; the obligation to safeguard, maintain and develop his or her assets; and the authority to represent the minor and determine the minor's place of residence.[12] Arguably, a parent's right to autonomously raise the child is not an absolute right and is always subject to the needs, rights and best interests of the child.[13] Situations can arise that warrant intervention by the state, primarily when a parent, as the legal guardian, does not fulfill this role properly, which might lead to revocation of guardianship or its restriction.[14] These rare legal exceptions to parental guardianship can be found in the Legal Capacity and Guardianship Law and the Youth Law (Care and Supervision), and they require special or exceptional grounds.[15] As shown in cases discussed later in this section, Israeli courts are cautious in applying these exceptions. The superior standing of biological parents' claims to guardianship renders it challenging for grandparents to legally limit or negate a father's right of guardianship over his children, even following such a horrendous crime as femicide. Moreover, from a legal standpoint, Israeli law has determined that every inmate has a right to have his children visit him, as such.[16] This principle reflects the Israeli legal system's general occupation with allowing a family to prosper and less with allowing a family member, like an orphan, to withdraw from it.

7 TMS 8250/07 A.B.I v. I.B.I (07.05.2012).
8 Barak, 2013: p. 43; Doron and Linchitz, 2010.
9 TMS 53687–07–13 Almonit v. Almoni (11.12.2014).
10 The Legal Capacity and Guardianship Law 1962: art. 14.
11 HCJ 3752/10 Amnon Rubinstein v. The Knesset (19.09.14): para. 59 (Justice Arbel).
12 Legal Capacity and Guardianship Law 1962: sec. 15.
13 HCJ 3752/10 Amnon Rubinstein v. The Knesset (19.09.14): para. 59 (Justice Arbel).
14 Legal Capacity and Guardianship Law 1962: sec. 27.
15 Legal Capacity and Guardianship Law 1962; Youth Law (Care and Supervision) 1960; HCJ 3752/10 Amnon Rubinstein v. The Knesset (19.09.14): para. 59 (Judge Arbel).
16 Barak, 2013: p. 44.

An Israeli study conducted in 2011 attempted to gather information on secondary victims of femicide, focusing on grandparents who lost their child to femicide and raised her children.[17] The study included interviews with the parents of 19 women who were murdered by their partners. Many of these grandparents brought to the fore the legal battles they faced following the murders of their daughters and the economic, emotional and physical problems that accompanied these legal issues.[18] Many grandparents spoke about the difficulty of handling the guardianship process in court and described "battling" in court for custody of their grandchildren against the father and his family as an exhausting experience. The grandparents were forced to overcome many hurdles during these legal battles, such as the financial burden of high legal costs and the emotional costs of undergoing strict and invasive parenthood and personality tests, which they were forced to take and pay for.[19] Guardianship legal battles also forced these secondary victims to relive the trauma of losing their daughter, and they described them as time-consuming and emotionally tiring. Apart from these complaints related to legal issues, grandparents experienced a major life change in becoming the main caregivers of their grandchildren. Some grandparents had to change their place of work or stop working altogether to care for their grandchildren once becoming guardians.[20] Most of the grandchildren in the study received psychological treatment or some sort of mental care, whereas most grandparents, who were in desperate need of guidance and support for raising and caring for their grandchildren and in need of care themselves, did not receive this help.[21] All grandparents contemplated what type of relationship, if at all, the children should have with their father, the murderer. One grandfather spoke in anger about their lingering legal proceedings. He explained that he and the grandmother had guardianship over their grandchildren, but the man who murdered their daughter was unwilling to give up his rights and essentially did not have to because of his legal status as the biological guardian of his children.[22] Obviously, this situation can be extremely frustrating and painful for grandparents, who are not only secondary victims themselves but must now care for and act in the best interests of their grandchildren.

Visitation Rights

Under regular circumstances, a child is compelled to maintain personal relations and participate in practices that will help a parent realize his visitation rights. In femicide cases, this obligation usually translates into a demand that the children

17 Sahar, 2011.
18 Sahar, 2011: p. 35.
19 Sahar, 2011: p. 37.
20 Sahar, 2011: p. 35.
21 Sahar, 2011: p. 36.
22 Sahar, 2011: p. 38.

visit their father in jail according to a court-ordered visitation arrangement.[23] Clearly, this can be difficult for the children, who must visit their father in jail, and difficult for the grandparents, raising the children, to cope with. In one Israeli case, the court decided to limit the frequency of a child's visits to his father in jail because these visits put a heavy burden on the child's ability to cope with the situation and because a jail is not a suitable environment for the child to spend extended periods of time.[24] Additionally, the father who committed the murder and his family may present to the children an alternate reality in which their father is not a murderer or will get out of jail soon despite his life sentence, as occurred in another Israeli case. In this case, the father and his family attempted to turn the children against their maternal grandparents while also describing the children's murdered mother in a negative light and disgracing her memory.[25] The psychologists and other experts in the case spoke extensively about the harm this can impose on the children.[26] Such a situation can be extremely difficult for the maternal grandparents to overcome, especially during a drawn-out custody battle or amid a shared-custody agreement with the paternal grandparents and court-ordered visits to the children's incarcerated father. Furthermore, maternal grandparents risk exposing themselves to a claim of "alienating a child," which has recently become salient and endorsed by Israeli family courts.[27] Under this doctrine, refusing to meet a father has been ruled out by the court as part of the child's autonomy. Alimony can also be revoked as a result of such refusal.[28] Ultimately, the children suffer the most, and it is difficult to heal the kind of mental and psychological damage that this can cause.[29]

The grandparents' testimonies and court decisions all reflect the family-status chaos inflicted on secondary victims and the failure of the legal system to provide them with determinative tools to settle the normative implications of the murder on their new family structure.

23 TMS 8250/07 A.B.I v. I.B.I (07.05.2012). In this case, the original visitation arrangement was reduced to a requirement that the child (a secondary victim of femicide) visit his father in jail once a month. This arrangement was then further reduced to once every 2 months, although experts in the case recommended the visits be limited to once every 3 months. This court's reasoning took into consideration the psychologist's recommendation, which discussed the heavy emotional burden these visits had on the child. The court decided that further lowering the frequency of these visits would negatively affect the quality of the relationship between the father and child and held that the visits continue no less than once every 2 months. However, the court emphasized in its conclusion regarding this decision that this visitation arrangement be reexamined from time to time (para. 38).

24 TMS 8250/07 A.B.I v. I.B.I (07.05.2012).

25 AM 464/03 Palmoni v. Almoni (08.08.2004): para. 15.

26 AM 464/03 Palmoni v. Almoni (08.08.2004): para. 15, 78.

27 www.globes.co.il/news/article.aspx?did=1001315512

28 Civ. Appeal 3761/10 Ploni v. Plonit (15.07.2010): para. 7–8 (Justice Rubinstein). The legal rule permitting reducing or revoking alimony in cases in which a child refuses to see their father is not controversial in Israeli law, although revoking alimony is seen as an extreme step that should only be taken in exceptional circumstances.

29 AM 464/03 Palmoni v. Almoni (08.08.2004): para. 22.

Israel's family and status laws respond to family structures affected by femicide on a case-by-case basis, thereby burdening secondary victims with endless court litigations against a person from whom they wish to detach. Their battle is twofold: First, they need to establish their aptitude to serve as the guardians and their superiority to the father's natural right; and second and subsequently, they need to prove that any relation to the murdering father should be terminated. On the substantive front, the murderer also has the upper hand vis-à-vis secondary victims, because he enjoys the automatic right to guardianship and visitation as the parent.[30] Absent the predetermination that the father loses his rights regarding his child due to murdering the mother, the maternal guardians carry the onus of "shifting" the familial relations in their favor, needing to transform the natural flow of order from the father to them.

The troubling Israeli legal constellation regarding post-femicide family relations is not a legal necessity. In other countries like the United States, statutes bolster the rights of child victims of domestic homicide and protect them from maintaining a relationship with the father or being subjected to forced visits to their incarcerated parent.[31] Lizzie's Law, a Massachusetts-state bill, states that "No court shall make an order providing visitation rights to a parent who has been convicted of murder in the first-degree of the other parent of the child who is the subject of the order, unless such child is of suitable age to signify his assent and assents to such order."[32] This law was the first of its kind in the country, and other states soon followed. California's Family Code Section 3030(c), for example, also protects children from their parent convicted of first-degree murder of their other parent by preventing the incarcerated parent from receiving custody or unsupervised visitation with their children unless the court finds that there is no risk to the child's welfare.[33] Another interesting and more strict example is Maryland Code of Family Law Section 9–101.1, which sees domestic violence against the other parent of the child as sufficiently grave to justify revoking a parent's child custody or visitation rights.[34]

Although the statutes presented here are a step in the right direction compared to Israel's lack of any statutory regulation of the matter, some of them are still too narrow in scope, primarily due to being contingent on having the parent convicted of first-degree murder, whereas intimate-partner killing is only rarely indicted with such a count, which is the hardest to prove in court.[35] Moreover, in many femicide cases, the courts apply a method of turning a defendant's claim that his crime was committed "in the heat of passion" into receiving a lesser

30 Blecher-Prigat, 2009.
31 Kowalczyk, 1998.
32 Massachusetts House Bill No. 4869 (1997): sec. 1.
33 Lowery and Redfield, 2003.
34 Maryland Code of Family Law Section 9–101.1.
35 Shen et al., 2011. In the United States murder has its own category of "super-intentionality." In almost every state, first-degree murder requires proof of not just an intentional killing, but a killing carried out after deliberation or with premeditation.

conviction or being exonerated from a murder conviction.[36] This is because most states in the United States recognize the heat of passion as a partial defense in murder cases, which results in the lesser conviction of manslaughter.[37] This legal doctrine showcases how this unfairness transfers to other aspects of femicide, harming secondary victims beyond the criminal conviction's outcome.

Another less formalistic approach to the femicide family aftermath is presented in another California statute that attempts to protect secondary-victim children. Family Code Section 7825(a)(2) allows for the termination of parental rights altogether for felony convictions, as long as the felonies "prove the unfitness of the parent or parents to have the future custody and control of the child."[38] This statute, which may be read as self-evident regarding femicide, still confers on Californian courts a wide discretion to determine which specific felonies prove the unfitness of a parent.[39] This broadly defined provision, as can be seen in a series of California cases, proved to be less productive to secondary victims, because the courts were inconsistent in their rulings as to what constitutes "unfitness."[40] In the James case, reiterating the "heat-of-passion" doctrine, the court ruled that a father who was convicted of second-degree murder of his wife would not lose his parental rights because a "crime of passion" does not reflect a criminal personality of violent nature.[41] In its reasoning, the court stipulated that the murder did not constitute direct neglect of the children, although the killing deprived them of the love and care of their mother, and hence failed to satisfy the statute's requirement of direct neglect of the parent in his relationship with the child. The court admitted that the murder of the mother in certain circumstances may prove the father's unfitness, such as when the child was present during the murder. Focusing on the "best interests" of the children and whether it be detrimental to them if the father were to retain his parental rights, the court discussed issues such as the children's will to maintain relations with the father (which was split between them) and the father's expected release time. In more recent cases, the court terminated parental rights following similarly grave felonies. However, certain elements of this James case are still cited in recent case law.[42] In 1979, three years after James, a California court used the statute to terminate the parental rights of a father who was convicted of voluntary manslaughter of his child's mother, but only after explaining that the killing of the

36 Dayan, 2018.
37 Fontaine, 2009.
38 California Family Code 7825.
39 Lowery and Redfield, 2003: p. 25.
40 Lowery and Redfield, 2003: p. 25.
41 James M., 65 Cal. App. 3d 254 (1976).
42 Nicholas K. v. John K., 2005 Cal. App. In this case, the court cites James M., 65 Cal. App. 3d 254 (1976), stating that the court may also consider the length of the remaining sentence of the father and how long it will deprive the child of a normal home. In Orenthal J. Simpson v. Louis Brown, et al. (Guardianship of Sydney Simpson, et al., Minors), 67 Cal. App. 4th 914, 920 (1998), the court cited James M., 65 Cal. App. 3d 254 (1976) at length.

mother was sufficient reason to negate guardianship and indicating the father's drinking problem as crucial to the decision as well.[43]

An opposite account of femicide as a proxy to custodial inaptness was expressed in California in 1985, when the court terminated a father's parental rights pursuant to his conviction of assault with a deadly weapon after stabbing his children's mother 17 times.[44] The court overturned James' prerequisite that the children be present or in danger when the felony occurred, because the nature of the conviction exhibited the violent personality and unfitness of the parent to have future custody of his children.[45] Another California court's demonstration of care for secondary victims' custodial ordeals was evinced in the infamous case involving the two children of O.J. Simpson and the deceased Nicole Simpson. Pursuant to his criminal acquittal, Simpson requested the termination of the children's maternal grandparents' guardianship over his children. The Browns were appointed formal guardians of the children following Simpson's arrest and during his 17-month incarceration, yet lost custody after his post-acquittal suit.[46] The appellate court reversed the order, ruling that the trial court should have considered evidence regarding the circumstances from the criminal trial, including evidence relating to domestic violence to which Nicole was subjected, as the "totality of the evidence" relating to Simpson's fitness as a parent.[47] They also opined that the trial court had erred in placing the burden of proof on the Browns to show that it would be detrimental to the children to be returned to the natural parent, because it was Simpson, from whom the custody had been previously taken, who should have shown his "overall fitness."

A threat to this more liberal approach toward secondary victims was recently removed by another California case of 2014, which pointed out one of the flaws of Family Code Section 7825(a)(2) in protecting secondary victims of femicide. This statute is practically inapplicable in cases where the father's conviction is appealed and awaits final judgement.[48] In this case, the father shot and killed the mother and her father (the child's grandfather) and was convicted of two accounts of first-degree murder. With his appeal at the time of this custody trial pending before the appellate court, the court ruled that the statute could not apply to the maternal grandmother's plea for guardianship.[49] Evoking the child's best-interest principle, the court stated initially that "the court should not be in

43 Geoffrey G. (1979) 98 Cal. App. 3d: "The murder of one parent by the other is not necessarily a felony showing the felonious parent to be unfit to have custody and control."
44 Arthur C., 176 Cal. App. 3d 442 (1985).
45 Arthur C., 176 Cal. App. 3d 442 (1985). Pursuant to Civil Code 323(a)(4), which is today Family Code Section 7825(a)(2).
46 Orenthal J. Simpson v. Louis Brown, et al. (Guardianship of Sydney Simpson, et al., Minors), 67 Cal. App. 4th 914, 920 (1998): p. 922.
47 Orenthal J. Simpson v. Louis Brown, et al. (Guardianship of Sydney Simpson, et al., Minors), 67 Cal. App. 4th 914, 920 (1998): p. 928.
48 T.F. v. R.L. (In re A.L.), 2014 Cal. App.
49 T.F. v. R.L. (In re A.L.), 2014 Cal. App.: p. 6–7.

the business of making victims out of victims. And here the child is not . . . only a victim once . . . because her mother was taken from her, but she also lost her father."[50] Ultimately, though, the court terminated parental rights pursuant to another Family Code section, number 7822, for intentional abandonment of his child, because the father did not attempt to emotionally or financially support his child from the time he was arrested for the killings.

The varying legal discussions and outcomes of these cases exemplify the lack of uniformity in determining the parental rights of felons convicted of violent crimes, which leads to courts' interpretational solutions, adding more stress and agony to secondary victims, even if ultimately deciding in their favor.

Inheritance Rights

By terminating the life of a woman, femicide raises considerable interest among secondary victims in the issue of heirship. Inheritance laws traditionally mandate that the husband, alongside the children, inherits his wife's estate upon her death. Unless indicated differently, even in femicide circumstances, the husband who murdered his wife will likely inherit her estate, leaving the secondary victims with as little as half the financial means they could have received but for his succession.[51] This injustice has been addressed by Israeli inheritance law, which created an exemption by mandating in its section 5 that it forbids anyone "convicted of intentionally causing the death of the testator or attempting to cause his death" from inheriting the estate of the deceased.[52] This command reflects the general principle that committing a crime and then benefiting from it is morally impaired, and was integrated in Israeli and American law pursuant to cases where people murdered their family members and expected to inherit their estate, at times murdering them with the aim to secure their inheritance.[53] These cases' normative difficulty, put against their ethical clarity, led to massive legislation of "slayer statutes" across the United States, which prohibit a murderer from benefiting from the crime.[54]

Israel adopted the "slayer-statute" clause as early as 1965. Limiting the right to inherit, however, proved complicated to apply, because it raised issues identical to those presented regarding guardianship, due to the precondition of "premeditated death," which is hard to satisfy in femicide cases.[55] Additionally, this formality remained blind to other forms of benefiting from abuse of a spouse, because

50 T.F. v. R.L. (In re A.L.), 2014 Cal. App.: p. 6–7.

51 Succession Law, 1965: art. 10(1), 11.

52 Succession Law, 1965: art. 5.

53 Riggs v. Palmer, 115 N.Y. 506 (1889); CA 3798/94 Plonit v. Ploni (03.10.1996, Israel).

54 Rhodes, 2007: p. 979; Scheppele, 1991. "The slayer statute is the most commonly enacted statute that strips heirship status. . . . All jurisdictions in the United States address inheritance by the decedent's slayer, with the overwhelming majority, 48 of 51, doing so by statute. The remaining three do so by case law" (2001: pp. 979–980).

55 Shen et al., 2011.

the law does not cover cases such as where the woman decides to take her own life to escape domestic abuse. One of the most telling cases in Israeli case law pertains exactly to this circumstance. In the Kenig case,[56] the claimant asked to revoke the inheritance rights of his brother-in-law – the husband of his late sister, who committed suicide by jumping from a hotel room while holding her baby in her arms. The woman, who was devastated due to her husband's abusive behavior and refusal to divorce her and set her free, left behind several handwritten notes that revealed her emotional grief, stemming from her abuse. One note was titled as "a will" and in it, she requested that her husband not inherit any of her estate and not attend her funeral. The court did not accept these notes as a valid will, because they failed to fulfill technical elements mandated by Israeli law. Consequently, the deceased woman's well-expressed wishes were not "honor"ed, and the formal written law, allowing her husband to inherit her estate, was applied. The court also failed to invoke the general idea reflected in section 5 – that a husband should not merit from his wrongdoing: Namely, from his abuse, which led to his wife's death and the formation of her estate.[57]

Another injustice regarding inheritance lurks for secondary victims in cases where the couple had a child. Traditional inheritance law mandates that the offspring share the mother's estate with the father in equal shares.[58] This result can be avoided by invoking section 5: Namely, the inheritance exemption, if the father was proven to have murdered the mother. However, if the child dies, the father is eligible to inherit his estate, thereby bypassing the prohibition on his direct inheritance. Even in cases where the secondary victims satisfied the strict preconditions of the exemption and block the father and husband from directly inheriting his murder victim's estate, under the circumstance of his child's death, he could still inherit her estate indirectly.

Summing up the inheritance legal position of the femicide perpetrator vis-à-vis the secondary victims, it is clear that only in rare cases can the former's automatic inheritance of the estate of the woman for whose death he is responsible be frustrated. Inheritance is, therefore, yet another front on which the well-being of secondary victims is unjustly abridged. Provided that legislatures have proved their inclination to punish people who murder others and seek their estate, the next natural and more realistically adapted rule should be that any criminal conviction for causing the death of a spouse as part of domestic violence should bar the perpetrator from inheriting his victim's estate, directly or indirectly.

56 40/80 Paul Koenig v. Joshua Cohen (28.07.1982).

57 To prevent such outcomes, though, the law in Israel was amended to bestow the court with the power to "honor" a will even if there was some sort of deficiency in its details or proceedings, as long as the will contains the necessary basic components laid out in the law and the court has no doubt that it reflects the true wishes of the testator. Succession Law, 1965: art. 25 (amended 2004).

58 Succession Law, 1965: art. 10(2).

Identity: Family Name

Another implication of the murder regards an ostensibly formal question, which touches on one of the most rudimentary components of the identity of the new orphan: Her or his family name. As part of the Jewish tradition and former (yet highly effective) Israeli law, upon marriage, the woman's maiden name is automatically changed to her new husband's surname. Although this law was repealed around two decades ago, now leaving the choice for the woman to decide how to be called after marriage,[59] adopting the husband's name is still the prevalent practice for married women, thereby turning the father's name into the couple's surname.[60] In some femicide cases in which the father murdered the mother, a child who wishes to detach from the father's legacy and change the family name to that end will be compelled to fight legally for this right. Such a child stood in the middle of a court decision in Israel.[61] The child and his maternal guardians requested to adopt his deceased mother's maiden name and erase his father's name from his records. The court had to find a balance between the desire of the child to change his last name and the expert opinions of different professionals, including social workers and a child psychologist, who maintained it was in the child's best interests in the long run to keep his father's last name while adding his mother's maiden name at best. Bravely, the court disagreed.[62] Given the child's unique situation, the court explained that what is in his best interest is also determined by the family unit in which he is raised and how the child perceives himself and his place in society. Additionally, the court favored the pain of the family members of the murdered woman who are now raising the child and who testified how the surname of the father is a constant reminder of his evil.[63]

Summary

The battles brought by secondary victims to family courts position them in an inferior position. They challenge family ties and the right to exercise them away from the reach of the law and the state, which is a socio-legal convention in democratic states. The U.S. Supreme Court has long established that a person's right to autonomy and freedom of choice in matters of family life is a constitutional right, thereby rendering the importance of preserving the relationships of parents with their children indifferent to whether they have been model parents.[64] In Israel, too, the right to a family is strongly guarded and in recent decades has been reinforced to a point of treating the family itself as a "constitutional unit," positioned at the heart of a person's dignity and against which the state should

59 See Names and Procedures Law, 1956: sec. 6a (1).
60 Rom, 2019.
61 (Name Change) 45797-07-11 Haifa District Attorney v. Y. D. (25.01.12)
62 (Name Change) 45797-07-11 Haifa District Attorney v. Y. D. (25.0112): para. 28.
63 (Name Change) 45797-07-11 Haifa District Attorney v. Y. D. (25.01.12): para. 28.
64 Santosky v. Kramer, 455 U.S. 745 (1982); Conner, 2008; Micek, 2000.

withhold its power.[65] Establishing the right to a family in Israel as constitutional, the Israeli Supreme court solemnly declared:

> In establishing his family, a person shapes the way in which he lives his life and builds his private world. Therefore, in protecting the right to family life, the law protects the most basic freedom of the citizen to live his life as an autonomous person, who is free to make his choices.[66]

These noble and inspirational words should also apply to people's wish to retract from the family, under the constellation of femicide. Autonomy should not only serve the "positive" element of building a family, but also the "negative" element of dissolving it, releasing secondary victims from the harm inherent to many of them in remaining attached to the person who destroyed their family.[67] It is a moral and legal imperative that the men's decision to terminate the family life with his own hands be answered with a reciprocal gesture by those who loved the person he killed.

Criminal Law's Implications for Secondary Victims

The criminal-law system is an institution designed to enable the state to prosecute an individual who failed to comply with its normative order as expressed in its criminal code. This system's interest is therefore focused on the perpetrator of the crime, rather than on its primary or secondary victims. Conceptually, the victims' interest, infringed by the criminal act, is undertaken by the state, thereby annulling its interest in prosecuting the case. Under common-law jurisprudence, victims have traditionally been unable to participate in criminal proceedings for these normative reasons and their structural implication, allowing no parties other than the state and the accused to bring their rivalry before the court. Thus, victims are widely perceived as "private parties" whose role should be confined to that of witnesses. Moreover, their specific and aggravated interest in the criminal trial was rejected because it was seen as an external threat to the objective and public nature of the criminal-justice system.[68] Notwithstanding this normative and practical bias against victims' right to represent their interest independently of the state, recent decades have witnessed both a major shift in the attitude toward the role of victims in the criminal-justice system and a breakdown in the public-private divide in criminal-justice discourse – frequently referred to as "the victims' revolution."[69]

65 Barak, 2013.

66 HCJ 7052/03 Adalah Legal Center for Arab Minority Rights in Israel v. Minister of Interior (14.05.2006): para. 7 (Justice Joubran).

67 The concept of a "negative" right to family life was conceptualized by Karin Carmit Yefet (2009).

68 Doak, 2005.

69 Pugach and Tamir, 2017: p. 46; Sebba, 1997.

During the past 3 decades, crime victims gradually became integrated into the criminal process as independent participants with standing rights.[70] Although not equals, they obtained novel core rights, including, inter alia: the right to be treated with fairness, dignity, sensitivity, and respect; the right to attend and be present at criminal justice proceedings; and the right to be heard during and informed of criminal proceedings. This cluster of rights is conferred on the victim and in the case that she is deceased, her immediate relatives. Our focus in this part is the right to compensation for the harm inflicted by the crime, because it sets a particular challenge for secondary victims.[71] Israeli law, drawing inspiration from this worldwide shift, also transformed to confer this bundle of rights on victims, respecting the simple fact that in addition to the public interest in the crime executed against them, they also possess a unique interest.

Status as Crime Victims

The relatively newly established status of victims yielded a special sub-status for a victim's relatives, when the crime's primary victim was deceased as a result of the crime. Generally speaking, relatives of people who die are rendered their substitutes for legal purposes, having no significance of their own other than speaking for those who can speak no more. However, when the death is a direct result of a crime, due to the importance of such a death, the relatives are not confined to being substitutes or representatives of the victims, but turn into victims themselves, having their own standing as such in their own right. This progressive shift in the status of secondary victims has been nurtured by psychological analyses of these relatives' experience, which indicated that the impact of the crime on them is different in its nature than in cases where the primary crime victim survives. The effects of homicide on family-member survivors are widespread and often debilitating.

A recent literature review analyzing nearly 30 years of research revealed the effects of homicide on surviving family members.[72] These secondary victims may suffer from posttraumatic-stress disorder (P.T.S.D.) and other psychological effects such as behavioral changes and negative emotional reactions like feelings of rage, guilt and blame.[73] It is common for these victims to reexperience the homicide through reoccurring dreams or thoughts about the event or the homicide victim as part of their P.T.S.D. symptoms. Symptoms such as "emotional anesthesia" (in which victims experience numbness toward their lost loved one), memory loss, sleep problems and a lack of interest in important life activities are also reported among such victims.[74] In addition, victims experience a loss of confidence in society, viewing the world as cruel and dangerous. In child

70 Aaronson, 2008.
71 Fordham, 2014.
72 Connolly and Gordon, 2015.
73 Connolly and Gordon, 2015: p. 497.
74 Connolly and Gordon, 2015: p. 498.

and adolescent victims, P.T.S.D. can affect development, moral reasoning, and external and internal behavior. Such behavioral changes differ according to the child's age and their ability to understand death.[75] The traumatic event can also have negative effects on children's academic and social successes in school. Adults also reported difficulty returning to work, and some victims reported quitting or being dismissed after the homicide and experiencing feelings of social alienation. The woman's parents constitute particularly vulnerable victims, due to the aggravated harm they endure with her death, and research indicates that there is extra burden for older people in losing an adult child.[76] Family dynamics may also be altered due to the homicide because families must adjust to their loved one's absence and the change this can bring to each family member's role and responsibilities. Moreover, families face increased financial burdens worsened by funeral fees and legal costs. Victims were especially worried about finances in cases in which the deceased was the primary breadwinner.[77] In addition to these short- and long-term effects, these victims also face numerous challenges in their experiences with the criminal-justice system as it relates to their loved ones' cases. Although secondary victims are officially eligible for protection of their rights as such, many of them report a lack of information regarding the case, insensitive treatment by prosecutors and judges, unfair sentencing of the perpetrator, and suffering from graphic and insensitive media coverage of the homicide.[78]

Realizing the immense devastation that death by a crime inflicts on the victim's relatives, victimology theories have gradually transformed their approach to them from "relatives" to "co-victims" and "murder survivors."[79] This shift has eventually permeated into the legal system, wherein the relatives of a deceased person's status almost fully matches that of her surviving victims.[80] The terminological use of the victim's immediate relatives as co-victims goes beyond its symbolic value. Victims'-rights systems address victims and are designed to affect them alone. Proving that one is a victim, hence, provides not only recognition of one's suffering but also a framework ensuring the fulfillment of their rights and the rectification of their harms. Israeli law defines victims as people "directly affected by the crime" or "immediate family members of a person killed by the crime." The American system, in contrast, defines a crime victim more broadly, referring to a person "directly and proximately harmed as a result of the commission of a

75 Connolly and Gordon, 2015: p. 498.
76 Hadad-Carmel and Doron, 2009.
77 Connolly and Gordon, 2015: p. 499.
78 Connolly and Gordon, 2015: p. 500.
79 Connolly and Gordon, 2015: p. 494; Van Dijk, 2008.
80 See, for example, the terminology shift expressed by the U.S. Office for Victims of Crime regarding homicide survivors and co-victims: "A homicide survivor or co-victim is anyone (such as a spouse or partner, child, sibling, extended family member, or friend) who has been impacted by the death of a loved one by homicide."In Israel, the Victims' Rights Act (2001) provides in article 2: "Victim: A person directly hurt by the crime and family members whose relative died as a result of the crime."

federal offense."[81] Read comparatively, the Israeli law's definition reflects a narrower perception of victimhood. Under the American scheme, both direct and indirect victims are recognized as such, and their acknowledgement is not mutually exclusive. This renders possible the recognition of multiple victims of a single crime, even if the direct victim survives the crime and the other victims are relatives harmfully affected by the same crime.[82] Under Israeli law, indirect victims are recognized only as substitutes for the direct victim, in the case that the latter died as a result of the crime. If the direct victim survives, they lose this status, as no accumulation of victims is allowed. The two victim types are mutually exclusive.

Limited Compensation for Limited Victims

Being recognized as victim is instrumental in realizing the right to receive compensation for the crime's harms. Compensation is available through either a statutory-crime victim-compensation fund, as some United States and European countries provide,[83] or a court compensation writ, ordered directly against the perpetrator, as part of the criminal proceedings. These monetary-relief mechanisms are distinguished from the secondary victims' right to sue for damages independently, using civil claims, spearheaded by tort law. As opposed to independent civil claims, a compensation plea in the scope of the criminal system is conditional on the state's decision to invoke it. In Israel, the criminal-compensation apparatus is promulgated in its criminal code and applies to the victim or to his or her immediate family, if the victim died.[84] The compensation is designed to allow the victims or their relatives immediate relief from burdens imposed on them by the crime and its harmful aftermath.[85] Under criminal law, both conceptually and procedurally, these damages are limited in several ways. Most notably, and in contrast to almost any other compensation scheme in Israel, the law sets a relatively low cap on the amount that can be issued by the court as damages.

The relevance of a cap on the compensation carries significance for secondary victims when it pertains to the question of whether the damages sum is limited per crime or per secondary victim. In the case the sum is available per crime, the total amount for compensating victims for a crime is destined to be low, because the extent of the harm caused becomes irrelevant once it exceeds the fixed amount set by the law. Conversely, if the other interpretation applies, what determines the amount of compensation is the number of victims it is destined to relieve. Under this proposition, the compensation sets a more just coverage of the harm, dependent solely on the number of relatives affected by the crime,

81 The Crime Victims' Rights Act (2004), 18 U.S.C. § 3771 E (2).

82 In the case of fatal crimes, the law specifically names those eligible to the victim's rights. See the Crime Victims' Rights Act (2004), 18 U.S.C. § 3771 B.

83 Mandatory Victims Restitution Act, 18 U.S.C. § 3663.

84 Criminal Law, 1977: art. 77. The application is to the spouse, children or parents, consecutively, as mandated by the Crime Victims' Rights Act, 2001: art. 22.

85 Miers, 2014.

with the cap affecting the amount ordered to each of them separately, not collectively. Note that different victims may be eligible for differing compensation sums, reflecting the scope of their specific harm.

The question regarding which interpretation prevails was recently discussed and decided by the Israeli Supreme Court in the Tweik case. After deliberating the case twice, due to its importance, the court decided on both issues previously raised: The eligibility to be recognized as a victim and the nature of the cap the law has set on damages for victims.[86] Regarding the first issue, the court adopted a liberal approach, expanding the definition of a victim to include people indirectly affected by the crime. On the second issue, it displayed a conservative approach, stating that the law's capped sum is limited per crime. Namely, the maximum compensable harm is unaffected by whether the woman left one orphan behind her or ten.

The facts in Tweik were indisputably ferocious: Tweik was the estranged spouse of a woman, Nava, whom he killed in a vicious slaying attack. Her three daughters, who were severely harmed by his crime, were the subjects of a compensation plea brought by the people on their behalf as part of the criminal-charge proceedings.[87] Beyond the pain and suffering they endured as a result of realizing the extensive cruelty involved in their mother's killing, one of the daughters was unfortunate to find her mother bleeding to death in the scene's aftermath. The people asked the court to exercise the daughters' right to compensation individually, as secondary victims of the killing. The district court that tried the case had convicted Tweik of voluntary manslaughter, sentencing him to 19 years in prison.[88] Proceeding to decide the compensation plea before it, the court declared the daughters were secondary victims and as such, were eligible for compensation under the law, individually and cumulatively. Namely, the court interpreted the statutory cap as applying to the victims, not to the crime. The court opined that its liberal approach emanated from society's obligation to defeat the prevalence of femicide and defend its victims. More particularly, it invoked the gravity of the harm femicide inflicts on a woman's children, whom the perpetrator, who is normally a close member of her family, is well aware of, as justifying this pro-victim approach.[89] The decision was appealed by Tweik to the Supreme Court, which accepted his appeal and made the crime victims lose on both fronts. The court held that crime victimhood applies to direct victims or their successors, subsequently and not cumulatively, in the case the crime victim died due to the crime. Additionally, the court adhered to the more conservative approach to the compensation limit, deciding that the cap be applied per crime and not per victim.[90] Per the importance of the issue and its implications for crime victims' rights, the prosecution asked for another deliberation of the two issues at hand, and the Supreme Court, in a rare step, agreed to redeliberate the case with an expanded bench.

86 CSA 5625/16 Assraf v. Tweik (13/9/17)

87 Because criminal proceedings do not allow the victims a separate standing right, as previously explained, the daughters' rights were represented by the state attorney's lawyers.

88 TPH 50330–11–13 People v. Ploni (29.12.2014): para. 51.

89 TPH 50330–11–13 People v. Ploni (29.12.2014): para. 50.

90 CA 1076/15 Tweik v. People (7.6.2016): para. 9

Aligning itself with American and European approaches to crime victims' rights, the bench deciding the case for the second time accepted the claim that indirect victims are entitled to recognition and protection under criminal law. Overriding its former decision, it maintained that secondary victims are to be treated as any other victims, regardless of whether the primary and direct victim has survived the crime. The court further held that secondary victims must prove that the crime affected them severely enough to render them in "great need of immediate relief."[91] Proceeding to the compensation-cap principle, the court maintained that it applies per crime and not per victim. Accordingly, the three orphans' compensation writ was now decreased almost by a third its trial-court worth. Justifying its decision, the court invoked four pillars: (1) The compensation mechanism should be confined primarily to the boundaries of civil law and therefore, should be simplified in criminal law – a rule mandating one cap for all the crime's victims better comports with this goal; (2) criminal compensation is set to bring immediate relief, which is reasonably attainable even with low sums of money; (3) assigning the cap per victim might yield, in a crime involving multiple victims, a substantial amount of money, which will insert into criminal law a civil venue, because it warrants prolonged complicated monetary litigation; and (4) crime victims, as any other wrongfully injured people, have the civil, torts-based claims system available for them to facilitate their pleas for greater compensation.

Notwithstanding the ultimate status of this court decision, it warrants scrutiny, because the rationales underlying it were considerably attacked by the dissenting judges. Reinforcing many of the rationales brought by the district court, the dissent indicated that the number of victims should not deter courts from recognizing and attaching the cap to each of them individually, because all of them are the natural result of the criminal's act and their number is defined primarily by it. The crueler the crime is, the more family members, and even others, are likely to be severely affected by it, rendering justifiable the obligation of the perpetrator to pay for any reasonably foreseen harms, regardless of how high the amount.[92] The dissent further ameliorated the majority's worry of allowing complicated deliberations to burden trial courts. The justices offered that the prosecution would undertake a preliminary assessment of the harms and their adequate compensatory value before bringing it to the court for consideration.[93] As for having a separate civil-claim path available for secondary victims, the dissent challenged the effectiveness of pursuing it and shed light on the reality that such claims are extremely rare and difficult to fully realize.[94]

91 CSA 5625/16 Assraf v. Tweik (13.9.2017).

92 CSA 5625/16 Assraf v. Tweik (13/9/17): para. 47 (Justice Solberg). Creatively, one of the justices suggested that at least in the case of minor orphans, the cap per crime will not apply. CSA 5625/16 Assraf v. Tweik (13/9/17): para. 14 (Justice Hendel).

93 CSA 5625/16 Assraf v. Tweik (13/9/17): para. 49 (Justice Solberg)

94 CSA 5625/16 Assraf v. Tweik (13/9/17): para. 9, 13, 17 (Justice Rubinstein). See also Kay, 2006.

Summary

The status of secondary victims of femicide has advanced along with the general victims'-rights revolution that has occurred in liberal legal systems across the world. In Israel, this progress has been halted in two ways. Firstly, the law protecting victims' rights conditioned the recognition of secondary victims as genuine victims upon the death of the crime's direct victim. Importantly, the Tweik decision removed this first barrier. The second limitation pertained to secondary victims' right to compensation in criminal proceedings. Instead of utilizing this eligibility as a vehicle to significantly address their miseries in the crime's aftermath, the compensation provision was narrowly and conservatively construed to a point where it de facto forces those seeking a reasonable amount of monetary recourse to pursue the long and winding road of independent tort claims. The third and last part of this chapter exposes the meager potentiality of this path.

Tort Law's Implications for Secondary Victims

Tort law – the law enabling people to sue for damages those who did them wrong – compensates for personal suffering, including the suffering caused through the killing of a person. Traditionally, it provides two recourse trails for suing damages: One for the victim herself and the other for her relatives. The victim's independent right to collect damages for her death is dependent on having a meritorious claim and, because she is deceased, is delegated to her successors – normally, her immediate relatives. The second recourse trail, and cumulative to the latter, concerns the harm inflicted on secondary victims, which is composed of a twofold claim: Most prominent is the claim for emotional distress, whereby the immediate relatives of the woman sue for being left with the emotional suffering emanating from having lost their loved one in a heinous crime. A second monetary claim arises in the case that the woman's relatives were financially dependent on her, rendering them exposed to a loss of her support. Of the two claims, it is the emotional-distress claim that presents significant difficulties for secondary victims, due to the gendered bias of tort law against protecting human interests such as care for the other and personal connectedness.

Emotional Harm and Tort Law's Biased Architecture

Feminists have long ago proven the argument that tort law's structure is masculine.[95] Interests such as "caring for others" and "personal connectedness," traditionally associated with women, are subject to lower legal recognition and protection resulting from gender bias.[96] Moreover, intangible losses are also

95 Chamallas, 1998.
96 Chamallas and Kerber, 1990; Chamallas and Wriggins, 2010.

considered under common-law tradition as inferior to tangible losses and, to some extent, are irrecoverable.[97] Lingering limitations have dictated tort law's attitude toward compensating for harms such as emotional distress or suffering, and these harms have never ceased to be the main target of legal attacks and liability restrictions, despite the rhetoric of acceptance and understanding of their societal importance.[98] Against this backdrop, the intangible harm associated with the loss of a close person – resulting from the brutal demise of care and connectedness relations, alongside the fact that this harm is considered intangible and indirect – overburden secondary victims with handicapping challenges.

Indirect emotional harm is tightly rooted in the basic notion of human feelings. It is identified as the emotional and mental suffering caused to a person in a care relationship setting. A prominent example is A's claim against C, who negligently harmed B. In this setting, A suffers emotional and mental pain arising from a physical injury to her loved one, B, with B's injury resulting from C's negligent behavior. This damage is intangible and indirect by virtue of not arising from a physical injury to the plaintiff (A) herself, but rather from injury to a third party, B, to whom she is closely and emotionally related. Although having a direct impact on the plaintiff, this damage is perceived in tort law as indirect, because it is the outcome of an injury performed against someone else's body and not against the plaintiff. A clear example of such harm, and the most common one, is that caused to a mother who suffers emotional harm as a result of an injury caused to her child in an accident, either by means of witnessing the accident or its immediate aftermath. In this setting, this loss relates more to emotions related to the care of others, which is typically considered a female virtue, because care work is typically performed by women.[99] Moreover, statistics show that plaintiffs with indirect-emotional-harm claims are predominantly women, thereby implying that women are also disproportionally affected by the stringent liability rules governing these claims.[100] It is the female-related trait of this loss that triggered the interest of feminist analysts of tort law in reframing the qualified recognition this loss has gained in negligence law as reflecting a gender bias against women. This feminist perspective becomes even more dominant in the case of femicide, whereby hypothetically, the family's matriarch's rather than patriarch's death is more likely to cause emotional distress to her close family members left behind. This idea is substantiated by the fact that the "ethics of care," namely nurturing and emotionally investing in offspring, are borne predominantly by mothers rather than fathers.[101]

97 Levit, 1992.
98 Handsley, 1996.
99 Research also indicates that most care work is burdened by women. See Wayne and Cordiero, 2003.
100 Chamallas and Kerber, 1990: p. 814.
101 Chamallas and Kerber, 1990; Gilligan, 1982.

Indirect Emotional Harm under Israeli Tort Law[102]

The Israeli tort-law domain is paradigmatically common law, reflecting and embracing the general conceptions and specific legal doctrines of Anglo-American law. Structured along the lines of the British Empire's colonial legal regime, the Israeli Tort Ordinance – the primary authoritative source of tort adjudication – practically functions as a legal transplantation in the Israeli legal system. Consequently, the bias embedded in common law against intangible harms applies to Israeli law. This dynamic led to an even more stringent rule against liability for indirect ethereal harms in Israel, as the following review demonstrates.

Constructing a narrow duty of care for indirect emotional harm, Israeli law has made problematic use of rules developed in Anglo-American case law in this area. Starting as early as the late 1950s, the Israeli Supreme Court discussed the notion of indirect emotional harm, identified as "nervous shock," in a case wherein a mother whose son had drowned in a cesspit sued for her resulting emotional distress.[103] Her claim, brought against the decisively negligent defendant, was that losing her sole child under such agonizing circumstance induced tremendous suffering. The suit was dismissed by the trial court, a decision the Supreme Court affirmed. It held that in Israeli case law, emotional harm is not subject to compensation unless it led to bodily injury or a notable illness. Additional grounds for denying compensation, set as a policy consideration, was that it was inconceivable to allow recognition of injury to someone whose harm arose from hearing of the disaster rather than witnessing it, as English case law had mandated at that time.[104]

It was only decades after American and English laws recognized indirect emotional harm that it became recognized by the Israeli Supreme Court. In 1990, in Al-Socha,[105] the court introduced a new "secondary duty of care" toward indirect parties injured as a result of the physical harm of their loved ones. In establishing the duty, however, the court was very cautious in delineating its boundaries, warning against the liability disaster likely to unfold if the duty was not strictly confined.[106] Narrowing the duty throughout its analysis, the court eventually presented a restricted and entirely modeled duty of care that allows imposing liability only under the following conditions: (a) The plaintiff holds substantial family ties to the directly-injured victim; (b) some closeness in place or time to the scene of the event is required – namely, it is sufficient to show that the harm was caused as a result of the other person's suffering; and (c) substantial emotional harm occurred to the plaintiff. The court's diversion from its former no-liability rule, although confined and conditioned, held hope for indirect secondary victims. Nonetheless, this hope was soon to be shattered because its legacy was construed in a fundamentally reductionist fashion.

102 For a detailed review of this harm, see Bitton, 2010.
103 SC 294/54 Stern v. Shamir, P.D. 12(i) 421 (1958).
104 SC 294/54 Stern v. Shamir, P.D. 12(i) 421, 443 (1958).
105 SC 87/452,444 Al-Socha v. The Estate of the late David Dahan P.D. 44(iii) 397 (1990).
106 SC 87/452,444 Al-Socha v. The Estate of the late David Dahan P.D. 44(iii) 397, 432 (1990).

Drawing from Al-Socha's conservative tone, courts in Israel persistently narrowed the scope of the duty of care set in this case for protection against indirect emotional harm.[107] At the center of this process stood the conceptual transformation of the parameters suggested as guidance to courts into rigid preliminary conditions. They were not perceived as discretionary any longer, but rather as means for judging the case's merits at preliminary stages, without allowing it to cross the court's threshold.[108] To date, almost no suit for compensation brought under indirect emotional harm of secondary victims has been accepted or approved by courts. Most of these suits fall short of fulfilling the liability prerequisite that secondary victims were left with an extremely notable, permanent malfunctioning mental disability, because most of them suffer from significant emotional rather than psychiatric harms.[109]

Part of tort law's reluctance to acknowledge a duty of care toward secondary victims is rooted in framing their position vis-à-vis the negligent party as "bystanders" seeking compensation for witnessing harm caused to others. Generalizing the issue as regarding "bystanders" ensued despite the involvement of plaintiffs who brought their grievances due to an accident that befell their close loved ones.[110] This legal framing, which prevails to this very day, triggered the courts to adopt a negative position on liability imposition originating from three considerations described as "central" to policy making: The risk of a flood of cases; the risk of fraudulent claims; and the fear of imposing an excessive burden on the behavior of tortfeasors who hurt one person but are required to compensate many more.[111] Against this backdrop that reinforces the need to limit the duty, one can only imagine how burdensome it is for secondary victims of femicide to successfully bring a case against the perpetrator for the emotional distress they have endured. The one relief that can be found in Israeli law for their hurt is the state-provided stipend assigned only to minor orphans of a domestic-violence victim of up to the median national wage.[112]

Alternatively, and more prone to winning, is the second recourse trail tort law affords secondary victims: Bringing a suit for the loss of monetary support resulting from the demise of the deceased woman. For this path, the claim is conditional on two elements: First, that the people suing for compensation are first-tier relatives, and second, that they relied on the deceased person for their living and thus were financially dependent on her at the time she died.[113] This claim, however preferred under traditional tort law, is subject to substantial prerequisites, ignores the emotional distress of the secondary victims, and is derivative rather than independent.

107 Bitton, 2010.
108 Mullaney and Handford, 1993.
109 Bitton, 2013.
110 Bitton, 2010: p. 107.
111 Bitton, 2010: p. 107.
112 Social Security Stipend Law (Minor Orphans of Domestic Violence Victims), 1995.
113 Tort Ordinance [New Form] 1968: art. 78.

Conclusion

Despite the positive traits embedded in tort claims,[114] this legal domain offers secondary victims only a limited scope of recognition. Under its auspices, the victimhood of those who loved the femicide victim – were deeply connected to her and therefore, substantially hurt by her killing – will be recognized and rectified only if stringent prerequisites are met. This desertion of secondary victims by tort law, read together with their inferior status under criminal law, creates a disillusioning reality for them. Their grief and need to be compensated for substantial injuries caused by the femicide are left unanswered and, more importantly and alarmingly, untreated. Unattended harm, as tort-law theory and reality have long proven, is doomed to expand into further tiers of harm and damages. The key to addressing this dead-end reality for secondary victims, as some Supreme Court justices in the Tweik case pledged, is to amend criminal law to allow compensation per crime victim, be they primary or secondary. At the same time, rights pertaining to secondary victims in the realms of family law and personal-status issues should be better protected and tailored around the peculiarities of femicide. Society must recognize that the crime perpetrator and his malicious behavior have effects far beyond the primary victim, affecting her immediate relatives as well. Such cases must be decided in favor of these secondary victims' interests, when balanced against the perpetrator's criminal behavior.

Having explored in this chapter various legal aspects of femicide's secondary victims, the next chapter, Chapter 8, focuses on the contribution of torts to femicide victims and the importance of eradicating this phenomenon altogether.

References

Aaronson, D. (2008). New rights and remedies: The Federal Crime Victims' Rights Act of 2004. *Pace Law Review*, *28*, 623–682.

Barak, A. (2013). The family constitution: Constitutional aspects of family law. *Law & Business*, 13–55.

Bitton, Y. (2010). Liability of bias: A comparative study of gender-related interests in negligence law. *Annual Survey of International and Comparative Law*, *16*(1), 63–128.

Bitton, Y. (2013). Pregnancy is no disease? Channeling pregnancy and labor harms down the birth canal. *Mechkarey Mishpat*, *107*, 29.

Blecher-Prigat, A. (2009). Rethinking visitation: From a parental to a relational right. *Duke Journal of Gender Law & Policy*, *16*, 1–36.

Chamallas, M. (1998). The architecture of bias: Deep structures in tort law. *University of Pennsylvania Law Review*, *146*, 463–531.

Chamallas, M., & Kerber, K. M. (1990). Women, mothers and the law of fright: A history. *Michigan Law Review*, *88*, 814–864.

Chamallas, M., & Wriggins, J. B. (2010). *The measure of injury: Race, gender, and tort law*. NYU Press.

114 Perry, 2009.

Conner, D. H. (2008). Do no harm: An analysis of the legal and social consequences of child visitation determinations for incarcerated perpetrators of extreme acts of violence against women. *Columbia Journal of Gender and Law*, *17*, 023575.

Connolly, J., & Gordon, R. (2015). Co-victims of homicide: A systematic review of the literature. *Trauma, Violence, & Abuse*, *16*(4), 494–505.

Costa, D. H., Njaine, K., & Schenker, M. (2017). Repercussions of homicide on victims' families: A literature review. *Ciência & Saúde Coletiva*, *22*(9), 3087–3097.

Dawson, M., Sutton, D., Carrigan, M., & Grand'Maison, V. (2018). *Call it femicide: Understanding gender-related killings of women and girls in Canada*. Canadian Femicide Observatory for Justice and Accountability.

Dayan, H. (2018). *Femicide and the law: American criminal doctrines*. Routledge.

Doak, J. (2005). Victims' rights in criminal trials: Prospects for participation. *Journal of Law and Society*, *32*(2), 294–316.

Doron, I., & Linchitz, G. (2010). The legal standing of grandparents to visitation rights with their grandchildren: The Israeli story. *The Elder Law Review*, *6*, 1–13.

Fontaine, R. G. (2009). Adequate (non) provocation and heat of passion as excuse not justification. *University of Michigan Journal of Law Reform*, *43*(1), 27–51.

Fordham, M. (2014). Psychiatric injury, secondary victims and the sudden shock requirement. *Singapore Journal of Legal Studies*, *2014*(1), 41–58.

Gilligan, C. (1982). *In a different voice: Psychological theory and women's development*. Harvard University Press.

Hadad-Carmel, S., & Doron, I. (2009). Bereavement in old age: A loss of a grown child: The meaning of losing an adult offspring in old age. *Gerontology and Geriatrics*, *4*(1), 51–76.

Handsley, E. (1996). Mental injury occasioned by harm to another: A feminist critique. *Law & Inequality Journal*, *14*, 391–488.

Jaffe, P. G., & Juodis, M. (2006). Children as victims and witnesses of domestic homicide: Lessons learned from domestic violence death review committees. *Juvenile and Family Court Journal*, *57*, 13–28.

Kay, J. W. (2006). Is restitution possible for murder? Surviving family members speak. In J. Acker & D. Karp (Eds.), *Wounds that do not bind: Victim-based perspectives on the death penalty* (pp. 323–348). Carolina Academic Press.

Kowalczyk, D. (1998). Lizzie's law: Healing the scars of domestic murder – An emerging national model. *Brooklyn Law Review*, *64*, 1241.

Levit, N. (1992). Ethereal torts. *George Washington Law Review*, *61*, 136–192.

Lowery, D., & Redfield, M. (2003). Criminal histories and parental custody and visitation rights. *Los Angeles Lawyer*, 25–29.

Micek, J. (2000). Termination of parental rights based on felony conviction. *Journal of Contemporary Legal Issues*, *11*(1), 565–569.

Miers, D. (2014). Offender and state compensation for victims of crime: Two decades of development and change. *International Review of Victimology*, *20*(1), 145–168.

Mullaney, N. J., & Handford, P. R. (1993). *Tort liability for psychiatric damage: The law of tort rules: OK?* Sweet & Maxwell.

Perry, R. (2009). Empowerment and tort law. *Tennessee Law Review*, *76*, 959–992.

Pugach, D., & Tamir, N. (2017). Nudging the criminal justice system into listening to crime victims in plea agreements. *Hastings Women's Law Journal*, *28*(1), 45–72.

Rhodes, A. (2007). Consequences of heirs' misconduct: Moving from rules to discretion. *Ohio North University Law Review*, *33*, 975–991.

Rom, M. (2019). *So what's your name now? Challenge and appropriation in the selection process of Israeli women of their surname after marriage*. Pardes.

Sahar, Z. (2011). "Sometimes she asks to call me dad": About grandparents raising their murdered daughter's children. *Meeting Point*, *3*, 33–40.

Scheppele, K. M. (1991). The interpretation of law: Riggs v. Palmer revisited. In R. Post (Ed.), *Law and the order of culture* (pp. 46–49). University of California Press.

Sebba, L. (1997). Will the victim revolution trigger reorientation of the criminal justice system? *Israel Law Review*, *31*(1–3), 379–428.

Shen, F. X., Hoffman, M. B., Jones, O. D., & Greene, J. D. (2011). Sorting guilty minds. *New York University Law Review*, *86*(5), 1306–1360.

Van Dijk, J. J. M. (2008). In the shadow of Christ? On the use of the word "victim" for those affected by crime. *Criminal Justice Ethics*, *27*(1), 13–24.

Wayne, J. H., & Cordiero, B. L. (2003). Who is a good organizational citizen? Social perception of male and female employees who use family leave. *Sex Roles*, *49*(5–6), 233.

Yefet, K. C. (2009). Unchaining the Agunot: Enlisting the Israeli constitution in the service of women's marital freedom. *Yale Journal of Law and Feminism*, *20*(2), 441–504.

8 Femicide Victims' Agency through Tort Law

Introduction

This last chapter in Part III of the book continues to explore secondary matters that relate to the legal treatment of femicide. This chapter illuminates such seemingly secondary issues that bear primary importance but remain in the shadows of scholarly research.

Femicide is perceived as a matter of public interest to society. Bearing important societal ramifications, it stands at the center of the criminal-justice system's attention, which fights homicide with the utmost dedication, utilizing its strongest punishment means and investigation tools.[1] In this chapter, we advance the idea that femicide should be of great interest to another distinctively different field of law: Tort law – the law designed to provide damages for harm by individually suing for compensation those responsible for that harm. Harnessing it to confront the "private" harm embedded in every femicide case and its individualistic implications, tort law may potentially redress, and ultimately abolish, the "public" harm endured by women through femicide. The path from a private tort claim to a public transformation of human behavior relies, in a nutshell, on the basic tort theory of large-scale personal deterrence. According to this theory, the plaintiff, rather than the state, is invited to create deterrence through a civil claim brought to court against a person perceived (and approved by the court) to be inefficiently injurious.[2]

To establish the contention that tort law is instrumental in fighting femicide, this chapter first presents the stages by which feminist legal scholarship has turned tort law into a bastion of women's rights protection. In its second part, the chapter analyzes Israeli femicide cases brought under tort law to present their functionality as complementing the shortcomings of criminal law in fighting against femicide, while allowing a critical view of the relations between the two fields as diverse and, at times, disharmonious. The last part of this chapter presents the disadvantages of the growing de facto relegation or referral of some femicide cases from the criminal to the civil legal system.

1 Capital punishment is almost exclusively assigned to murders.
2 Hackney, 1997.

DOI: 10.4324/9781003333272-11

Feminist Analysis of Tort Law's Gender-Based Protectionism

Three evolutional stages facilitated tort law's contemporary compatibility to protect women's gender-related interests – namely, interests that are typical to women's life experiences, some by nature such as birth or miscarriage and some by social construction such as rape and femicide. The gradual evolution of tort law's protectionism inclinations spans three consecutive periods: The period of "conceptual traditionalism" that treated tort law as apolitical and as having no distributive account; the "enlightenment" period that exposed tort's masculine tendencies and discriminatory neglect to protect women's interests; and the "transformative" period, whereby the demand for protecting women's interests encouraged the modification and expansion of tort law to include women's rights under its auspices.[3]

First Stage: Conceptual Traditionalism

From both a conceptual and traditional perspective, tort law is considered an integral part of "private law" that is based on a bilateral and apolitical foundation. This characterization of tort law took shape toward the end of the 19th century, during the advent of modern tort law. Because tort law is located conceptually on the "private side" of the infamous dichotomy between private law and public law in Blackstonian and libertarian legal philosophy,[4] two obstacles impeded its feminist-analysis potential. First, feminist analyses of the law are generally hindered by a traditionalist inclination to preserve the legal system as formal, scientific, apolitical and even antipolitical. Under this premise, feminist analysis of law is considered political and hence estranged from legal reasoning. According to this argument, the goals of feminist analysis are not to achieve egalitarian distribution of resources among minority groups and equate the unequal balance of power in society, but rather to advance women's interests in protecting "women's rights."[5] The second obstacle that the feminist analysis of tort law encounters under this traditional guise is its function as private law, which provides for the vindication of concrete rights in a bilateral, private-like dispute. As such, political considerations that seek to redress the unequal gender-driven distribution of wealth in society should not be considered when determining whether to impose liability for harm.[6] Allowing distributive considerations into tort law would violate, according to the traditional contention, the rights of the parties to have their dispute adjudicated according to their bilateral considerations alone.[7] Indeed, this notion was considered so fundamental to the construction and character

3 Bitton, 2014.
4 Hall, 1943.
5 Bitton, 2014.
6 Keren-Paz, 2007b.
7 Weinrib, 2012.

of tort law, it also persuaded feminist legal scholars, who failed to apply their own criticism of the private public dichotomy and focused their substantial legal analyses beginning in the 1980s on arenas identified as belonging to public law. It is, therefore, understandable that feminist analysis of tort law was substantially delayed during this conceptual traditionalism period and occurred significantly later, during the "enlightenment" period.[8]

Second Stage: Enlightenment

To overcome torts' traditional perception as apolitical, the primary goal of feminist analysis in its initial stages was to expose torts' non-private and political character. Critical approaches toward tort law, which portrayed it as both politicized and public by nature, facilitated such a view. As early as the 1930s, several American realist intellectuals voiced their criticism of the politicization of private law. Their successors – primarily critical legal-studies scholars – added to the political function of tort law the claim that this field of law, in and of itself, reflects clear political aspects.[9]

Against the background of this progressive analysis, the establishment of a feminist analysis of tort law was substantially facilitated. Drawing on this sentiment, feminists contended that the political slant of tort law was self-evident, setting the conceptual stage for a second layer of analysis, whereby the pro-masculine tendency in tort law was exposed.

One of the first feminist scholars to reject this approach to tort law was Leslie Bender, who decided to forego the traditional analytic approaches that differentiated between private and public law, choosing instead to apply traditional "feminist questions" to tort law.[10] Initially, Bender posed two basic questions: First, does tort law address the unique needs of women, and second, do tort law doctrines have a unique influence on women? She answered these questions with "no" and "yes," respectively. Subsequently, she deepened her research to determine the extent to which tort-law doctrines have disregarded the needs of women and the repercussions of this disregard. Other feminist legal scholars followed Bender's pioneering analysis, many of whom extended the intended impact of their feminist analysis beyond women to all groups disadvantaged by tort law, rendering their critique universal and hence more legitimate.[11]

This solid critique gained gradual respect when, in the early 1990s, articles presenting it were awarded a satisfying academic stage in reputable journals. Among other topics, these articles focused on the central doctrine of negligence, liability for actions that cause indirect emotional damage, the definition of "a reasonable man," patterns of recognition for the principle of foreseeability, and

8 Bitton, 2014.
9 Horwitz, 1992.
10 Bender, 1993.
11 Bitton, 2014.

the limitations of compensation for intangible interests. The articles argued that tort law reflected masculine patterns of thought and life experiences and did not account for women's gendered life experiences and tort-related needs. These articles established two notions: First, they affirmed that injured women bear an unequal burden due to sustaining uniquely feminine harms, and second and more importantly, they emphasized that these inequalities extended into and were reinforced by tort law. In other words, despite the primacy of feminist analysis in law, many complex measures that influenced women stood in the way of exposing the gender bias in tort law. In the realm of tort liability, women suffered bias and had less legal protection than their male counterparts. Outside of the boundaries of tort law, this was used to reproduce and deepen androcentric stereotypes in society, which were integral parts of the disadvantaged position in which women were placed. With the advancement of this focused analysis of tort law, a wider meta-theoretical critique of tort law began to take shape. This analysis that united a body of recognized and consistent critics, such as Martha Chamallas,[12] Lucinda Finley,[13] Anita Bernstein[14] and others, did not limit itself to one doctrine or another, but began to express itself in more inclusive language that exposed the systemic masculine biases in tort law and the need to adapt it to women's needs.

Pursuant to the influence that U.S. feminist analysis of law had on Israeli general legal analysts, it was not surprising to discover that similar patterns of masculine biases existed in Israel, and in some cases even more intensely. Like their U.S. counterparts, Israeli feminists first explored branches of public law and then, two decades later, expanded their critique to branches of private law.[15] American influence was also evident in the initial preoccupation with detailed doctrines of tort law, which only subsequently developed into a broader analysis of the field. As it grew deeper, the analysis pointed out that tort law did not recognize intangible harms, which women predominantly incur, nor did it provide compensation for such damages.[16] The analysis also criticized "neutral" tort patterns that demonstrated gender biases when considered in the framework of female life experiences, such as giving birth.[17] In the final stage, the analysis called for a reevaluation of tort liability to account for the gender power relations in shaping its doctrines and for the acknowledgment that tort law should serve more prominently as recourse for alleviating the systematic suffering that characterizes women's lives.[18] Once feminist analysis penetrated Israeli tort law, the field started taking a traceable new turn in its development to better protect women's human rights.

12 Chamallas, 1998.
13 Finley, 1989.
14 Bernstein, 2001.
15 Bilsky, 2001.
16 Bitton, 2007.
17 Keren-Paz, 2007a.
18 Bitton, 2008.

Third Stage: Transformative

If it were possible to rank the importance and virtue of the stages presented here separately, the third stage would undoubtedly be ranked the highest. Its distinction lies in the fact that it enabled the modification and expansion of tort law in a way that not only deepened the influence of feminist analysis and the protection of women's rights, but also allowed for a greater understanding of it and for the formation of new, creative and important areas in tort law for the betterment of women.

Aimed at integrating the feminist analysis of torts, this advanced stage warranted both theoretical and practical entrenchment work in the field, which was particularly feasible under contemporary tort law in Israel. Israeli tort law experienced a dramatic expansion during the last two decades, with the last decade being almost unparalleled in the rest of the world in terms of its willingness to accommodate the changing reality.[19] The time was ripe to treat women's human rights anew and provide them fair protection under tort law, equal to that traditionally provided to men.[20] Several fundamental processes were prompted to avail this rudimentary shift. With its transformative shift toward protecting women's rights, a growing practice has been developed to use it to protect women against violence and the violation of their right to integrity. More particularly, femicide cases were now brought before the courts under a tort claim for compensation. In the following part of this chapter, we present these cases according to their role in the fight against femicide. Most notably, we focus on how these cases were instrumental in complementing substantial shortcomings the criminal system demonstrates in holistically and effectively addressing femicide and demolishing it as a social phenomenon. In this respect, femicide cases initiated by tort law also serve as critical artifacts of the criminal system.

Summary

Tort law has undergone substantial shifts in its protection of women's rights, from an androcentric field of law to a law that attends to women's interests and compensates women for the violations thereof. This shift did not happen as part of some natural development of the law alongside society's progress, but rather resulted, at least in Israel, from an orchestrated effort by academics on one hand and activists on the other.[21] Additional to feminist ideology and scholarly creativity that triggered and encouraged this development, practical advantages of tort law enabled it. Tort law appeals greatly to practitioners due to its potential to yield a substantial stipend for the representing lawyer. Inherent in tort proceedings and uniquely characteristic of tort law is the possibility of the transfer of a

19 Bitton, 2014.
20 Bitton, 2016.
21 Bitton, 2014.

significant amount of money to the plaintiff.[22] This benefit strongly incentivized feminism-motivated private lawyers to undertake litigation cases in the field. It also encouraged the development of civil society organizations to be based on a unique budget model whereby the organizations finance their social-change activities using a proportion of the funds awarded to successful plaintiffs. Combined with theoretical feminist analysis of the law, bringing these cases before the courts enabled such practical change to develop rapidly. Israeli courts, to their credit, responded very positively to the new legal trend, and the mission of turning tort law into a bastion of protecting women's rights began its realization process.[23]

Torts' Agency: Filling the Gaps in Criminal Law

This part introduces the complexities emanating from utilizing tort law as a tool to fight femicide. The former part presented the nature of tort law as challenging for such usage and the feminist approach that opened it to this utilization; this part takes the question of tort law's aptitude to fight femicide vis-à-vis the primarily tool addressing it, criminal law. In light of the overarching perception that criminal law is where all forms of homicide should be addressed, the question remains: What need exists in utilizing tort law for this end? Despite their acknowledged distinctiveness, soon to be elaborated here, torts and criminal law are perceived as having the potential to contribute to and support each other. This approach reflects the familiar paradigm of positive relations between these branches of law as being based on mutual complementarity and endorsement. Alongside this harmonious paradigm, the interplay between these two legal systems also carries problematic and negative aspects. This part first introduces the prevailing paradigm of complementarity between the fields, then proceeds to the paradigm that sees tort law as standing at times in grave and acute tension with the criminal law. To illustrate these paradigms, this part presents the challenges faced throughout litigation proceedings of tort suits brought by victims of femicide against their perpetrators. In these suits, criminal actions of femicide are "translated" into civil claims for liability, in what is often termed "crim-tort." Looked at as special torts, crim-torts are of primary importance to femicide civil plaintiffs and warrant scholarly attention as such.[24]

Under common law's analysis by Blackstone,[25] the division of labor between tort law and criminal law is crystal clear: Criminal law relates to issues of public interest and is located at the public front of legal affairs, whereas positioned at the private front, tort law is designed to resolve private disputes between two (or more) parties, whereby one party harmed the other. This explains the practice of the state

22 Kritzer, 1997.
23 Bitton, 2014, 2016.
24 Koenig and Rustad, 1998.
25 Blackstone, 1765/1769.

to bring criminally disobedient individuals to justice, whereas the abridgement of tort obligations is left to the discretion and execution of individuals. Tort law rectifies in retrospect what criminal law is aimed at preventing in advance; for this reason, tort law applies only when the harm materializes as a result of an ill behavior, whereas the application of criminal law is ignited by the criminal behavior itself, with even an attempt to execute it sufficing at times. Financial concerns underly tort liability imposition, whereas punishment considerations occupy criminal-law decisions. Although some of the lines demarcating these fields' scope have blurred with time, these prominent conceptual and practical disparities still shape the two fields as distinctively different and separate from each other.[26]

The differences between tort and criminal law have led to their development as having divergent legal functions that are nevertheless associated. Broadly put, tort law has become the assistant in criminal law's mission. Namely, next to criminal law's primacy as a lead tool in achieving social order, in cases of crim-torts, tort law holds a secondary yet significantly important role. Aligned with theories of legal harmony as characterizing healthy legal systems,[27] this notion of crim-torts envisions tort law as having the power to strengthen the impact of or add another layer of effectiveness to criminal law.

Strengthening the criminal-law process is achieved mainly through tort law's compensation imposition trait, which puts a price tag on the behavior, signifying society's resentment of the crime as harmful to others who suffered a loss because of it.[28] Tort law here seconds criminal law's normative signifiers, reiterates the behavior as being wrongful and utilizes its exclusive money-based relief to create a deterring effect.[29] The monetary relief of tort law serves yet another important social aim that criminal law mostly lacks: Providing the victim of a crime with compensation for injuries. Enabling the rectification of the harm and remedying its results are goals that go, at least de facto, beyond the individual's well-being and involve an overarching social interest. It allows people the opportunity to get back to the point where they were prior to the occurrence of a tort, where they can function independently and contribute to society as injury-free people. In this capacity, tort law reinforces criminal law in a more significant, complementary manner. Namely, it complements criminal law, where the latter lacks the power to have a similar effect by civil enforcement.

The harmonious coexistence of tort law and criminal law, whereby the latter enjoys reinforcement by the former, also flows in the other direction. Tort law's liability imposition may be substantially aided by criminal law's determinative nature. A plaintiff bringing a crim-tort plea before the court is hardly as burdened as the regular tort plaintiff. Once the factual basis of the tort has been officially identified by a criminal court as a crime and the defendant has been found guilty in court,

26 Coffee, 1991; Hall, 1943; Katz, 1996; Simons, 2008.
27 Holmes, 1881.
28 Coffee, 1991.
29 Heriot, 1996.

the plaintiff carries very little burden in proving eligibility for tort relief in the civil proceedings that follow. Various laws stipulating this legal leverage for a civil plaintiff render this complementary relation between the fields particularly valuable.[30]

The alleged reciprocal harmony between the two legal fields is not consistent, and its discrepancies might yield devastating effect on the victim's well-being from a tort-based perspective. Take, for example, cases in which a civil plea is halted until the criminal proceedings are due or in which the criminal proceedings exhaust the perpetrator's financial means. In both scenarios, the victim is left with no monetary remedy at a time when it is needed most.[31] In the following paragraphs, we showcase both the harmonious and disharmonious ramifications of the relations between the two legal fields for femicide cases and their victims' ability to receive recourse using civil actions.

Harmonious Relations between the Fields: Lack of Liability for Peripheral Enablers of Femicide

Many femicide cases are facilitated and enabled by agents positioned in the penumbra of the main perpetrator's action. Take, for example, premises on which the victim has been attacked because security measures were unreasonably maintained. A condominium management company neglecting to safeguard the victim's key to her apartment, thereby enabling attackers to duplicate it, invade her residence and brutally rape her, is the enabler of the rape.[32] Cases of this type raise the issue of holding enablers accountable for their negligent and harmful behavior. As a general rule, enablers fall outside the scope of criminal law's auspices, which is rooted in and limited to individual guilt emanating from its insistence on proving mens rea. Neither the management company nor its operators, in this example, can be attributed such criminal characteristics to be held liable. Tort law, on the other hand, can. Despite its reluctance to impose liability on peripheral tortfeasors – namely, parties that were not the direct inflictors of the harm – tort law has eventually transformed its approach to cover such indirect liability. By embracing this capacity, tort law fulfills its complementary role in the tort-criminal-law dyad, by adding another layer of accountability to the perpetrator's criminal guilt for femicide. The following examples demonstrate this transformation in Israel and its limits.

The Beitili *Case*[33]

Establishing peripheral liability to protect women against femicide in public places is compatible with our changing social order. Due to the capitalist nature of society, companies pervade the public area of life, and the classic liberal account

30 The Evidence Ordinance, 1971: sec. 42A-42D.

31 Bitton, 2013.

32 See, e.g., the facts stated at Doe v. Linder Const. Ltd. 845 S.W.2d 173 (Tenn 1992).

33 CC 2271/04 Brez v. Beitili Ltd., (7.4.2010).

they hold as private entities should not shield them from liability that carries public meaning. Demonstrative of this understanding is the Israeli case of Beitili, whereby the court imposed liability on the privately owned company Beitili, a successful chain of home-design stores, to compensate the estate of Tamar Brez, a woman who was raped and murdered in 1997 on the roof of Beitili's flagship premises.[34] Brez went to the shop in search of furniture, and store personnel directed her to the top-floor display, which was an area isolated from the rest of the store.[35] Confident in the safety inherent in every business premise that welcomes the public with a security guard at its entrance, Brez went to the top floor.[36] However, upon her arrival, an employee who had been lurking behind her attacked her and locked the door to the main floor behind her.[37] Undisturbed, he implemented a sadistic premeditated plan of rape and murder of a woman patron.[38] The perpetrator, as he later testified during his criminal trial, carried out the rape and murder after having searched for months for a site suitable for his vicious plan, eventually finding his unsupervised workspace most apt for the mission.[39] The plaintiff claimed Beitili, by focusing solely on maximizing its premises' profitability as its main priority, failed to create a safe retail environment for women, although women constitute its lion share of customers.[40] This strategy led Beitili to negligently operate the store roof as part of its retail space, despite realizing that it lacked any supervisory coverage and functioned, de facto, as ex-territory.

Accepting the suit, the district court acknowledged the negligence claim and refurnished the notion of duty shaping it. The court's position was that the business owners' category of duty liability, normally confined to actions directly influencing customer safety, should be expanded to include safety concerns emanating from third parties' actions, thereby incentivizing business owners to invest in security measures for shoppers. Although couched in gender-neutral terms, the verdict had far-reaching implications for women. It utilized tort law to shift the responsibility that women have traditionally assumed to ensure their own safety in public spaces – with which they were burdened due to structural gender disparities – to society as a whole. The judgment revolved on the axis of business owners' responsibility to prevent the risk of creating "secluded spaces" in business premises, thereby reinforcing the case's gender significance, because women alone incur the additional risk of being raped in these secluded spaces, due to what sociologists identify as the "existential feminine fear of being raped" that is common to women of different origin, social status and age.[41] This persistent fear

34 *Id.*: p. 3.
35 *Id.*: p. 4.
36 *Id.*
37 *Id.*
38 *Id.*: pp. 4–5.
39 *Id.*: p. 10.
40 CC (TA) 2271/04 Brez v. Beitili Ltd., PM, 23–26, 35 (2010) (Isr.).
41 Gordon and Riger, 1989; Russell, 1975.

also causes women to incur the costs of exercising precaution and measurements, which will be greatly lessened if taken by business owners.[42]

The radiating effect this ruling has on the safety of women stems not only from the foregoing contentions but also from the case's far-reaching influence, both symbolically and materially. From a symbolic point of view, the court condemned the outrageous neglect of retailers to ensure safe shopping environment for women, which resonates with the commonly held perception that women alone are required to limit their personal freedom and quality of life to reduce their risk of becoming victims of male sexual attack.[43] From a materialistic perspective, though the verdict was directed against the specific defendant company, it directly affected insurance companies across the national business market that provide insurance for on-the-premises damages. The court's liability-insurance paradigm increased the efficacy of the concept of changing social burdens and responsibilities in relation to injuries women incur. To protect their financial interests, insurance companies accommodating the court's decision, under a premise of simple rational economic calculus, changed their safety requirements for business premises as prerequisites for issuing insurance policies.[44] These requirements are likely to change personal-safety-assuring patterns of businesses in Israel and accordingly, influence the allocation of responsibility for women's safety. As such, they may substantially enhance the tort-driven social-change initiative introduced by feminist critics of tort law.

Despite its celebrated traits, it is important to note that Beitili's rhetoric did not contain innovative interpretations of tort law, but rather employed conventional analysis. Thus, it demonstrated that the power to impose liability on peripheral tortfeasors – which bears significant value for identifying entities that facilitate systematic materialization of potential social vulnerability – is embedded in tort law. Here lies the significance of the case in terms of internal tort law as well: It demonstrates that tort law is suitable for modern social systems under which the evolution of damage may reach far beyond the injured party and the direct tortfeasor.[45] Applying this notion to Beitili, it can be argued that the day the business space of Beitili was designed, minimal security arrangements were made. Long before Beitili opened its doors to the public, Brez's rape and murder were determined. Tort law takes us to this preliminary point in the planning phase to identify the determination of Brez's fate as an injustice, and it does so exactly where criminal law is unable.

42 Bitton and Shavit, 2015.

43 Beyond shouldering the costs of rape itself, women also incur the costs of preventing it. More to the point, they are put in a contradictory condition, in which they are taught to fear men and at the same time expected to rely on them for protection from other men (Madriz, 1997).

44 In Beitili, the insurance company was one of Israel's most prominent companies, Migdal Group, which occupies the largest share of the market and insures many private business premises in Israel. *Beitili*, *supra*: note 148.

45 Fletcher, 2008.

The Jacobov *Case*[46]

Another sphere in which the protection of women's life is most needed and criminal law's shorthandedness is particularly apparent is policing. Police officials, positioned at the frontline of protecting women from femicide, occasionally yet repeatedly fail to do so, to an extent that they become instrumental in facilitating the femicide. Regardless of the extreme malfunction of their actions, however, criminal law has no bearings on their professional failures, unless they were intentional aiders or accomplices, which happens only in extremely rare circumstances. Here again, tort law's complementarity is evident and necessary, as the Jacobov case demonstrates.

Sonia Jacobov was a young woman introduced to a man as a match by a family friend. From the outset, she disliked the man and notified him of her decision not to proceed with the relationship. The man, in retaliation, began harassing her. Terrified and seeking protection, Jacobov filed 11 complaints against the man, alerting the police about his escalating actions and threats. The police reacted with ineffective protective measures and the man's obsession culminated in an attack on Jacobov, which resulted in her severe injury and the killing of her younger sister who rushed to her assistance. As expected, criminal charges were brought against the man and culminated in his conviction in murder. Frustrated by the criminal system's shortsighted approach, Jacobov decided that the police officials who were negligent in addressing her complaints should also be held accountable and filed a tort suit against them. The lawsuit was denied by the district court, with the main contention that Jacobov didn't prove that the murder would have been prevented had the police acted properly. On appeal, Jacobov contended that the opposite can't be proven either and that the negligent inaction of the police contributed to her inability to do so. The civil attorney representing the state decided to pay the compensation due to the solid weight of her claims and the fear of having a precedent set.

Jacobov's tort suit against the police illuminated the important role police officials have in protecting women against femicide, at least in cases wherein prior to its execution, escalation unfolds and authorities have the power to act in the threatened women's interest. This role is easily overlooked in the aftermath of the femicide, especially with the focus resting on criminal proceedings. Tort law, therefore, complements criminal law in a fundamental manner, coercing governmental authorities to internalize the cost of their negligence regarding broader feminine suffering resulting from femicide. The benefit of such a feminist course of action is threefold: It enables women or their heirs to demand justice in a system that provides them little protection before and after the violent acts they sustain. At the same time, it aims to induce changes in the conceptual framework of legal tort rules by injecting feminist epistemology into them. In other words, using tort claims to compensate women for femicide encourages altering

46 TA 2841/98 Jacobov v. Israel Police Force (23.3.2005)

the current tort-law apparatus, which is rooted in a masculine epistemological framework in which feminine suffering is still left unchallenged. And last, the tort claim helps dismantle the private-public dichotomy by extenuating the role of law enforcement and its public agents as nurturers of the patriarchal structure in which the private harm of femicide is executed. The use of tort law, hence, reveals through a private mechanism this discriminating public social construct of power-disparity exploitation and calls for a revisiting of police protocols in future similar cases.[47]

Disharmonious Paradigm: Femicide–Suicide, Lack of Criminal Guilt, and Tort Liability

As previously mentioned, not all relations between the two fields are fertile. In many cases, they result in extra burden on femicide victims or their survivors seeking compensation for their injuries. Two close circumstances are brought here to demonstrate this difficulty, which stands in sharp contrast to the commonly held predetermination as to the positive influence of criminal law on tort claims. The first example relates to cases of femicide followed by suicide, wherein the criminal system refrains from establishing the guilt of the deceased murderer. The second relates to cases wherein the criminal system allows the perpetrator to invoke a legal excuse to exempt him from criminal guilt.

Cases of femicide followed by suicide are not uncommon. Although homicide–suicides account for a relatively small share of total homicides, they are likely to involve men who committed femicide of their former or current intimate partners, in a phenomenon known as femicide–suicide[48] or intimate- or domestic lethal violence–suicide.[49] A common characteristic of these cases is that due to the men's suicides, no criminal proceedings are taken, pursuant to the murders. The reason for this is prosaic: A dead person cannot be charged with criminal counts and figuratively, with the death of the perpetrator, society's interest in the case also dies. Under Israeli law, and as common sense dictates, police's broad discretion rather than the law dictates whether and to what extent the murder should be investigated.[50] Given the general heavy burden of such an undertaking for police forces globally, it is more likely that these cases will be closed without any substantial investigative measures taken. Moreover, in Israel, such a decision is commanded by the "lack of public interest" justification promulgated by law.[51]

Lack of criminal conviction, however, affects not only the criminal aspect of the cases, but also other affected fields. In tort law, the absence of a formal conviction results in the inability to pursue a compensation suit that relies on the murder,

47 Bitton, 2009.
48 Dayan, 2021.
49 Harper and Voigt, 2007: p. 307.
50 Sec. 62 to Criminal Proceedings Law and sec. 6(b)(2) to the police orders (issued, 14.1.01).
51 Sec. 62(a) to Criminal Proceedings Law.

wherein the murder is the axle around which the suit revolves. Any compensation suit relaying on the harm done to the woman, even if the case has been investigated, would still depend on the suing estate proving the murder first, and only if it manages to do so could it proceed to the tort claim itself.

The ramifications of this criminal–tort law discrepancy are substantial, as in Israel alone, in the decade from 2005 to 2015, at least 34 clear-cut cases of femicide–suicide occurred. This implies that 34 murdered women's relatives' right to sue for compensation has been severely impaired. Comparably, cases in which women's murder or attempted murder was followed by the indictment of their perpetrators could proceed directly to the compensation stage, having the leverage of a criminal conviction on their side, as mandated by the Israeli Evidence Ordinance. The ordinance provides that in the case a tort suit follows a conviction, the plaintiff may use the verdict given against the defendant in the criminal proceedings to set the facts of blame regarding his wrongful behavior. This allows the plaintiffs to proceed directly to the question of harm quantification.[52]

The following tort cases, emanating from a femicide–suicide case and an attempted femicide–suicide case, demonstrate how burdening the reality of no conviction is to surviving women or the femicide victim's estate when they sue for compensation.

The Elimelech *Case*[53]

Anat Elimelech's femicide–suicide case has been introduced in length in Chapter 6. To recap, Anat was murdered by her former spouse after she separated from him. The perpetrator committed the murder in his apartment and then killed himself immediately thereafter. His brother, who managed to enter the murder scene prior to the police due to their negligent failure to secure it, tampered with the evidence and staged the murder scene to look like Anat was not the victim of the crime, but rather its perpetrator. Moving the killing weapon from the man's hand to hers, it seemed, at first glance, as if Anat has murdered her ex-spouse and proceeded to suicide.[54] Investigating the case, the police considered the option of declaring the case unsolved, and it was only due to Anat's family members' relentless pressure that the investigation resumed. Only three weeks after her death, and after Anat's guilty narrative spread throughout the nation, the police decided to change the initial conviction and determined that Anat had been murdered and that her spouse committed suicide pursuant to murdering her. At this stage, the announcement ignored the obvious staging of the murder scene.

52 The Evidence Ordinance, 1971, sec. 42A-42D.

53 TMS 29170/05 The Late Elimelech v. The Late Afuta (20.2.2011 – Part I) (8.8.2011 – Part II).

54 Elimelech, part I: para. 60–75; Elimelech, part II: para. 263–275 (made to exonerate his brother of all guilt).

According to criminal law, once the murderer took his own life, there was no reason to proceed with the case. Furthermore, the prosecution also decided not to press charges against the brother for murder-scene staging, and the case against him was closed.[55] Anat's family's appeal to the general attorney was subsequently dismissed, under the reasoning that being derivative of obstruction to justice, the charges could not stand. Given that doing justice had been frustrated by the murderer's suicidal act, the obstruction thereof became impossible, from a conceptual and practical perspective, the police posited, despite the fallibility of this claim.[56] The heinous crime of Anat's murder and the crime of scene staging were both left unpunished and, more importantly, undetermined. The family, having gone through the agony of having people doubt Anat's innocence, sought compensation in her name for both the murder and the outrageous slander of her memory. It was only when the murderer's estate and his brother's answer to their suit was served that they realized the long and winding path they needed to take to obtain recourse for their loved one.

To deliberate the case, the court decided to divide it into two consecutive and conditional stages: The first stage was dedicated to conducting a semi-criminal trial aimed at concluding how Anat died and whether she was indeed murdered. The second stage was set to discuss, in the case that she was proven to be murdered, the damages for her estate. The effect of a lack of formal legal declaration regarding Anat's reason for death was particularly felt. The family was burdened with proving her death cause, though having neither authoritarian nor financial means to investigate it. It was only due to pro bono representation that they managed to do so.[57] After deliberating the case for eight years, in three different settings including the Supreme Court, and 15 years after the murder, finally, an Israeli court legally formalized the assertions required for the tort claims: That Anat was murdered by a shot to her heart; that her former spouse was the person who shot her; and that the murder scene had been staged by his brother. Unfortunately, though not unexpectedly, at this stage, the murderer's estate was already insolvent and no order of pay was issued against it, although Anat's claim was accepted by the court.

The Malada *Case*[58]

The following case reveals how even failed femicide–suicide cases could turn out to be poorly managed by the legal system, despite the survival of the parties. Frehut was the estranged spouse of Malada. A few years after the couple divorced, Malada, the ex-husband, who was a police officer, began threatening Frehut. Her recurring complaints to the police's Internal Affairs Department were loosely

55 Elimelech, part I: para. 74.

56 Shohetman, 2001.

57 The family sought representation from Tmura Center, a legal nongovernmental organization fighting for women's rights using tort lawsuits. The organization was founded and managed by Dr. Yifat Bitton. See www.tmura.org.il/ (last visited April 16, 2020).

58 TMS 30009/10 Malada v. Malada (20.12.2015).

investigated and eventually dismissed based on a "he said, she said" justification. In the process, though, a decision was informally provided by the Internal Affairs Department not to allow the husband access to a weapon. Upon being a sui generis decision, not documented and unformalized, once Malada was restationed to a new police county, he obtained the weapon that he used against Frehut on his first day of deployment. Bursting into her home, he shot her in her bedroom, while the kids shouted for help from the window. Subsequently to shooting her in the neck, Malada shot himself in the head, inflicting a brain injury upon himself. Miraculously, both Frehut and Malada survived the gunshot wounds. Malada's injury was not severe enough to prevent him from physically functioning independently, yet it sufficed to exempt him from criminal guilt. Bringing her tort claim to court against Malada and the police that allowed him access to the gun, Frehut was asked to prove that she was shot by her ex-husband and not vice versa, like his lawyers contended. Here, again, it took pro bono lawyers seven years to prove what should have been proven by the police.[59]

The fact that the perpetrator didn't die as a result of the crime but was extremely injured encouraged the prosecution to withdraw from charging him. It was only when the tort-lawsuit courier came to the hospital – where Malada was supposed to be hospitalized with a coma – to serve him that Frehut learned that Malada came out of his coma and became physically self-sufficient to a degree he was sent home. If not for her tort claim, no one would have known that a former police officer, suspected of attempting to murder a woman, had been set free, discharged of any accountability for his actions. It was tort law, in this case, that exposed the lawlessness of criminal law toward women and enabled some doing of justice vis-à-vis Frehut, even if partial and only ex post. More importantly, during the trial proceedings, the police eventually admitted malfunction in handling her complaints and compensated her for part of her damage, after an out-of-court deliberation with the head of its Internal Affairs Department led to a settlement. More importantly, Frehut became an agent of change in the process, by illuminating the shortcomings of the department and forcing it to reconsider its protocol under similar circumstances.

Summary

Femicide–suicide cases such as Anat's and Frehut's give names to these victims and shed light on their hidden additional hurts induced by the legal system. Like their death or injury, this additional harm is preventable. Adopting a legal rule that dictates a mandatory investigation to fully explore these cases and turn these findings into a legal determination is imperative. Having a declaration of legal validity as to the woman's murder would be of useful and effective value to tort claims brought against their dead murderers and anyone else whose liability derives from the murder and should be held accountable.

59 Here, too, Tmura Center represented the woman plaintiff.

Pitfalls of Utilizing Tort Law

Notwithstanding the clear empowering effect of utilizing tort law as an agency tool for femicide victims to fight femicide and put a monetary price tag on it, this tool carries caveats associated with the tort route that are worthy of acknowledgement. This section presents the twofold argument endorsing the growing use of torts to legally address femicide cases: First, it introduces the main problematic consequences of using tort lawsuits and negating the almost exclusive legal treatment of these cases by criminal law. This is done by delineating the hierarchy between the two routes. Second, this section calls for the employment of critical caution when endorsing this development, presenting theoretical and practical tools designed to enable and justify it in the most positive manner.

The tort and criminal routes differ so much from each other that it seems almost unnecessary, and to some extent impossible, to compare their scopes of protection for women's right to life and freedom from gender-based violence. Our intuitive recognition that criminal protection is far preferable to women needs only little explanation, rendering the distinctive rudimentary and quintessential elements of each legal field as positioned in a clear hierarchical structure in which criminal protection is dominant and crucial.[60] Given this hierarchy, it is certainly possible to argue that the referral of a matter of significant public interest from the criminal to the tort route is a downgrade, which causes the claims in question to become depoliticized and weakened in several important ways needed to acknowledge and seek tools to ameliorate harm.

Claims Undergo a Definitional Transformation

When a matter becomes the subject of a tort claim, it transforms from a substance of public importance to one of a private nature.[61] In other words, this is a situation wherein the court essentially privatizes a public problem. To solve this difficulty, the idea behind torts being used to affect public change should be re-promulgated by the concept of private recourse. Under this theoretical stance, the plaintiff operates as a kind of private attorney general who exacts a monetary cost on the undesirable behavior and thus, as formerly explained, deters potential defendants from carrying out this behavior in the future.[62] Although this approach of transforming a public matter into a private claim in tort may seem benign and morally neutral, it is important to stress that this model of deterrence, by using private plaintiffs, resonates with another preexisting, highly acceptable and conservative theory of economic efficiency in tort law. According to this theory, the plaintiff, rather than the state, is invited to create deterrence

60 CA 6821/93 Bank Ha'mizrachi Hameuchad v. Migdal, PD 49(4) 221, 292–319, 353 (1994).

61 Weinrib, 2012.

62 See Goldberg and Zipursky, 2010, for the similarity between a prosecutor and a tort claimant; see Goldberg, 2003, for deterrence.

through a civil claim brought to court against the person perceived as inefficiently injurious.[63] Under this guise, by addressing the case through the tort route, the civil court decides, using economic-efficiency analysis, who is the cheapest agent to prevent[64] the harm caused by femicide. In the Beitili case, for example, it announced that a retailer is that agent.[65] Such broad-reaching reasoning, taken in private lawsuits, demarcates the cases as having public importance, though relegated to private law ordering of the kind that only tort law offers.

Another theory that can relax this conceptual effect sees tort law as a tool for enhancing human rights in a manner beyond a private dispute between two parties and involving broader social meaning. A social-change theory of tort law known as the vulnerability theory – developed and advocated elsewhere – offers a conceptual and practical home to social struggles such as the fight against femicide. Premised on the notion that tort law should serve to eliminate social-power relations of abuse and compensate their inferred harms, the theory advocates for compensating those whose harms were sustained through the abuse of one person's power relations over another. The theory renders central the fact of the power relations in which rival parties are set vis-à-vis each other, as is the case of the patriarchy-induced harm of femicide. Whenever the abuse of power relations triggers a dispute, it commands the imposition of liability on the abuser and parties enabling it due to their negligent behavior.

Claims Undergo a Hierarchical Transformation

The interception from the criminal system, addressing homicide cases at district courts, to the tort system, addressing compensation claims mainly at magistrate courts, implies marginalization of the issue at hand. Moreover, it is detrimental not only to the plaintiff, but also puts pressure on judges of this lower instance, who are now compelled to decide the tort case in a complicated position. On one hand, the system has referred the plaintiff to these courts to seek a remedy via torts; on the other hand, by dismissing the femicide perpetrator or other facilitators thereof from their criminal liability, the system is seen as giving the case some seal of lesser importance, which makes it difficult for judges of the lower instance to be determinative. Deciding these tort cases, therefore, these judges face the need to decide on a tort claim regarding an act of femicide that was just deemed, at least in some cases, noncriminal. Analytically, this alleged discrepancy comports and is compatible with the law, but in practice, this requires judges, unfamiliar with conducting criminal proceedings, to entertain criminal-law reasoning and practices in their civil courtrooms. Indeed, this problem manifested in the Elimelech and Malada cases, wherein family courts deciding tort-compensation lawsuits

63 Hackney, 1997.

64 Calabresi, 1970.

65 Dotan, 1999; see regarding the court's use of either rhetoric or settlement tactics to protect human rights.

had to first pretend to have criminal-ruling skills to establish that the femicide and attempted femicide occurred, because there was no prior decision taken by a criminal court against the perpetrators.

Claims Undergo a Resources Transformation

Developing a field of claims via the tort route is not without significant practical and financial consequences for the plaintiffs. As argued, pursuing tort claims demands the investment of considerable time and financial resources by the plaintiffs, who are normally at a stage where their emotional availability and capability is greatly limited.[66] In this respect, the need to fund legal representation would probably significantly burden any mourning family. Moreover, when compared to the perpetrator's right to an attorney in the criminal proceedings, the expectation from the victim's side to incur the costs of managing a civil lawsuit for years seems as unfair as it is unequal. To this end, securing representation in femicide cases will provide a fairer, more equal opportunity for femicide-victim families to undertake the pursuit of civil justice. Some states, like Israel, have indeed established such funded representation in a manner similar to the public-defense mechanism, which greatly enhanced the access of femicide victims to civil justice.[67]

To sum up, the power embedded in the decision to utilize the tort system can bestow "power" on victims of femicide and their families, although at the same time, it might render these women "powerless."[68] Courts and litigating parties should cautiously try these cases and consciously address the difficulties of the tort path. An example can be seen in the Malada case, wherein the plaintiff, upon realizing she was required to prove that she was the victim of a failed femicide, demanded that the people prosecute the perpetrator, regardless of his mental capacity, which rendered him excused of criminal guilt. Her insistence was that the indictment be done, and the excuse invoked pursuant to it proved resourceful, because it allowed her to prove much more easily, with the aid of the police's investigative means, that she was the victim of a premeditated murder attempt.

Conclusion

The cases presented here are demonstrative of a larger trend of feminist influence over the boundaries of tort law's protection. Judgments that addressed feminine life experiences, such as femicide, reshaped these boundaries and tort law's most fundamental concepts. For example, the elements of reasonability, foreseeability, and the causal nexus in negligence law were reconsidered in a case whereby a

66 Normally, in Israel, court fees for a civil suit amount to 2.5% of the total sum sought by the plaintiff for compensation, as stipulated in article 6 of the Court Regulations. Court Regulations (Fees), 2007, KT 6579 p. 720 (Isr.). Attorney fees are also paid in advance.

67 www.justice.gov.il/Units/SiuaMishpaty/OurScopes/Pages/VictimsOfCrimesDead.aspx (last visited April 13, 2020). Representation is provided to all victims of homicide.

68 Pratt, 2005: p. 1062.

woman committed suicide after enduring continuous suffering at the hands of a violent spouse.[69] The husband claimed that he could not be found responsible for the harm embodied in the woman's death, due to a breach of the causal chain between his violent actions and his wife's "voluntary" decision to kill herself. His claim was declined by the court, which declared that the husband's violence was the main reason for the woman's suicidal act. At this stage, it is sufficient to pinpoint cases of this type as signifying the great potential embedded in feminist analysis of tort law to become a new tool accommodating the special needs of women suffering from gender-based violence.

This tort-liability mechanism allows the legal system a holistic treatment, in which it operates against femicide not only through the criminal system, which makes it punishable for the murderer, but also ensures that femicide can be looked at from a broader perspective of civil accountability. The fact that these two legal fields interact in harmonious and disharmonious manners is a reminder of the further exploration required to pave a path that will offer more holistic and coherent means to abolish femicide.

Having presented the revolution tort law underwent in recent decades to protect women's needs, this last chapter demonstrated its aptitude to become instrumental in compensating women and their heirs for femicide and holding accountable its enablers. Discussing the harmonious and disharmonious interplay between tort and criminal law regarding femicide, the chapter shed light on the advantages and pitfalls of the growing use of tort law in femicide cases. The next chapter, the last chapter of the book, offers concluding remarks, presenting a meta-crimino-legal overview of the phenomenon of femicide and its expansive aspects and ramifications.

References

Bender, L. (1993). Overview of feminist torts scholarship. *Cornell Law Review*, *78*, 575.

Bernstein, A. (2001). Restatement (third) of torts: General principles and the prescription of masculine order. *Vanderbilt Law Review*, *54*, 1367.

Bilsky, L. (2001). Cultural translation: The case of Israeli feminism. *Tel Aviv Law Review*, *25*, 523.

Bitton, Y. (2003). Feminine life-experience and the foreseeability of harm. *Mishpatim*, *33*, 585.

Bitton, Y. (2007). The price of tears. In D. Barak-Erez, Y. Bitton, D. Pugatch, & S. Yanisky-Ravid (Eds.), *Readings in law, gender and feminism*. Nevo.

Bitton, Y. (2008). Bringing power relations within the scope of negligence liability. *Mishpatim*, *37*, 145.

Bitton, Y. (2009). Public hierarchy – Private harm: Negotiating divorce within Judaism in (re)interpretations. In L. Peterson & L. Desdner (Eds.), *The shapes of justice in women's experience* (pp. 115–135). Cambridge Scholars.

69 HCJ 7832/00 Yaakobov v. The State of Israel, 56(2) PD 534 [2002] (Isr.). The transformative element embedded in the case analysis the court provided is presented in Bitton, 2003.

Bitton, Y. (2013). Harm and punishment: The tortious-criminal systems' intersection in representing victims of sexual crimes. *Iyuney Mishpat*, *36*, 657.

Bitton, Y. (2014). Transformative feminist approach to tort law: Exposing, changing, expanding – The Israeli case. *Hastings Women's Law Journal*, *25*, 221.

Bitton, Y. (2016). Discriminatory religious practices, compensatory hu(wo)man rights laws: Suspensions and exclusions in remedying feminine suffering. *Seattle Journal of Social Change*, *14*(1), 1–60.

Bitton, Y., & Shavit, T. (2015). The differences between men's and women's monetary valuation of crime avoidance behavior. *Feminist Criminology*, *10*(2), 115–139.

Blackstone, W. (1765/1769). *Commentaries on the laws of England* [photo reprint 1979]. Clarendon Press.

Calabresi, G. (1970). *The costs of accidents: A legal and economic analysis*. Yale University Press.

Chamallas, M. (1998). Architecture of bias: Deep structures in tort law. *University of Pennsylvania Law Review*, *146*, 463.

Coffee, J. C., Jr. (1991). Does "unlawful" mean "criminal"? Reflections on the disappearing tort/crime distinction in American law. *Boston University Law Review*, *71*, 193.

Dayan, H. (2021). Sociocultural aspects of femicide – suicide: The case of Israel. *Journal of Interpersonal Violence*, *16*(4), 494–505.

Dotan, Y. (1999). Judicial rhetoric, government lawyers, and human rights: The case of the Israeli High Court of Justice during the Intifada. *Law & Society Review*, *33*(2), 319–363.

Finley, L. M. (1989). A break in the silence: Including women's issues in a torts course. *Yale Law Journal*, *1*(1), 41.

Fletcher, G. P. (2008). *Tort Liability for Human Rights Abuses*. Hurt Publishing.

Goldberg, J. C. P. (2003). Twentieth-century tort theory. *Georgetown Law Journal*, *90*, 513.

Goldberg, J. C. P., & Zipursky, B. (2010). Torts as wrongs. *Texas Law Review*, *88*, 917.

Gordon, M. T., & Riger, S. (1989). *The female fear: The social cost of rape*. University of Illinois Press.

Hackney, J. R., Jr. (1997). Law and neoclassical economics: Science, politics, and the reconfiguration of American tort law theory. *Law and History Review*, *15*(2), 275–322.

Hall, J. (1943). Interrelations of criminal law and torts. *Columbia Law Review*, *43*, 753.

Harper, D. W., & Voigt, L. (2007). Homicide followed by suicide: An integrated theoretical perspective. *Homicide Studies*, *11*(4), 295–318.

Heriot, G. (1996). An essay on the civil-criminal distinction with special reference to punitive damages. *Journal of Contemporary Legal Issues*, *7*, 43.

Holmes, O. W., Jr. (1881). *The common law*. Little, Brown & Co.

Horwitz, M. (1992). *The transformation of American law, 1870–1960: The crisis of the legal orthodoxy*. Oxford University Press.

Katz, L. (1996). A look at tort law with criminal law blinders. *Boston University Law Review*, *76*, 307.

Keren-Paz, T. (2007a). A feminist-distributive gaze over the duty of care of pregnant women: Ideology, symbolism and pragmatism. In D. Barak-Erez, Y. Bitton, D. Pugatch, & S. Yanisky-Ravid (Eds.), *Law, gender and feminism*. Nevo.

Keren-Paz, T. (2007b). *Torts, egalitarianism, and distributive justice*. Ashgate.
Koenig, T., & Rustad, M. (1998). "Crimtorts" as corporate just deserts. *University of Michigan Journal of Law Reform*, *31*, 289.
Kritzer, H. M. (1997). Contingency lawyers as gatekeepers in the civil justice system. *Judicature*, *81*, 22.
Madriz, E. (1997). *Nothing bad happens to good girls: Fear of crime in women's lives*. University of California Press.
Pratt, G. (2005). Abandoned women and spaces of the exception. *Antipode*, *37*, 1052.
Russell, D. E. H. (1975). *The politics of rape: The victim's perspective*. Stein and Day.
Shohetman, E. (2001). On the Crime of Interfering with Investigation. *Shaarey Mishpat Law Review*, *2*, 383.
Simons, K. W. (2008). The crime/tort distinction: Legal doctrine and normative perspectives. *Widener Law Journal*, *17*, 719.
Weinrib, E. J. (2012). *The idea of private law* (rev. ed.). Oxford University Press.

9 Femicide, a Crime of Distinctive Nature

Introduction

Femicide warrants academic research from myriad perspectives: Political, cultural, legal, geographical, racial, religious, economic and other relevant elements. This book, however, limited its scope of analysis to contemporary crimino-legal aspects, using Israel as a case study. Additionally, while acknowledging that femicide spans women's lives at various stages, this book focused on adult women, mainly regarding the subtype of intimate-partner femicide. Notwithstanding this rather limited scope of analyses of such a multifaceted, complex phenomenon, the interdisciplinary approach it entertains provides an innovative contribution to the understanding of femicide through a sophisticated and nuanced analytical mapping of adult femicide as a "crime of distinctive nature."

Identifying femicide as a "crime of distinctive nature" stems from both its criminological and legal traits. Criminology-wise, it intersects with criminal behaviors, and law-wise, it carries various legal implications that are not necessarily applicable to other crimes. This last chapter focuses on the quintessential characteristics of both fronts: First, using criminological tools, it establishes the peculiarity of femicide as overlapping with many other criminological behaviors and criminal acts; and second, it lays out primary legal mechanisms designed to answer the overarching implications of femicide as a "crime of distinctive nature."

Mapping Femicide's Multiple Criminological Intersections

Femicide is a crime of distinctive nature primarily on account of how it intersects with other criminological phenomena, as shown by various chapters in this book. The book's main chapters showcase how femicide crosses into no fewer than six other criminal acts. In Chapter 1, we demonstrated how femicide and homicide intersect; in Chapter 3, we discussed the way intimate-partner homicide intersects with femicide; in Chapter 4, we demonstrated how "honor" crimes intersect with femicide as shown by the phenomenon of "honor" femicide; in Chapter 5, we demonstrated how homicide–suicide acts intersect with femicide, as manifested in the phenomenon of femicide–suicide; and last, in Chapter 6, we

DOI: 10.4324/9781003333272-12

demonstrated how staged crimes intersect with femicide, as shown by the phenomenon of concealed femicide. Additional criminal intersections may exist too, such as attempted murder, etc., yet the six discussed herein are the main criminal intersections found in adult femicide in Israel. These multiple intersections, taken separately, are not new to the study of femicide, yet their exact contours and realms haven't been discussed in the holistic manner that renders femicide a crime of distinctive nature.

This last chapter aims to mark and delineate the contours of adult femicide's intersections with these six criminal phenomena, as a means to justify the demand to treat it as a distinctive crime, not only by virtue of its severity, but also by virtue of its complexity and singularity. In doing so, we describe the realms in which the various criminal phenomena intersect with adult femicide and identify the contours of each intersection. Namely, we delineate the intersecting criminal realms with femicide in each criminal phenomenon and identify in each intersection the realms falling outside the scope of the intersection with femicide, which therefore should be excluded from each respective overlapping, intersecting realm. We believe that such mapping is needed to better clarify femicide and how, from a criminological standpoint, it is a multifaceted phenomenon of an idiosyncratic nature, additional to its apparent gendered disposition.

First Intersection: Homicide

Femicide is part and parcel of the larger criminal phenomenon of homicide, where one or more person takes the life of another. Yet the two crimes should not be equated. Homicide and femicide intersect in the sense that both result in fatal casualties. However, the two phenomena divert in their gendered aspect. While homicidal crime is squarely situated in the male gender, femicide is distinctively outside of it, from a victimological vantage point. In other words, most homicides are carried out by men, and most homicide victims are men as well.[1] In femicide, contrary to homicide, women are targeted. Similarly to homicide, though, they are targeted mostly by male perpetrators. Indeed, the gendered criminological characteristic of femicide is in stark contrast to the worldwide homicide patterns in which male homicide victims outnumber female victims, normally comprising no more than 10% of global homicide victims.[2]

The clear gendered difference femicide bares, compared to homicide in terms of the identity of the parties involved, affects other aspects of these two crimes. Most homicides are committed by acquaintances and are executed in the public sphere. Femicide, instead, is situated in close proximity to the familial context, given that most perpetrators come from the victim women's nuclear- or extended-family circle. Accordingly, the killing often takes place in the private sphere of the victim's

1 UNODC, 2019(1): pp. 18, 23.
2 UNODC 2019(5): p. 21; UNODC 2019(2): p. 69.

home rather than in some public space or even private space of someone other than the victim's own home.[3] The similarity in the perpetrator's gender in both crimes is overtaken though by their victims' different gender, affecting their criminological characteristics. Homicide perpetrators generally tend to share common traits, such as: Problematic childhood, under-education, likelihood of unemployment, previous criminal convictions and a tendency to abuse alcohol and drugs.[4] Contrastingly, the typical profile of femicide killers differs: They are heterogeneous in age, often lack prior criminal records and have much greater representation among the middle classes than most killers.[5] Thus, overall, though seemingly belonging to the same criminological category, homicide and femicide have less in common than expected. The two phenomena share an overlap in their intersection only in relation to the fatal violence inflicted on the victim and the perpetrator's gender.

Second Intersection: Domestic Violence

An additional notable criminal phenomenon with which femicide intersects is domestic violence. Domestic violence is often treated in the broader perspective of violence against women, because most victims of domestic violence are women.[6] Thus, similar to femicide, the criminal phenomenon of domestic violence intersects in the common victim's gender. It also intersects with the gendered asymmetry characterizing femicide: It is rare for women to violently abuse men or kill them. Given that in most cases of domestic violence, the perpetrators are men and the victims are women, most domestic violence cases are, in fact, equivalent to gender-based domestic violence (G.B.D.V.), targeted at women.[7]

G.B.D.V. is not particularized and does not depend on any specific class, because it cuts across all strata and social groups.[8] G.B.D.V. toward women tends to include rape, repeated sexual offenses and severe physical injury, which is typically more hazardous than that caused by attacks committed by strangers.[9] The American Medical Association's Council on Scientific Affairs, for instance, reported that G.B.D.V. is more violent than attacks committed under other circumstances: Whereas approximately 50% of the attacks committed by strangers end in significant injury, the rate is as high as 80% for attacks perpetrated against intimate partners, resulting in real injury. These injuries also demonstrate a high rate of physical severity, including damage to internal organs and loss of consciousness.[10] Thus, G.B.D.V. intersects with femicide in the sense that they both

3 Campbell et al., 2003, 2007.
4 See Dobash et al., 2004: pp. 599–601.
5 Ben Ze'ev and Goussinsky, 2008: p. 90.
6 Siegel, 1996.
7 Farr, 2002; Koss et al., 1994; Websdale, 2003; Zorza, 1991.
8 MacKinnon, 2001: p. 717.
9 MacKinnon, 2001, pp. 744, 869; Siegel, 1996: p. 2173.
10 Siegel, 1996: p. 2173.

inflict severe – and at times fatal – violence on women.[11] G.B.D.V. and femicide also intersect regarding the common victim–perpetrator relationship, because as in femicide, the vast majority of G.B.D.V. is directed against women by their past or present partners.[12]

It is important to emphasize, however, that although in some cases femicide is the culmination of an existing pattern of G.B.D.V. toward the woman, femicide is, nevertheless, distinct from G.B.D.V. While G.B.D.V. is directed at a female partner with the aim of achieving control and dominance over her, femicide intends to bring about her ruin – and more specifically, her death.[13] Killing and violence in this specific context should thus be treated as separate phenomena due to the different motivations underlying the two behaviors. Violence toward women is a means of controlling her and the act serves as a display of power against her, while the femicide killer aims to achieve another purpose: The utter and complete destruction of the woman. This distinctiveness bares implications for myriad accounts. Understanding the boundaries of femicide vis-à-vis G.B.D.V. is important for obtaining a more precise assessment of each phenomenon's prevalence. Failed femicide attempts, for example, might easily be mistaken for severe G.B.D.V. cases. Similarly, cases of concealed femicide might escape criminal investigation, due to the lack of previous G.B.D.V. incidents between the intimate partner and the dead woman.

Third Intersection: Intimate-Partner Homicide

As revealed in Chapter 3, femicide intersects with intimate-partner homicide (I.P.H.). Both phenomena intersect by way of displaying lethal and fatal forms of violence. An additional realm of intersection relates to the typical identity of both the victim and the killer and to the typical killing scene. As in femicide, in most I.P.H. cases, the victim is the woman partner, and the killer is almost always her male intimate partner. Indeed, I.P.H. is estimated to account for the vast majority of femicide cases[14] and is distributed evenly throughout various racial and social strata.[15] They intersect also in the sense that the sociodemographic data on femicide killers and I.P.H. killers suggest that they are almost always "ordinary guys."[16]

However, despite their many intersections, femicide should not be equated with I.P.H. As demonstrated in our discussion of "honor" femicide in Chapter 4, femicide is not always an I.P.H. criminal phenomenon. In non-Western societies, femicide is often perpetrated by the woman's extended-family members, rather

11 Gillespie, 1989: pp. 59–60, 148–149; La Fond, 1982: pp. 276–277.

12 Browne, 1987: pp. 9–10; Siegel, 1996: p. 2172.

13 Ben Ze'ev and Goussinsky, 2008; Goussinsky and Yassour-Borochowitz, 2012.

14 Campbell et al., 2007: pp. 246–269; Serran and Firestone, 2004: pp. 1, 12; Smith and Zahn, 1998: pp. 156–157.

15 MacKinnon, 2001: p. 717.

16 Dobash et al., 2004.

than her former or current intimate partner. Furthermore, whereas in femicide, most killers are men and victims are women, in the I.P.H. phenomenon, women occasionally fill the role of perpetrators. In these cases, women kill men, in the homicidal phenomenon known as "battered women syndrome."[17] Such killings are delineated from femicide not only because of the different gender of the victim and perpetrator, but also because of the different motives and modus operandi in these killings, triggered by prolonged and severe domestic abuse the woman faced from the abuser she kills.[18] Thus, despite the substantial intersection, I.P.H. and femicide are delineated by femicide killings in non-Western societies and battered-woman-syndrome I.P.H.

Fourth Intersection: Homicide–Suicide

As noted in Chapter 5, femicide and homicide–suicide (H.S.) intersect in the sense that all typologies of H.S. include the category of femicide–suicide as the primary phenomenon subtype, accounting for most H.S. events.[19] An additional realm of intersection of the two phenomena relates to the nature of the relationship between the perpetrator and victim, because as in femicide, H.S. perpetrators are predominantly the victim's current or former intimate partner.[20]

The similarities and intersections of femicide and H.S. led to a scholarly tendency to perceive them as a unified homicidal phenomenon.[21] Some scholars, for example, argued that H.S. is more similar to suicide than cases that only involve homicide, viewing it as a kind of "extended suicide."[22] Furthermore, although femicide commonly involves the killing of a female intimate partner, many other H.S. forms involve non-female victims, such as in cases of filicide (killing of children by their parents) and familicide (killing of the family by the perpetrator). Apart from these apparent differences, the two phenomena differ also in the homicide motives. While most femicide cases are post-separation killings of the female intimate partner, intended not to allow her freedom as an independent autonomous person, many H.S. cases derive from diverse emotions. Consider, for example, H.S. cases stemming from interpersonal conflict, altruism (merciful action), extreme mental abnormality, accidental/mistaken killing, and acts of terror.[23] Moreover, although femicide usually targets a specific particular victim, H.S. includes other homicidal forms that may target multiple victims, such as

17 Browne, 2008; Walker, 1985.
18 Dayan, 2017, 2018; Walker, 1985.
19 Berman, 1996: p. 343; Liem, 2010: p. 158; Liem et al., 2011: p. 72; Marzuk et al., 1992: p. 3180; Wallace, 1986: pp. 180, 182.
20 Banks et al., 2008: p. 1070, 1075; Flynn et al., 2009: p. 313; Harper and Voigt, 2007: p. 312; Liem, 2010: p. 156; Liem et al., 2011: p. 72; Milroy, 1995: p. 119; Scott, 2009: pp. 372–373; Saleva et al., 2007: p. 206; Warren et al., 2010: p. 1595.
21 Harper and Voigt, 2007: p. 299; Milroy, 1995: p. 64.
22 Rosenbaum, 1990: pp. 1036–1039; Van Wormer, 1999: pp. 361, 364–365.
23 Wallace, 1986: pp. 183–184.

cases of public-killing-spree-suicide for reasons of revenge.[24] Thus, overall, the intersection of femicide and H.S. seems to be limited to the particular H.S. subtype, which of intimate-partner H.S., wherein the victim is the woman and the motivation for killing her is to prevent her from realizing her selfhood.

Fifth Intersection: "Honor" Crimes

As demonstrated in Chapter 4, femicide and "honor" crimes (H.C.) intersect. The two phenomena resemble each other in the sense that both are perpetrated in the familial arena and the perpetrators are often the victim's male family members. They also share similarity in the sense that the victims tend to be women, rather than men. Femicide's homogenous nature changes, though, where key characteristics of femicide under circumstance of H.C. become heterogeneous in relation to their familial, collective and "honor"-related nature.[25] "Honor" femicide, for example, may be perpetrated by more than one perpetrator, whereas femicide is normally committed by sole actors. The heterogeneous nature of femicide is also manifested in the collective nature of "honor" femicide, in the sense that perpetrators often belong to the extended family, whereas common femicide perpetrators are traditionally the victim's former or current intimate partner.

The prevalence of the notion of "honor" in some of the femicide cases, even if this part alone is taken as the subtype of reference, does not render the two phenomena similar. First and foremost, H.C. cases are not gender-specific, although women are their predominant victims. H.C. may target a wide range of family members, male included.[26] Furthermore, H.C. do not necessarily involve homicides. Acts of "honor" killings in general, and "honor" femicide in particular, represent only a small portion of the total cases of H.C. Abu Rabia lamented the fact that a host of statistics refer to women killed in the name of family "honor," yet no statistics exist that refer to other forms of honor crimes perpetrated against women who were allegedly engaged in what is perceived as promiscuous sexual behavior. According to Abu Rabia, the possibility of finding a nonfatal resolution will normally surpass the killing of the woman, pushing most H.C. cases outside the homicidal scope, as in the case of forcing a woman to marry her rapist, etc. At the same time, many women might be killed for reasons other than "honor," while their death is presented under the guise of "honor."[27] Consequently, "honor" killings in general and "honor" femicide in particular are the exception to the social rules of "honor."[28] This realization must serve to tell one phenomenon from the other and fight them separately.

24 Harper and Voigt, 2007: p. 307.
25 Abu-Odeh, 1997; Chesler, 2010.
26 Kressel et al., 1981: pp. 145–146.
27 Abu Rabia, 2011: p. 36; Baxter, 2007: p. 753; Dodd, 1973: p. 43; Hasan, 2002: p. 4; Kulwicky, 2002: p. 85.
28 Abu Rabia, 2011: p. 43.

Sixth Intersection: Staged Crimes

The last criminological phenomenon with which femicide intersects, as demonstrated in Chapter 6, is staged crimes (S.C.), namely, crimes where the perpetrator changes or alters a crime scene. Staging is exercised through the taking of precautionary actions by the perpetrator by intentionally moving, adding or taking away items of physical or forensic evidence in an attempt to avoid detection and prosecution and focusing the investigation away from himself.[29] In particular, as elaborated in Chapter 6, staging behaviors are specific types of acts intended to suggest an alternative scenario to the death that had occurred.[30] The two phenomena intersect particularly in homicide cases, because S.C. homicide victims and perpetrators are usually involved in a domestic relationship of an intimate nature. As indicated, most staged-homicide victims are women and most perpetrators are men. Furthermore, S.C. killings share commonalities with femicide in that they are often carried out at the victim's home, commonly against the backdrop of relationship dissolution.[31] However, the shared realm of intersection is only partial. To begin with, and in stark contrast to femicide, the most prevalent incarnation of S.C. are cases of fraud committed to gain monetary benefits rather than homicides. As such, S.C. victims do not tend to be of female gender or have an intimate relationship with the perpetrator, but rather nonfamilial individuals or, more likely, insurance companies. Only a relatively small share of S.C. are of a homicidal nature. Thus, despite their intersection, the two phenomena should be delineated.

Femicide: A (Criminological) Crime of Distinctive Nature

The myriad realms of intersections, overlaps and similarities of femicide with other criminological phenomena are unprecedented and render them as integrative as they are quintessential. The following graphic presentation of the various realms of intersection and their resulting delineating contours showcase its peculiar nature as a "homicide subtype" (figure 9.1 below). This graphic model also aims to depict the relative size of each intersection, to enable better understanding of their effect over femicide. Notice, for example, how most S.C. are excluded from femicide, because they are nonfatal, nonfamilial and gender-random. Contrastingly, the size of the intersection between I.P.H. and femicide is relatively larger, given that most I.P.H. cases are also femicide cases, targeting the woman intimate partner as their victims.

Some reservations must be made to the graphic model's architecture, all resulting from the need to maintain its analytical clarity. Firstly, the mapping of

29 Chancellor and Graham, 2014, 2017: p. 3.

30 Bitton and Dayan, 2019.

31 Bitton and Dayan, 2019; Eke, 2007; Ferguson, 2015; Hazelwood and Napier, 2004; Keppel and Weis, 2004; Petherick and Ferguson, 2015; Pettler, 2016.

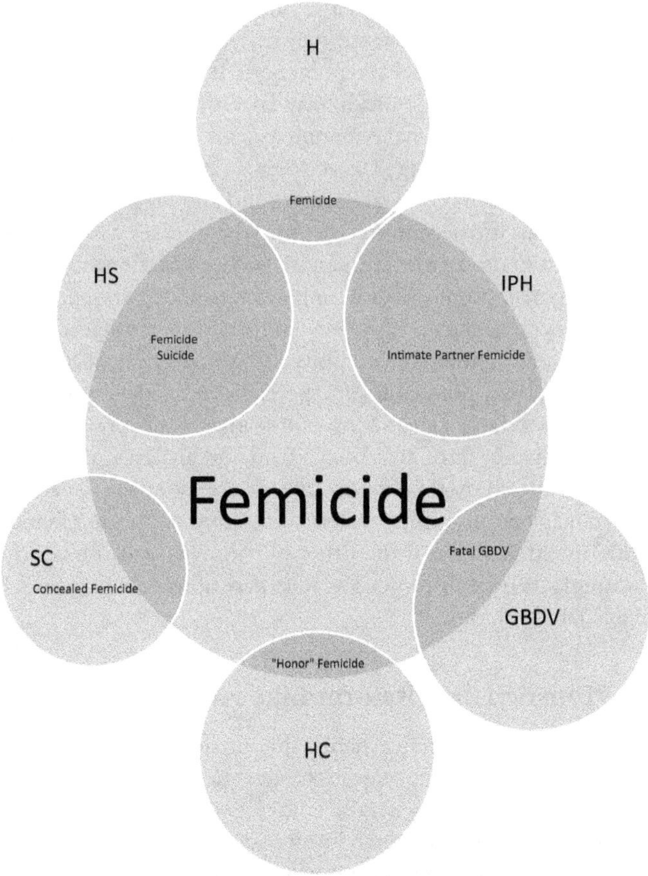

Figure 9.1 The Intersections of Femicide and Other Crimes.

Source: GBDV = gender-based domestic violence; H = homicide; HC = "honor" crimes; HS = homicide–suicide; IPH = intimate-partner homicide; SC = staged crimes.

femicide's various intersections somewhat simplifies the nature of other possible intersections among the six criminal phenomena. The model presents the various intersecting criminal phenomena as separate from one another, although they may possibly intersect in reality. For example, H.C. may intersect with G.B.D.V. in cases of nonfatal H.C. executed through domestic violence; likewise, G.B.D.V. may intersect with I.P.H. in cases wherein the battered woman kills her abusive intimate partner, and may intersect with S.C., in cases whereby the killing of a woman is camouflaged as an accident or suicide. However, in our model, we focused only on femicide's intersections with these phenomena, as our analysis indicates how overarching they are due to the specific nature of femicide.

Another complexity excluded from our graphic model for analytical clarity is the fact that the various intersections are limited in the presentation to bilateral interaction with femicide in the sense that each presents convergence between femicide and one other criminal phenomenon. In reality, however, as demonstrated throughout the book, femicide may encompass multilateral intersections with multiple concurrent criminal phenomena. For example, femicide may intersect with S.C. in cases camouflaged as accidental deaths,[32] while also intersecting with H.C. when the victim is of Arab background and killed for alleged breach of family "honor." It can further intersect with I.P.H. in cases wherein the perpetrator who kills his intimate-partner woman is also her agnatic family member.

The analytic, spatial, criminological, integrative model presented here for the first time demonstrates femicide's all-encompassing, multifaceted heterogenic nature. Ultimately, its various intersections with other criminal phenomena form and construct a distinct homicide subtype characterized first and foremost by one common denominator: The killing of a woman. Thus, reiterating our point of departure in Chapter 1 of this book, femicide analyses, crimino-legal ones included, cannot but study this homicide with a gender-sensitive framework of analysis. Nor can any public policy makers committed to fighting femicide assume that methods aimed at fighting the other phenomena will suffice to abolish it. Femicide warrants its own antidote. The next part of this chapter responds to this need from a legal standpoint.

Femicide: Holistic Legal Reform Like No Other

Femicide is a crime of distinctive nature by virtue of the need to holistically address its overarching legal implications no less than by virtue of its criminological complexities. Being an idiosyncratic crime, it warrants specific legal rules and tools which must be tailored to match its myriad peculiarities, including: Identifying the risk factors for femicide victimization and perpetration to effectively prevent it, inter alia, through a matching penalty approach; designing investigative tools to ensure effective enforcement; attending to needs and necessities of the victim's family; and more. Against the backdrop of these overarching peculiarities, the law's dull set of tools to address femicide are primarily fractured, fragmented and decontextualized, gender-wise. This discrepancy renders it imperative to set out the guidelines for a legal reform that will utilize rudimentary crimino-legal accounts and analysis to effectuate the transformation required to fight femicide effectively and to address its detrimental results more fairly. The second part of this chapter is designed to reconstruct the legal proposition of femicide to achieve this goal.

Being a crime of distinctive nature, femicide should be legally addressed accordingly. Yet, an overview of femicide-related legislation reveals that this approach is not prevalent. Rather, femicide is treated as if it were any other crime that the

32 Dayan, 2022.

legal system addresses according to the crime's characteristics and its particular circumstance. Reviewing the Israeli legal system throughout this book exposes its utter obliviousness toward femicide's peculiarities, as is common in most legal systems. Although this seemingly neutral stance aligns with the law's natural adherence to broad applicability – namely, that murder is murder, regardless of its characteristics – the law's ability to treat a crime differently due to its distinctive social importance is not unprecedented. Legal systems entertain an array of apparatuses designed to illuminate the severity of crimes, among these: Defining the crime as particularly heinous so as to name it a "hate crime"; aggravating the legal response toward its perpetrators; allocating specific legal powers to authorities fighting it; altering existing legal doctrines to accommodate a more nuanced yet structured struggle against it, etc. Given the special status of femicide as a crime of distinctive nature, these legal tools should be made available and restructure the legal battlefield over women's right to live.

First Tool: Defining Femicide as Hate Crime

One of the main tools to acknowledge the socially destructive nature and overarching negative effects of a crime is to identify it as a hate crime. This limited category of crimes is narrowly designated to denounce a crime motivated by hate of the person against whom the crime is perpetrated, due not only to that person's personal traits, but also to their group-based association. Although femicide meets the requirements of this widely accepted definition of hate crimes, crimes motivated by gender hatred were initially not included in most antibias crime legislation, despite relentless feminist efforts.[33] With the advent of the millennium, these decade-long efforts finally proved fruitful, and many states – in the United States, for instance – began incorporating gender-biased motivated violence in their hate-crime bills. This hopeful development was soon shattered by reality. While feminists hailed the commendable achievement of having femicide formally acknowledged as a hate crime, femicide cases failed to enjoy these statutes' application and they soon proved to be no more than empty shells.[34] Massachusetts' hate-crime statute, for instance, conditions the inclusion of the statute in an indictment against a femicide perpetrator upon two requirements: First, that the perpetrator used epithets uttered during the commission of the crime that denigrate women as a class, and second, that at least two restraining orders were filed against the perpetrator by two people for previous hate crimes he allegedly committed. These two requirements barely allowed any utilization of this statute for the benefit of women victims of gender-based violence in Massachusetts, as it excluded from its scope of application even cases of mass shootings of women, rapes by strangers, etc. Applying these criteria to femicide by an intimate partner, the fit seems to be even less plausible. Notwithstanding its rigidity and rare

33 Copeland and Wolfe, 1991.
34 McPhail, 2002.

applicability, Massachusetts' legal system endeavors to allow some femicide cases the privilege of being termed hate crime. Other legal systems, such as Israel, failed to provide even this formal façade of apparent importance, excluding gender altogether as basis for identifying a crime as motivated by hate.[35]

Legally defining a criminological phenomenon "hate crime" yields myriad implications – financial, symbolic and more – that benefit the fight against the phenomenon and render the law more effective and uncompromising in ultimately decreasing if not abolishing it. This labeling creates a chain of effects primarily advantaging the crime's victims: First and foremost, it mandates the designation of state financial resources required to fight against the phenomenon; it normally requires mandatory structured data collection, which is particularly meager in femicide cases; mandatory data collection, in turn, encourages consciousness raising; which motivates public authorities to better monitor and control the phenomenon, using measurable means. Public awareness and data-collection actions naturally motivate professional exploration of the hate crime's risk factors and their analyses. Analytically reviewed data allows developing tools to identify risk factors, prevent their realization and so on. Additionally, on the penal front, given that hate crime entails mandatory punishments, often tripling the penalty set by the original legal provision, the materialistic effects are aggregated in terms of deterrence and prevention.

Hate crimes also have symbolic bearings by conferring virtues on their victims, portraying them as completely innocent and blameless. Premised on the notion of a public problem and not a private one, these crimes manifest how the hate held by one group against another is realized in a specific criminal act, in a random, almost depersonalized manner. Under this guise, the specific perpetrator and victims are private merely in the sense that they serve the realization of some public problem, larger than their own selves. The victims, more specifically, are also freed of any judgement of their choices or behaviors, given the depersonalization they undergo at the hands of the perpetrator. The judgement process and public condemnation are channeled toward the structural harms the crime inflicts on society, rather than on the specific parties involved in it.

Femicide seems to stand in sharp contrast to the reasoning underlying the legal constellation offered by hate crime. Socially and criminologically, it is still perceived as a private account of criminality. The growing acknowledgment in its gendered structure and social harm has no bearing on its conventional association with the "private" realm of living as well as with interpersonal interactions. Namely, femicide, at best, is seen as "the problem" in and of itself, rather than a signifier of a larger social problem of unjust gendered power relations. For the most part, it reflects men's dominance over women in the family, rather than patriarchy as a whole. Moreover, patriarchy itself is not targeted as a social harm and problem warranting categorical abolishment the way racism does, for example. This is one of the reasons all hate crimes encompass race-based criminal acts,

35 Sec. 144(f), Israeli Criminal Code, 1977.

while only part of them similarly attend to gender-based criminal acts. These wrongly held conventions distance intimate-partner femicide from being recognized by legal systems as a hate crime in the first place and from motivating prosecutors to apply hate-crime charges on them in legal systems that do include gender bias as a basis for such recognition.

To sum up, labeling intimate-partner femicide as a hate crime could and should be applied to all legal systems entertaining this mechanism. Hate crimes are designed to more effectively fight an intolerable systemic social phenomenon of which the crime is merely its punishable incarnation. They allow the harnessing of the criminal-law system for the betterment of a group compelled to sustain the harms inflicted upon it by individuals belonging to the dominant group. Notwithstanding the aptitude of femicide to hate crime's proposition, the challenges of thus labeling femicide are apparent either in the legislative or the prosecutorial stages. Moreover, even if realized, identifying intimate-partner femicide as a hate crime would not suffice to redress the overarching effects and harms materializing outside the realm of the criminal affair.

Second Tool: Legal Specification of Femicide: By Definition

Legal reforms are the main mechanism used by legislatures to accommodate new perceptions as to the nature of crimes. Affected by feminist legal critique, criminal law gradually became more attentive to the life experiences of women as different from that of men and as having been overlooked by myriad legal doctrines underlying crimes that are quintessential to women's lives. Our analyses indicate the need for a more nuanced legal structure treatment that would prevent women from being unequally affected by what are only seemingly neutral legal rules. As a result, the criminal system has questioned some of its most rudimentary doctrines and its general ostensibly neutral approach of "one (criminal) rule fits all." Instead it underwent reforms designating specific provisions to encompass the scope of these gendered life-experience-based differences. In some cases, it did so by newly naming a socially tolerated behavior a crime – such as in the case of sexual harassment. In others, it omitted prerequisites for establishing guilt that stood in sharp discrepancy with women's experiences – such as in the case of rape and its notorious prerequisite that a woman fight back her rapist in order to establish that the intercourse was forced on her against her will. These legal reforms, though driven by women's outcry and designed to adapt to women's life experience, adhered nevertheless to the law's gender-neutral façade, where applicable. An example of such legal reform is the special criminal mechanisms set to meet the need to contextualize homicide executed by women who kill their abusers. Following feminist critique of the irrelevance of self-defense preconditions as the only defense for women accused of homicide of their abusive men, the law in some states has been reformed to judge these women more fairly.[36] In Israel, for

36 Dayan, 2017.

instance, the 2019 criminal-law reform provides that a person who kills another person due to substantial mental distress following persistent extreme abuse can enjoy a lesser mandatory punishment.[37] Regardless of how fair such reforms are to women, this legislative tool can also serve to differentiate femicide from other crimes and treat it in a more nuanced and hence more effective manner.[38]

Naming the gendered phenomenon to which the reformed provision applies is of crucial effect due to its pivotal role in creating the chain of advantaging effects to the victims – in both the legal and the policy making fronts, as previously elaborated. Moreover, as opposed to hate crimes, wherein the gendered basis of the harm is what surfaces as a basis for aggregation, naming femicide as such draws focus to this specific phenomenon, allowing it the attention it deserves.[39] Despite its clear advantages, such legal specification of femicide is barely exercised. Following the specification of femicide in 1994 by the Inter-American Convention on the Prevention, Punishment and Eradication of Violence Against Women, some Latin American states were inspired to apply such law reforms. The Dominican Republic was one of the first states to adopt as early as the late 1990s a specific gender-based legal recognition of homicide, called "feminicide."[40] In Chile, a bill was brought to congress classifying femicide as a subcategory of parricide, with the stiffest sentences allowable, and a legal definition of this crime reflecting its gender-related reasons. It was mainly public pressure that allowed it to be enacted.[41] With time, other Latin American and Caribbean states joined in, and as many as 18 countries have thus far specified "feminicide" as a crime of a unique domain.[42] Other states have thus model cases to look up to.

Third Tool: Legal Specification of Femicide: By Aggravation

A more covert version of the overt naming of femicide as such would be the treatment of femicide as an aggravation of general homicide rules. This version is more common worldwide, being easier to apply since it simply mandates considering circumstances characterizing femicide – such as the killing of a spouse – in aggravating the punishment calculus. Israel, too, has adopted this aggravation model in its recent criminal-law reform, stipulating that the killing of a spouse is an aggravating circumstance of homicide, commanding mandatory life sentence for the defendant.[43] On its face, this aggravation rightfully uses neutral language. The killing of a spouse, be it male or female, is equally condemnable in terms of the social disgust from the betrayal of trust between spouses. However, given the fact that femicide alone is known to be significantly more prevalent than the

37 Sec. 301B(a), Israel Penal Code, 1977.
38 Dayan 2018.
39 Felstiner et al., 1980; MacKinnon, 1979.
40 María Jesús, 2009.
41 Bravo, 2009.
42 See the table of states specified by the United Nations Office on Drugs and Crimes, 2019.
43 Sec. 301A (a)(6), Israel Penal Code, 1977.

killing of a man by his female spouse, and given that most victims of domestic abuse are women killed by their male spouses, the wisdom in utilizing gender-neutral language is questionable at best. Moreover, many of the few women who kill their male spouses do it following persistent abuse, and thus present a very contextualized killing, rarely found in opposite cases. Refraining from using gendered language renders the law oblivious to this gendered atrocity and, consequentially, to women's suffering. In this regard, it is worth noting that some states, such as Belgium and Canada, have added the circumstance of hate, bias or discrimination in relation to the victim's sex as an aggravating factor, rebutting any gender neutrality of this kind.[44] Besides the symbolic negative effect it bestows on women,[45] the law's disregard of women's disproportionate suffering as a result of spousal killing carries more detrimental materialistic effect.

A careful inquiry into the reform's allegedly neutral language reveals its bias. It does not revolve around the peculiarities of femicide nor does it acknowledge its typical risk factors. For instance, it conditions the aggravated conviction with proving a set of elements, stipulating: "The victim is the defendant's spouse, and the killing followed a systematic or persistent physical or mental abuse of the spouse by the defendant". These elements, as shown repeatedly in this book, are not necessarily associated with intimate-partner femicide. Preconditioning the invocation of this aggravated conviction clause with physical or mental abuse systematically inflicted on the spouse prior to the killing renders it inapplicable to many intimate-partner femicide cases, significantly lowering its ability to cover a more varied reality of femicide cases and decreasing its relevance to fighting it. Going back to risk factors for femicide, indeed, the majority of intimate-partner homicides involve physical abuse of the woman by the man prior to the murder. However, it does not necessarily indicate that the abuse was "systematic" nor "persistent," as the clause requires. Moreover, the law seems to omit other factors that characterize intimate-partner femicide, regardless of the precondition enumerated by it. Controlling behavior, such as stalking, prior domestic abuse of a former spouse, refusal to undergo abortion, child abuse and the perpetrator's suicidality are all such risk factors. In some cases, the point of greatest risk of violence is when victims decide to leave their partner.[46] Notice that not all these factors are necessarily correlated to prior, let alone systemic and persistent, abuse.[47]

The reform, therefore, seems to reflect meager understanding of risk factors for femicide victimhood and perpetration, which is likely to limit its ability to be effectively applied. According to its reason, a man who killed his wife after she threatened to leave him will be punished as a femicide killer only if he has abused her before, although by killing her, he executes his dominance over her in the same manner he does if he kills her "only" because she decided to leave him.

44 United Nations Office on Drugs and Crimes, 2019: p. 48.
45 Dayan, 2014.
46 Fleury et al., 2000.
47 Campbell et al., 2000.

What is the reason for this mistreatment of femicide under a newly shaped legal reform where femicide persists to exist? It may be hypothesized that the use of seemingly neutral language led to that poor result or vice versa, that disregard of femicide as a gendered phenomenon led to this neutral promulgation. Be the reason as it may, women pay the price for this legal approach. Naming a phenomenon as such can instead facilitate a more nuanced premise on which the legal treatment of femicide will be administered. Using a more overt legal mechanism to fight femicide as its sole target can have the required corrective effect on the system.

Fourth Tool: Reconsidering Existing Legal Rules, Institutions and Doctrines

All crimes should be treated by the criminal legal system alike, with the same diligence and dedication as dictated by their severity and prevalence, and femicide is no different. However, protocols for the treatment of crimes by the criminal legal system reflect the preoccupation of criminals as related to some degree of preexisting criminal patterns. Given the peculiarity of femicide, however, employing existing crimino-legal protocols of murder may result in blindness to crimes and eventually to justice. As shown throughout the book, femicide should be looked at with a gendered lens, in a manner affecting basic perceptions as to its components and essence as a crime. This, in return, warrants reconsideration of existing legal rules and doctrines to incorporate more nuanced crimino-legal readings of femicide cases.

An example for such reconceptualization is demonstrated in the case of concealed femicide. Our analysis demonstrates how the usual protocol of identifying suspicious death, which automatically ignites a thorough investigation of the death, is much less effective in femicide. Being a crime of strong "domestic" nature, coupled with the opportunity to stage it uninterruptedly, renders it more susceptible to becoming concealed and unrevealed. It simply is a crime that lacks the façade of a classic homicide. Accordingly, our analysis calls for the restructuring of investigation protocol set to establish "suspicion" in cases of possible femicide. These cases include circumstances wherein a woman is found dead at her home as either: Prematurely dead, when in apparent good health; situated in a suicidal death scene; known to have been involved in separation from her intimate partner; in a relationship with an intimate partner involved with previous domestic violence; or found dead by her current or previous intimate partner.

Upon these circumstances, we have suggested to adopt a few investigative tools that will provide prosecutorial authorities with the power needed to ensure such cases do not remain unattended or even only loosely investigated. In Victoria, for example, a law reform simply recommended that homicide-investigation squads be trained to notice the close association between domestic homicides and family violence.[48] It is imperative, as we further suggest, to enhance investigative

48 Victorian Law Reform Commission, 2004: p. 257.

institutions designed to reveal concealment of homicide, specifically in women's-suspicious-death cases, which can be mistakenly camouflaged as natural or non-criminal deaths. Institutionalizing a coroner in the legal system reflects society's obligation to its members to clear any suspicion that a person's death was affected through some form of crime. Having similar medical-examiner systems is particularly important to women, because they are excellent resources for identifying female homicide victims, because they test all death cases, ensuring the inclusion of cases not pursued by the criminal-justice system. The North Carolina Medical Examiner System, for example, routinely identifies about 12% more homicides than the State Bureau of Investigation.[49] Applying a mandatory autopsy to all these suspicious deaths, regardless of the spouse's consent, would support the ability to reveal the true criminal nature of the death. Postmortem criminal inquests will ensure investigations are not discontinued in cases of an undetermined medical cause of death, wherein the death scene as it appears is ruled out by the postmortem medical examination, and wherein circumstantial nonmedical evidence points to possibly suspicious aspects related to the death. And last, we suggest establishing fatality review boards empowered with the ability to take a panoramic view of certain types of women's deaths, with the aim of monitoring and investigating their frequency and patterns.[50]

Alongside the reconsideration of legal institutions, as presented here, the criminal legal system must reevaluate the effect of its traditional conceptions of legal doctrines on femicide. Some doctrines, seemingly neutral, such as the evaluation of circumstantial evidence, have to be reconsidered vis-à-vis femicide and put on the same ground as that assigned to direct ones, as some reforms suggested.[51] As shown in our analysis of concealed femicide, prosecutorial and judiciary officials tend to invoke the use of this evidence to rationalize convictions of intimate partners in femicide. Their invocation, nonetheless, renders the conviction less powerful than if based on direct evidence. To rebut such delegitimization of the verdict, judges must use their rhetorical and justificatory tools more effectively and with the aim of not allowing such de-legitimacy to thrive.

The Meta-Tool: Maintaining a Holistic Approach

Important and pivotal to doing justice as they are, the tools introduced above would not address the peculiarity of femicide unless they do it in a holistic fashion. As the chapters concerning secondary victims and tort claims have shown, the harms of femicide are widespread and overarching. In contrast to common perceptions of homicide as relevant mainly to its direct victim and as involving primarily criminal matters, femicide expands beyond the boundaries of the individual victim and the realm of criminal law. Femicide, particularly when

49 Winyomo, 2009: p. 14.

50 Bitton and Dayan, 2019.

51 Victorian Law Reform Commission, 2004.

perpetrated by the victim's spouse, normally affects broader family cycles. It does not confine itself to the regular devastating effect homicide has on the victim's relatives. Pertaining more closely to family ties and relationships, such as when the father kills the child's mother and then asks for visitation or custodial rights while the child is under the supervision of the murdered woman's parents, it has lingering effects on the involved parties' close surrounding. This specific trait of secondary victimhood in femicide cases furthers the legal entangles and encounters that regular homicide cases normally yield. With femicide, the legal affairs reflect the crime's entailments, spanning family matters, inheritance and visitation questions, victims' rights and tort compensation claims. A more effective, just and humane legal approach to these ordeals warrants attending to these traits collectively, in a holistic framework. Here, as opposed to the focus on criminal systems' need to adapt to the severe peculiarity of femicide, law reforms are less widespread but not completely absent. Countries have started to take a tough stance on femicide perpetrators' reclaiming of custody rights and contacting their children once they are out of prison. Argentina, for example, adopted a law in 2017 removing parental authority from such perpetrators. A year later, Italy adopted a similar law protecting minors orphaned by domestic violence, giving priority to family members and relatives other than the father as guardians and availing them to change their family name. To facilitate its implementation, the new reform additionally provides the orphans with legal aid to manage their femicide-related grievances and render them eligible for state-funded psychological assistance.[52] It is our hope and recommendation that other similar law reforms follow.

The holistic approach to femicide should reach beyond the scope of promulgating a legal reform that uses the correct language. Rather, it should expand to the training of investigative officials alongside legal and judicial agents on the peculiarities of femicide and the nuanced treatment they require. These officials also need to change their traditional and well-entrenched misconceptions leading to engagement with ineffective practices, through training processes. No law reform will materialize without the transforming of the minds of those executing it. Consequently, law reforms must include in their transformation not only the law's alternation but also the agents of change they inspire to impact. The following recommendation from the Victorian Law Reform Commission exhibits that:[53]

> 35. Bodies which offer continuing professional development or judicial education, including Victoria Legal Aid, the Law Institute of Victoria, the Office of Public Prosecutions, the Victorian Bar and the Judicial College of Victoria should include sessions on family violence.

52 United Nations Office on Drugs and Crimes, 2019: p. 49.
53 Victorian Law Reform Commission, 2004: p. 258.

36. Professional legal education sessions on family violence should aim to assist judges and lawyers practicing in criminal law to understand the nature of family violence and could include discussion of issues such as:

common myths and misconceptions about family violence;

the nature and dynamics of abusive relationships.

It is imperative that the multifaceted complexity of femicide be recognized by the law through adopting a holistic approach toward it. While some law reforms pledged to apply such an approach, even they seem to interpret this notion narrowly, by not including all – or at least most – relevant legal implications of femicide under one legal reform's roof. The Victorian Law Reform concerning domestic violence, often hailed as a model reform openly committed to achieving "significant and holistic cultural change," has done so only in one, albeit important, field: Family law. As the analyses throughout this book suggest, to effectively counter a crime of distinctive nature, a legal reform like no other is in need, one that will span criminal law, family law, tort law and evidence law.

Summary

The crime of femicide is a distinctive crime that tells a very specific story about our society. It doesn't simply reflect, as all homicide cases do, that hatred and evil are still widespread within human nature. Rather, it reflects the realization that hatred and evil are not affecting society randomly, neither do they harm people similarly. Being "a crime of distinctive nature," femicide reflects the vulnerability of women to male dominance and its heinous lethal consequences. It further signifies the multifaceted harmful impact femicide inflicts on its surrounding, which calls for the promulgation of a legal reform that will address these peculiar harms appropriately. Our analyses throughout the book bring to the fore unique and newly introduced recommendations and proposals for public policy intended to prevent femicide and promote actions the state should take to fight femicide and restore justice to its victims using crimino-legal tools. We believe adopting them will save women's lives and dignity in Israel and elsewhere.

References

Abu-Odeh, L. (1997). Comparatively speaking: The 'honor' of the 'East' and the 'passion' of the 'West'. *Utah Law Review*, 287–307.

Abu Rabia, A. (2011). Family "honor" killings: Between custom and state law. *The Open Psychology Journal, 4*, 34–44.

Banks, L., Crandall, C., Sklar, D., & Bauer, M. (2008). A comparison of intimate partner homicide to intimate partner homicide-suicide, one hundred and twenty-four New Mexico cases. *Violence Against Women, 14*, 1065–1078.

Baxter, D. (2007). 'Honour Thy Sister': Selfhood, gender and agency in Palestinian culture. *Anthropological Quarterly, 80*(3), 737–775.

Ben Ze'ev, A., & Goussinsky, R. (2008). In the name of love: Romantic ideology and its victims. Oxford University Press.

Berman, A. (1996). Dyadic death: A typology. *Suicide and Life-Threatening Behavior, 26*, 342–350.

Bitton, Y., & Dayan, H. (2019). 'The perfect murder': An exploratory study of staged murder scenes and concealed femicide. *The British Journal of Criminology, 59*(5), 1054–1075.

Bravo, S. R. (2009). Femicide in Chile. In *Strengthening understanding of femicide.* World Health Organization.

Browne, A. (1987). *When Battered Women* Kill. New York: Free Press

Browne, A. (2008). *When battered women kill.* Simon and Schuster.

Campbell, J. C., Glass, N., & Sharps, P. W. (2000). Risk assessment for intimate partner violence. In G. F. Pinard & L. Pagani (Eds.), *Clinical assessment of dangerousness: Empirical contributions* (pp. 136–157). Cambridge University Press.

Campbell, J. C., Glass, N., Sharps, P. W., Laughon, K., & Bloom, T. (2007). Intimate partner homicide: Review and implications of research and policy. *Trauma, Violence, and Abuse, 8*(3), 246–269.

Campbell, J. C., Webster, D., Koziol-McLain, J., Block, C., Campbell, D., Curry, M. A., & Sharps, P. (2003). Risk factors for femicide in abusive relationships: Results from a multisite case control study. *American Journal of Public Health, 93*(7), 1089–1097.

Chancellor, A. S., & Graham, G. D. (2014). Staged crime scenes: Crime scene clues to suspect misdirection of the investigation. *Investigative Sciences Journal, 6*(1), 19–35.

Chancellor, A. S., & Graham, G. D. (2017). *Crime scene staging: Investigating suspect misdirection of the crime scene.* Charles C Thomas.

Chesler, P. (2010). Worldwide trends in "honor" killings. *Middle East Quarterly*, 3–11.

Cooper, M., & Eaves, D. (1996). Suicide following homicide in the family. *Violence and Victims, 11*(2), 99–112.

Copeland, L., & Wolfe, L. R. (1991). *Violence against women as bias motivated hate crime: Defining the issues.* Center for Women Policy Studies.

Dayan, H. (2014). Mine or dead: Femicide and a bill to amend Article 301 of the Israeli Penal Code. *Hukim, 6*, 205–232.

Dayan, H. (2017). 'To kill or not to kill': (When) that is the question? A legislative treatise on battered Israeli women facing a dead-end road. *William and Mary Journal of Women and Law, 23*(2), 219–247.

Dayan, H (2018). *Femicide and the law: American criminal doctrines.* Routledge.

Dayan, H. (2022). Ethnocultural Aspects of homicidal crime scene staging. *Homicide Studies* (Forthcoming).

Dobash, R. E., Dobash, R. P., Cavanagh, K., & Lewis, R. (2004). Not an ordinary killer – Just an ordinary guy: When men murder an intimate woman partner. *Violence Against Women, 10*, 577–605.

Dodd, P.C. (1973). Family honour and the forces of change in Arab society. *International Journal of Middle East Studies, 4*, 40–54.

Eke, A. (2007). *Staging in cases of homicide: Offender, victim and offence characteristics* [doctoral dissertation, York University].

Farr, K. A. (2002). Battered women who were "being killed and survived it": Straight talk from survivors. *Violence and Victims, 17*(3), 267–281.

Felstiner, W. L. F., Abel, R., & Sarat, A. (1980). The Emergence and transformation of disputes: naming, blaming, claiming. *Law & Society Review, 15*, 631.

Ferguson, C. (2015). Staged homicides: An examination of common features of faked burglaries, suicides, accidents and car accidents. *Journal of Police and Criminal Psychology*, *30*(3), 139–157.

Fleury, R. E., Sullivan, C. M., & Bybee, D. I. (2000). When ending the relationship does not end the violence: Women's experiences of violence by former partners. *Violence against Women*, *6*(12), 1363–1383. https://doi.org/10.1177/10778010022183695

Flynn, S., Swinson, N., While, D., Hunt, I., Roscoe, A., Rodway, C., Windfuhr, K., Kapur, N., Appleby, L., & Shaw, J. (2009). Homicide followed by suicide: A cross-sectional study. *The Journal of Forensic Psychiatry & Psychology*, *20*(2), 306–321.

Gillespie, C. K. (1989). *Justifiable homicide: Battered women, self-defense and the law*. Ohio State University Press

Goussinsky, R., & Yassour-Borochowitz, D. (2012). "I killed her, but I never laid a finger on her" – A phenomenological difference between wife-killing and wife-battering. *Aggression and Violent Behavior*, *17*(6), 553–564.

Harper, D. W., & Voigt, L. (2007). Homicide followed by suicide: An integrated theoretical perspective. *Homicide Studies*, *11*(4), 295–318.

Hasan, M. (2002). The politics of honour: Patriarchy, the state and the murder of women in the name of family honour. *Journal of Israel History*, *21*, 1–37.

Hazelwood, R. R., & Napier, M. R. (2004). Crime scene staging and its detection. *International Journal of Offender Therapy and Comparative Criminology*, *48*(6), 744–759.

Keppel, R. D., & Weis, J. G. (2004). The rarity of "unusual" dispositions of victim bodies: Staging and posing. *Journal of Forensic Science*, *49*(6), 1308–1312.

Koss, M. P., Goodman, L. A., Brown, A., Fitzgerald, L. F., Keita, G. P., & Russo, N.F. (1994). *No Safe Haven: Male Violence against Women at Home, at Work and in the Community* (p. 44). American Psychological Association.

Kressel, G. M., Bausani, A., Ginat, J., Joseph, R., Khazanov, A. M., Landau, S. F., & Shokeid, M. (1981). Sororicide/filiacide: Homicide for family honour [and comments and reply]. *Current Anthropology*, *22*(2), 141–158.

Kulwicky, A. D. (2002). The practice of honour crimes: A glimpse of domestic violence in the Arab world. *Issues in Mental Health Nursing*, *23*, 77–87.

La Fond, John Q. (1982). The case of liberalizing the use of deadly force in self defence. *University of Puget Sound Law Review*, *6*, 276–277.

Large, M., Smith, G., & Nielssen, O. (2009). The epidemiology of homicide followed by suicide: A systematic and quantitative review. *Suicide and Life-Threatening Behavior*, *39*(3), 294–308.

Liem, M. (2010). Homicide followed by suicide: A review. *Aggression and Violent Behavior*, *15*, 153–161.

Liem, M., Barber, C., Markwalder, N., Killias, M., & Nieuwbeerta, P. (2011). Homicide-suicide and other violent deaths: An international comparison. *Forensic Science International*, *207*, 70–76.

MacKinnon, C. A. (1979). *Sexual harassment of working women: A case of sex discrimination*. Yale University Press.

MacKinnon, C. A. (2001). The logic of experience: Reflections on the development of sexual harassment law. *The Georgetown Law Journal*, *90*, 813.

María Jesús, P. Z. (2009). Feminicide in the Dominican Republic. In *Strengthening understanding of femicide*. World Health Organization.

Marzuk, P. M., Tardiff, K., & Hirsch, C. S. (1992). The epidemiology of murder-suicide. *Journal of American Medical Association*, *267*, 3179–3183.

McPhail, B. A. (2002). Gender-bias hate crimes: A review. *Trauma, Violence, & Abuse*, *3*(2), 125–143.

Milroy, C. M. (1995). The epidemiology of homicide-suicide (dyadic death). *Forensic Science International*, *71*, 117–122.

Petherick, W., & Ferguson, C. (2015). False reports. In W. Petherick (Ed.), *Applied crime analysis: A social science approach to understanding crime, criminals, and victims.* (pp. 123–147). Academic Press.

Pettler, L. G. (2016). *Crime scene staging dynamics in homicide cases.* CRC Press.

Rosenbaum, M. (1990). The role of depression in couples involved in murder-suicide and homicide. *American Journal of Psychiatry*, *147*, 1036–1039.

Saleva, O., Putkonen, H., Kiviruusu, O., & Lonnqvist, J. (2007). Homicide-suicide – An event hard to prevent and separate from homicide or suicide. *Forensic Science International*, *166*, 204–208.

Scott, E. (2009). Murder-suicide: A review of the recent literature. *The Journal of the American Academy of Psychiatry and the Law*, *37*, 371–376.

Serran, G., & Firestone, P. (2004). Intimate partner homicide: A review of the male proprietariness and the self-defense theories. *Aggression and Violent Behavior*, *9*(1), 1–15

Siegel, R. B. (1996). The rule of love: Wife beating as prerogative and privacy. *Yale Law Journal*, *105*, 2117–2207.

Smith, M.D., & Zahn, M. (1998). *Homicide: A sourcebook of social research.* Sage

United Nations Office on Drugs and Crimes. (2019). *Global study on homicide: Gender-related killing of women and girls.* United Nations.

Van Wormer, K., & Odiah, C. (1999). The psychology of suicide-murder and the death penalty. *Journal of Criminal Justice, 27*, 361–370

Victorian Law Reform Commission. (2004). *Defenses to homicide.* Victorian Government Printer.

Walker, L. E. (1985). *The battered woman syndrome.* Springer.

Wallace, A. (1986). *Homicide: The social reality.* New South Wales Bureau of Crimes Statistics and Research, Attorney General's Department.

Warren-Gordon, K., Byers, D. B., Brodt, S. J., Watak, M., & Biskupski, B. (2010). Murder followed by suicide: A newspaper surveillance study using the New York Times index. *Journal of Forensic Science, 55*, 1592–1597.

Websdale, N. (2003). Reviewing domestic violence deaths. *National Institute of Justice Journal, 250*, 26–31.

Winyono, M. (2009). Conceptualizing femicide. In *Strengthening understanding of femicide.* World Health Organization.

Zorza, J. (1991). Woman battering: A major cause of homelessness. *Clearinghouse Review*, *25*, 421–430.

Appendix

Foreword

Preface

Part I: An Overview of Femicide

CHAPTER 1: A THEORETICAL OVERVIEW OF FEMICIDE

The introduction lays the groundwork for a comprehensive analysis of the various theoretical and empirical crimino-legal aspects of femicide that are examined throughout the book.

CHAPTER 2: EMPIRICAL CRIMINOLOGICAL INSIGHTS ON FEMICIDE

This chapter presents empirical observations on the phenomenon of femicide in Israel and its various criminological characteristics.

Part II: Femicide Subtypes

CHAPTER 3: A CRIMINO-LEGAL PERSPECTIVE ON INTIMATE-PARTNER FEMICIDE: THE "REASONABLE" ISRAELI WIFE KILLER

This chapter explores the most prevalent femicide subtype, intimate-partner femicide, from a socio-legal aspect. It focuses on the Israeli application of the common law's doctrine of "provocation." The chapter shows how the process of "transplantation" into the Israeli legal system resulted in the nurturing of the doctrine by Israeli religious law's patriarchal perceptions of marriage and possession.

CHAPTER 4: (DIS)"HONOR" FEMICIDE

This chapter explores theoretical and empirical issues relating to unique socio-criminological aspects and patterns of family "honor" femicide in Israel and its modus operandi, including causes, methods and precipitating factors.

CHAPTER 5: FEMICIDE–SUICIDE

This chapter presents a theoretical and empirical analysis of femicide–suicide, a phenomenon accounting for the majority of homicide–suicides. Exploring empirical data from Israel and analyzing the sociodemographic and criminological characteristics of such killings, the chapter points out that the distribution of the phenomenon varies across immigrant ethnic-minority groups in the country.

CHAPTER 6: CONCEALED FEMICIDE: FEMINIST THEORY AND CIRCUMSTANTIAL EVIDENCE

Presenting cases in which Israeli women died under circumstances identified here as proxies to crime, the chapter utilizes crimino-legal analysis to identify and discuss other killing methods staged as noncriminal death, overlooked by both the criminal system and academic researchers. To better understand this subtype of femicide and its unique implications, the chapter lays out the feminist theory underpinning it and concentrates on the evidentiary ramifications that concealment yields – lack of direct evidence to prove the murder.

Part III: Femicide's Secondary-Tier Effects

CHAPTER 7: SECONDARY VICTIMS AND THE IMPLICATIONS OF FEMICIDE

This chapter offers a critical crimino-legal analysis of the most overlooked victims of femicide: The victims' extended families, and more specifically, the victims' parents and children. These secondary victims are often exposed to the horror of the killing of their daughter or mother, and the legal implications of such a profound experience and loss accounts for various aspects of their lives in the aftermath of the femicide act.

CHAPTER 8: FEMICIDE: VICTIMS' AGENCY THROUGH TORT LAW

This chapter challenges the common perception that criminal law alone is the venue to pursue justice for femicide victims. It uncovers the potential embedded in tort law to undertake both a compensatory and transformative role in waging the fight against femicide. Discussing the harmonious and disharmonious interplay between tort and criminal law regarding femicide, the chapter sheds light on the advantages and pitfalls of the growing utilization of tort law in femicide cases.

CHAPTER 9: FEMICIDE: A CRIME OF DISTINCTIVE NATURE

Integrating the various book chapters, this part offers a multifaceted crimino-legal meta-overview of the phenomenon as peculiar by virtue of the myriad criminal acts it intersects with. Identifying it as "a crime of distinctive nature," it further proposes a holistic approach to furnishing the guidelines for policy recommendations to effectively abolish it.

Index

Page locators in *italics* indicate a figure

For Product Safety Concerns and Information please contact our EU
representative GPSR@taylorandfrancis.com
Taylor & Francis Verlag GmbH, Kaufingerstraße 24, 80331 München, Germany

www.ingramcontent.com/pod-product-compliance
Lightning Source LLC
LaVergne TN
LVHW021128300926
849160LV00010B/904

9781032366883